MW00852076

Naturalism, Realism, and Normativity

Naturalism, Realism, and Normativity

Hilary Putnam

EDITED BY MARIO DE CARO

||| Harvard University Press

Cambridge, Massachusetts
London, England
2016

Acknowledgments on pages 227–228 constitute an extension of this copyright page.

Library of Congress Cataloging-in-Publication Data

Names: Putnam, Hilary, author. | De Caro, Mario, editor.
Title: Naturalism, realism, and normativity / Hilary Putnam ; edited by Mario De Caro.
Description: Cambridge, Massachusetts : Harvard University Press, 2016. | Includes
    index.
Identifiers: LCCN 2015033370 | ISBN 9780674659698 (alk. paper)
Subjects: LCSH: Realism. | Naturalism. | Perception (Philosophy) | Normativity
    (Ethics)
Classification: LCC B835 .P86 2016 | DDC 191—dc23 LC record available at
    http://lccn.loc.gov/2015033370

Contents

IV. NAIVE REALISM, SENSATION, AND APPERCEPTION

V. LOOKING BACK

Naturalism, Realism, and Normativity

Introduction

PUTNAM'S PHILOSOPHY AND METAPHILOSOPHY

BY MARIO DE CARO

$\mathcal{T}$HE TITLE OF THIS VOLUME, which is taken from the first essay collected here, is meant to direct the reader's attention to three main philosophical questions with which Hilary Putnam has been dealing for very many years. The questions grow out of, on the one hand, the conclusions reached in Putnam's early papers, collected in the first two volumes of his *Philosophical Papers*,[1] in which he criticized logical positivist accounts of the meaning of scientific terms and the nature of scientific theories, in part because they were "incompatible with a rather minimal scientific realism,"[2] and, on the other hand, Putnam's return to a more nuanced version of those early realist views after a fourteen-year (1976–1990) swerve in a direction that, notwithstanding his original intentions, substantially leaned toward antirealism (Putnam's "internal realist" years).[3] The questions thus presuppose Putnam's realism (prescinding from the aforementioned "swerve") as well

---

1. *Mathematics, Matter and Method*, vol. 1, and *Mind, Language and Reality*, vol. 2 of *Philosophical Papers* (Cambridge: Cambridge University Press, 1975).

2. As Putnam says in "What Theories Are Not," a lecture delivered to the 1960 International Conference on Logic, Methodology and Philosophy of Science at Stanford University, and collected in Putnam's *Mathematics, Matter and Method*, 215–227. "Rather minimal scientific realism" occurs on p. 224. (This is the first time Putnam recalls calling his position "scientific realism.")

3. The clearer exposition of Putnam's internal realism is in his *Reason, Truth, and History* (Cambridge: Cambridge University Press, 1981).

1

as his more recent interest in what he calls the "entanglement" of fact
and value.[4]

1. Assuming that one accepts the arguments that Putnam has
   given for many years, that antirealism, in its many forms, is an
   unacceptable view, what form of realism should one embrace?
2. Assuming that the philosophies that appeal to the supernatural
   are not acceptable, what form of naturalism should one endorse?
3. Assuming that normativity is an essential component of our
   rational and moral practices, should or could we assume that, at
   least in principle, it is reducible to the non-normative components of such practices?

All these questions, besides being of primary philosophical interest,
presuppose deep metaphilosophical reflections regarding the nature,
role, goals, and methods of philosophy. Let's examine them in turn.

1. Realism

In 1983 Michael Devitt wrote an article very unsympathetically titled
"Realism and the Renegade Putnam."[5] In that article, Devitt—a student of Putnam's during his graduate years at Harvard—complained
that, by opting for "internal realism," Putnam became a "renegade"
from philosophical realism, which he had previously defended in the
papers collected in the *Philosophical Papers* volumes.

Indeed, in 1990 and subsequently, Putnam granted that internal
realism—a view based on an epistemic conception of truth—leaned
too much in an idealistic direction.[6] But while acknowledging that internal realism was a mistake, one can easily see that Devitt's harsh
judgment was quite unfair. As a matter of fact, Putnam never completely renounced realism. First of all, in his entire career (*including* his

---

4. Putnam used the term "entanglement" in *The Collapse of the Fact / Value Dichotomy and
Other Essays* (Cambridge, Mass.: Harvard University Press, 2002), but the idea, if not the
term, was already present in his *Renewing Philosophy* (Cambridge, Mass.: Harvard University Press, 1992) and in his subsequent essays on Dewey's philosophy, such as those published in *Words and Life*, ed. James Conant (Cambridge, Mass.: Harvard University Press,
1994).

5. Michael Devitt, "Realism and the Renegade Putnam: A Critical Study of Meaning
and the Moral Sciences, *Noûs* 17, no. 2 (1983): 291–301.

6. See Chapters 4, 7, and 8 in this work for some discussions on internal realism.

internal realist period) Putnam maintained that the theoretical terms of our best scientific practice do refer to real entities, even if such entities are in principle unobservable (i.e., electrons and black holes), and this means that he always rejected all forms of scientific antirealism, such as instrumentalism, conventionalism, operationalism, and relativism.[7] Second, when he moved away from his early physicalistically oriented realism toward internal realism, Putnam was motivated by his desire to shape a satisfying philosophical realism—that is, a realism able simultaneously to (1) accept the approximate and revisable correctness of the scientific worldview *and* (2) accept the approximate and revisable correctness of the commonsense worldview, which Putnam then thought (and still thinks) was threatened by the reductionist conceptions of reality. In this light, at least since 1976 Putnam has rejected all positions that are unable (or worse, do not even try) to do full justice, at the same time, to science and common sense. Arguably, Putnam's painstaking and uninterrupted efforts to shape a version of realism able to acknowledge the partial and revisable but very real verisimilitude of both the commonsense and the scientific images of the world, without privileging one over the other, is one of his most relevant bequests to the next generations of philosophers.

Before entering in more detail into Putnam's views on these issues, some remarks can be useful. First of all, it should be noted that the problem of realism does not have an "all or nothing" form. No serious philosopher has ever been a complete realist or a complete antirealist: even Alexius Meinong, perhaps the most realist of all philosophers, denied that a round square could be real; and even bishop Berkeley, a champion of antirealism in regard to the material world, was an arch-realist as to the mind (in particular the divine mind). In a word, all relevant philosophical conceptions are a mix of realistic and antirealist components: one can be a realist in one sense, without being a realist in another sense.[8]

Moreover, as has frequently been noted, there is not one form of realism, but many, which can be grouped in three main families:

---

7. See Hilary Putnam, "On Not Writing Off Scientific Realism," in *Philosophy in an Age of Science: Physics, Mathematics, and Skepticism*, ed. Mario De Caro and David Macarthur (Cambridge, Mass.: Harvard University Press, 2012), 91–108.

8. The themes of this section of the introduction are analyzed more in depth in Mario De Caro, "Realism, Common Sense, and Science," *The Monist* 98 (2015): 197–214.

1. *Ontological realism.* The views that belong to this family claim the reality of certain sorts of things: concrete (trees, galaxies, or atoms) or abstract (numbers, universals, or disembodied minds), properties (redness, goodness, electric charges, or freedom of the will) or events (the Big Bang, transubstantiation, the Moon landing). Moreover, the theories of the ontological-realist family can be general (such as when they claim the existence of the external world or of time) or particular (when they claim the existence of specific things or classes of things).[9]

2. *Semantic realism.* In a taxonomy due to the late Michael Dummett,[10] the views of this family claim that the meaning of a sentence is given by the conditions under which it is true, and that truth requires the reality of the entities to which the terms of that sentence refer (whereas semantic antirealist views claim that the meaning of a sentence is given by the conditions under which speakers are justified in asserting it).

3. *Epistemological realism.* The views of this family claim that there may be real facts and truths that are, in principle, unknowable (a possibility that is denied by epistemological antirealists).

Often the discussions of these three forms of realism are interconnected—and this is certainly the case for Putnam—but this is not necessarily so. However, besides this formal taxonomy, the different versions of realism can also be distinguished in virtue of their substantial claims. In particular, today the two most important versions of realism (in the general sense of the term), taken in their purest forms, are (1) *commonsense realism,* the view that acknowledges as real only the things we can experience directly (with our senses, such as Eddington's famous commonsense table)[11] or indirectly (by using the instruments that extend our senses, such as microscopes or telescopes), and (2) *hyperscientific realism,* the view that claims that (1) we should accept as real *only*

9. When discussing the independent existence of an entity, one should not pose the question in genetic or causal terms. The table in front of me obviously exists because someone built it; however, once it is built, the table exists independently of whoever built it.

10. The most complete discussion of metaphysical realism and antirealism by Dummett is in his *The Logical Basis of Metaphysics* (Cambridge, Mass.: Harvard University Press, 1991).

11. Eddington spoke of "two tables," the commonsense table and the physicist's table, in *The Nature of Physical Reality* (Cambridge: Cambridge University Press, 1929). On this, see Putnam, "On Not Writing Off Scientific Realism."

the entities and events (both observable and unobservable) to which our best scientific theories are ontologically committed, and none of these has the properties that our commonsense objects are supposed to have (Eddington's physicists' table was not solid, not smooth, etc.). When taken in their purest forms these two forms of realism are incompatible because each of them is drastically antirealist in the field in which the other assumes a firmly realist attitude.

It could be argued that the origin of this opposition can be tracked back to Aristotle's defense of the commonsense view of the world against Plato's peculiar idealism (which actually was a strong form of realism regarding ideal forms!). More safely, however, one can claim that the discussion opposing commonsense realism to hyperscientific realism became explicit when the scientific revolution obtained a foothold. As early as 1597, Jacopo Mazzoni—a philosopher who was a colleague and a good friend of Galileo in Pisa and influenced his intellectual development—wrote an important book in which, among other things, he opposed the Aristotelianism of his own time, which defended the commonsensical, perception-based view of the world, in favor of a version of Platonism according to which the natural world is mathematically structured.[12] A few years later, expanding on that view, Galileo offered the basics of the modern scientific worldview by claiming that only the mathematizable properties of the bodies investigated by physics are real, while the so-called secondary qualities—the qualitative properties that we get through perception and commonsensically attribute to the external bodies—have no independent existence:

As far as concerns the subject in which these tastes, smells, colours, etc. appear to us as inhering, they are nothing other than mere names, and they inhere only in the sentient body. Consequently, if the animal were removed, all these qualities would disappear and be annihilated.[13]

12. Jacopo Mazzoni, *In Universam Platonis et Aristotelis Philosophiam Praeludia, sive de comparatione Platonis et Aristotelis* (Venezia, 1597); English translation in Alexander Koyré, "Galileo and Plato," *Journal of the History of Ideas* 5 (1943): 400–428, quotation on p. 421.

13. Galileo Galilei, in *Le Opere di Galileo Galilei*, repr. ed. Antonio Favaro, *Edizione Nazionale*, vol. 6 (Firenze: G. Barbèra, 1968), 197–372; *The Assayer*, trans. S. Drake, in *The Controversy of the Comets of 1618* (Philadelphia: University of Pennsylvania Press, 1960), 151–336. It should be noted that for Galileo "mathematizable" meant "geometrizable." On

But Galileo did not only defend a rigorous mathematical realism that relegated secondary properties to the realm of the subjective and credited as real only primary properties; he also claimed that atoms, the unobservable entities whose existence he postulated in order to explain the changes of material states, were real.[14] What we have here called "hyperscientific realism" was born.

In the next centuries, hyperscientific realism was not unchallenged (idealists and empiricists, for example, rejected it), but it remained an important presence in Western culture. In his *The Crisis of European Sciences and Transcendental Phenomenology* (1936), Edmund Husserl offered an influential genealogical account of the antirealist view of the commonsense world produced by modern science. In his opinion, Galileo was responsible for

> the surreptitious substitution of the mathematically substructured world of idealities for *the only real world*, the one that is actually given through perception, that is ever experienced and experienceable—our everyday life-world. This substitution was promptly passed on to his successors, the physicists of all succeeding centuries.[15]

According to Husserl, then, the only real world is the "life-world," that is, the world of human experience in which the secondary qualities do belong to the external objects in which we commonsensically locate them, and values and meanings may be objective.[16] In Husserl's view, the life-world is the "forgotten meaning-fundament of natural sci-

---

Galileo's scientific realism (which in his case was a form of Platonism), see Mario De Caro, "On Galileo's Platonism, Again," in *Hypotheses and Perspectives within History and Philosophy of Science. Hommage to Alexandre Koyré 1964–2014*, ed. Raffaele Pisano, Joseph Agassi, and Daria Drozdova (Dordrecht, the Netherlands: Springer, forthcoming).

14. In the last years of his life, Galileo might have abandoned atomism in favor of a continuous conception of space: see Michele Camerota, "Galileo, Lucrezio e l'atomismo," in *Lucrezio, la natura e la scienza*, ed. Marco Beretta and Francesco Citti (Firenze: Biblioteca di Nuncius / Istituto e Museo di storia della scienza, Leo S. Olschki, 2008).

15. Edmund Husserl, *Die Krisis der europäischen Wissenschaften und die transzendentale Phänomenologie: Eine Einleitung in die phänomenologische Philosophie*, 1936; published in English as *The Crisis of European Sciences and Transcendental Phenomenology*, trans. David Carr (Evanston, Ill.: Northwestern University Press, 1970), 48 (emphasis added).

16. Husserl's "life-world" is a refinement of the everyday, subjective experience of individuals, obtained through the "phenomenological reduction." See Dermot Moran, *Hus-*

ence,"[17] and scientific concepts are mere idealizations with practical uses, such as measurement and prediction, but do not refer to any unobservable reality. In this light, science can only be interpreted operationalistically—that is, in antirealistic terms.

Husserl's *Crisis* did not offer the first exposition of a pure form of realism centered on the ontological primacy of the ordinary image of the world (Pierre Duhem, for example, was reported to have called himself "the unceasing apostle of common sense");[18] but certainly it was one of the purest, for its explicit refusal to accept scientific ontology. Many continental philosophers have followed Husserl in this direction, but not only continental philosophers have done so.

The philosopher of science Bas van Fraassen, a leading analytic philosopher, offers an excellent example in this sense. His "constructive empiricism" (which should be not confused with the most common versions of empiricism)[19] explicitly attempts at reconciling commonsense realism and scientific antirealism. On the one hand, van Fraassen takes as completely unproblematic the reference of "language . . . to trees and mountains, people and books."[20] On the other hand, he is a strict antirealist with respect to scientific theories that appeal to unobservable entities, even when they produce accurate explanations and predictions of observable evidence.[21] Van Fraassen's view represents one of the most consistent expressions of commonsense realism because it limits the scope of our ontology to what is observable and, accordingly, assumes an antirealist position with regard to scientific theories insofar as they make reference to unobservable entities.

Putnam is very sympathetic to the positive side of commonsense realism as long as it wants to protect the ordinary view of the world from the reductionist and eliminationism campaigns that are so common

---

serl's Crisis of the European Sciences and Transcendental Phenomenology: An Introduction (Cambridge: Cambridge University Press, 2012).

17. Husserl, *Crisis*, 48.

18. R. N. D Martin, *Pierre Duhem: Philosophy and History in the Work of a Believing Physicist* (La Salle, Ill.: Open Court, 1991).

19. Van Fraassen's constructive empiricism is very different from the more traditional empiricism of, say, Hume and the neopositivist philosophers, according to which our knowledge of the external world coincides with the knowledge of our sense data.

20. Bas van Fraassen, "On McMullin's Appreciation of Realism," *Philosophy of Science* 70 (2003): 479–491, quotation from p. 480.

21. Bas van Fraassen, *The Scientific Image* (Oxford: Oxford University Press, 1980).

nowadays. He, however, strongly disagrees with the negative side of commonsense realism—let us call it "hypercommmonsense realism"—with its antirealism concerning science. In this perspective, he has been a tireless proponent of the so-called no-miracles argument, which is based on the idea that the only way of explicating the great explanatory and predictive success of the best theories of modern science is to acknowledge that these theories are true (or approximately true) in regard to the natural world and refer to real entities, even when those are unobservable.[22] From the point of view of antirealism, on the contrary, the fact that science works so well in offering comprehensive explanations and extremely precise predictions of observable phenomena is an inexplicable mystery, if not a sheer miracle. Consequently, for Putnam we should take our best scientific theories as approximately true and the entities those theories refer to as real. Unsurprisingly, antirealists have tried to attack the miracle argument in various ways, but Putnam and others have responded to their arguments in convincing ways.[23]

In maintaining that scientific theories can be true or approximately true, Putnam insists that they are not necessarily verifiable under epistemically ideal conditions, as he instead believed during his internal realist period.[24] A convincing supporting example of why truth is not epistemically constrained is the conjecture "There is no life outside the earth," which, if true, would be unverifiable even in ideal epistemic conditions. Therefore, according to Putnam (apart from the internal realist period), scientific theories can be true (or approximately true) even if we are never able to verify them.

22. Hilary Putnam, "Do True Assertions Correspond to Reality?" in *Language and Reality*, vol. 2 of *Philosophical Papers* (Cambridge, Mass.: Cambridge University Press, 1975), 70–84.

23. The main charges against the miracle argument are that it is based on an inference to the best explanation (which allegedly is either doubtful in itself or not applicable at this meta-explanatory level); that different theories can account for the same sets empirical data; and that the history of science shows that false theories (such as Ptolemaic astronomy) can offer excellent predictions. Against these arguments, see Stathis Psillos, "The Scope and Limits of the No Miracles Argument," in *Explanation, Prediction, and Confirmation*, ed. Dennis Dieks et al. (Dordrecht, the Netherlands: Springer, 2011), 23–35; Hilary Putnam, "On Not Writing Off Scientific Realism"; Mario De Caro, "Review of J. Ritchie, *Understanding Naturalism*," *International Journal of Philosophical Studies* 19 (2011): 527–531; Mario Alai, "Novel Predictions and the No Miracle Argument," *Erkenntnis* 79 (2014): 297–326.

24. See Chapter 5 here.

But the story of contemporary realism gets more complicated. In fact, many scientific realists today take the extreme stance that we called hyperscientific realism, claiming not only that scientific realism is correct, but also that the reality described and explained by science is the only reality there is. Consequently, according to those philosophers scientific realism is the only realism worth defending. This is not a view that Putnam shares. For him, scientific naturalism and commonsense realism are to be reconciled, and this leads him to the belief that we have to work within the framework of "liberal naturalism."

2. Naturalism

The vast majority of scientific realists, including Putnam, defend philosophical naturalism—the conception that stresses the indispensability of the scientific worldview and rejects any appeal to the supernatural.[25] Among these philosophers, however, many combine naturalism with "hyperscientific realism," the previously mentioned view according to which every element of the commonsense worldview that cannot be reduced to the scientific worldview is to be rejected. The resulting conception has been called "scientific naturalism" or "strict naturalism," and Putnam has relentlessly criticized it for the last four decades.

In this battle, Putnam has not been alone: the list of philosophers who have tried to shape more tolerant forms of naturalism—forms that have been grouped under the label "liberal naturalism"[26]—includes Donald Davidson, John McDowell, Jennifer Hornsby, P. F. Strawson, Barry Stroud, and Tim Scanlon and is growing fast. However, liberal naturalism is still a minority view because most of the philosophical scene in analytic metaphysics continues to be occupied by scientific naturalism.

It is ironical that, at least in part, scientific naturalism stemmed from Husserl's *Crisis*. In fact, Wilfrid Sellars, one of the founders of scientific naturalism, found inspiration in that book (with the mediation of

25. See Chapter 1 here.
26. Mario De Caro and David Macarthur, *Naturalism in Question* (Cambridge, Mass.: Harvard University Press, 2004) and *Naturalism and Normativity* (New York: Columbia University Press, 2010).

his mentor Marvin Farber, who had been a student of Husserl's in Freiburg) for his famous distinction between the "manifest" and the "scientific image of the world" and for his "stereoscopic vision" (i.e., a unified view of those two images).[27] Sellars, however, interpreted the opposition between the two worlds in a way that was diametrically opposed to Husserl's. While Husserl was a realist about common sense and an antirealist about science, Sellars took the opposite stance, which he expressed with the famous neo-Protagorean motto:

> Speaking as a philosopher, I am quite prepared to say that the common sense world of physical objects in Space and Time is unreal—that is, that *there are no such things.* Or, to put it less paradoxically, that in the dimension of describing and explaining the world, science is the measure of all things, of what is that it is, and of what is not that it is not.[28]

Sellars and the other founding father of scientific naturalism, V. W. Quine (who insisted on the thesis that only our "first-grade conceptual system"—that is, physics—is in charge of describing reality as it really is),[29] generated a "puritanical" ontological attitude according to which only scientifically describable phenomena are real.[30] As a consequence, scientific naturalists face what has been called a "location problem" or "placement problem"[31]—that is, they have to show how to reduce the features of the commonsense world to the scientifically acceptable features or to show that that they are mere illusions. Unfortunately, as Putnam sardonically put it once, "None of these ontological reductions

27. Wilfrid Sellars, "Philosophy and the Scientific Image of Man," in *Frontiers of Science and Philosophy*, ed. R. Colodny (Pittsburgh: University of Pittsburgh Press, 1962), 37–78. On the influx of Husserl on Sellars, see Moran, *Husserl's Crisis*, 292–293.

28. Wilfrid Sellars, *Empiricism and the Philosophy of Mind* (1956; Cambridge, Mass.: Harvard University Press, 1997), 83 (emphasis added).

29. W. V. Quine, *Word and Object* (New York: Columbia University Press, 1960), and "Epistemology Naturalized," in *Ontological Relativity and Other Essays* (New York: Columbia University Press, 1969), 69–90.

30. This term is due to Stephen Stich, *Deconstructing the Mind* (New York: Oxford University Press, 1996), 199.

31. Frank Jackson, *From Metaphysics to Ethics* (Oxford: Oxford University Press, 1998), 1–5; Huw Price, "Naturalism without Representationalism," in De Caro and Macarthur, *Naturalism in Question*, 71–105.

gets believed by anyone except the proponent of the account and one or two of his friends and / or students."[32]

Putnamian liberal naturalism, instead, has a pluralistic attitude both in ontology and epistemology. In his view, not all the real features of the world can be reduced to the scientifically describable features, and the natural sciences are not the only genuine source of knowledge to which all the other apparent sources should hand over their epistemic pretensions. Obviously, this approach gives rise to what could be called a "reconciliation problem"—the problem of showing how the different kinds of features of the world can all be real without conceptual tension or even contradiction.[33] On this problem, Putnam has a number of interesting things to say.

In the last few years, he has started to make his reflections on liberal naturalism explicit,[34] but many important, if scattered, reflections in that direction can also be found in his previous works. Here is a list of the most important features that, according to Putnam, a satisfying liberal naturalism should encompass.

1. Liberal naturalism should incorporate scientific realism. It should assume a realistic attitude toward the unobservable entities postulated by our best scientific theories and consider those theories as true (or as approximately true, pending the appearance of better theories). This means that, in regard to the realism / antirealism debate concerning science, liberal naturalists should assume neither an instrumentalist attitude nor a quietist one (i.e., a noncommitting attitude regarding the realism / antirealism debate on science).[35]

2. The different sciences should not be interpreted monistically, as if they were one thing in content, method, and goals. From a philosophical point of view, pluralism is the right intellectual attitude in dealing with the sciences (but not only with the sciences).[36]

---

32. Hilary Putnam, "The Content and Appeal of 'Naturalism'," in De Caro and Macarthur, *Naturalism in Question*, 59–70, quotation from p. 62.

33. Mario De Caro, "Putnam's Liberal Naturalism," in *Themes from Putnam*, ed. Michael Frauchiger (Berlin: Ontos Verlag, forthcoming).

34. See Chapter 1 here.

35. Putnam, "On Not Writing Off Scientific Naturalism," and Chapter 5 here.

36. Putnam, "The Diversity of the Sciences: Global versus Local Methodological Approaches," in *Metaphysics and Morality: Essays in Honor of J. J. C. Smart*, ed. Philip Pettit,

3. It has to be acknowledged that both the scientific and the commonsense view of the world are only approximately correct and, consequently, are constantly revised. For Putnam, the key concept in this regard is that of *fallibilism*, which he takes from the pragmatist tradition: any of our beliefs could be wrong, but (contrary to what the skeptic claims) we need context-specific reasons to start doubting them.[37]

4. Contrary to a common opinion, not all objective knowledge should be seen as object-based. In particular, there is no need of assuming that mathematical or ethical statements refer to peculiar, abstract objects (such as sets or the Good) in order to be true or, in the case of ethics, for being better or worse than other competing claims.

5. It is our epistemic duty to try to resolve the contradictions and conceptual tensions between the commonsense and the scientific worldviews, but science does not necessarily have the last word here, even if it is frequently the case that it does. For example, Copernican astronomy initially posed many problems for common sense, and the first attempts to formulate the differential and integral calculus raised so many contradictions and inconsistencies that the whole enterprise looked commonsensically unacceptable; but the attempt to resolve those inconsistencies led to enormous mathematical progress.

6. Liberal naturalism, like all other forms of naturalism, should not make any supernatural assumptions. However, contrary to another very common opinion and in the spirit of the pragmatist tradition, according to Putnam this does not mean that all religious experience should be condemned as irrational or futile (not all religious people believe in divine dictation or in divine properties that violate the laws of nature, for example).[38]

Richard Sylan, and Jean Norman (Oxford: Basil Blackwell, 1987), 137–153; repr. "The Diversity of the Sciences," in *Words and Life*, ed. James Conant (Cambridge, Mass.: Harvard University Press, 1990), 463–480.

37. Putnam, *Pragmatism: An Open Question* (Oxford: Blackwell, 1995), *passim*.

38. Hilary Putnam, "Wittgenstein on Religious Belief," in *On Community*, ed. Leroy Rouner (Notre Dame, Ind.: University of Notre Dame Press, 1991), 56–75; repr. in Putnam, *Renewing Philosophy* (Cambridge, Mass.: Harvard University Press, 1992), 134–157.

7. As to the epistemological status of philosophy, it should be noted that philosophy has a double face: one is the scientific face (which interacts with the natural and social sciences), and the other is the moral face (which "interrogates our lives and our cultures as they have been up to now, and that challenges us to reform both").[39] Both are essential. Pluralism plays a role also in metaphilosophy, then.

8. The commonsense worldview is not in need of legitimation from science, although commonsense beliefs that turn out to be incompatible with scientific findings have to be given up. (Sometimes science does have the last word.) However, philosophers who claim that belief in the real existence of colors or of solidity (for example, the real existence of pink ice cubes) or the existence of *referring* is incompatible with science are simply wrong. Color realism and realism about representation[40] are respectable scientific positions according to Putnam, as well as commonsense positions, even if color predicates and the notion of representation are not reducible to predicates of physics. The placement problem is a false problem. There is no need to reduce all the ordinary features of the world to features describable in the vocabulary of the exact sciences.

9. Regarding the reconciliation problem (how the commonsense and the scientific views of the world can coexist without one being prior on the other or delegitimatizing it), it should be noted that, contrary to a view that is common nowadays in many philosophical quarters, the world cannot be entirely described by physics—obviously not by present physics, but arguably not even by an ideal physics. In this sense, a favorite example of Putnam's is literary criticism: how could a physical theory do ever so much as discuss the many aspects of Shakespeare's plays that sensitive readers and critics discern? As Putnam wrote,

---

39. Putnam, "Science and Philosophy," in De Caro and Macarthur, eds., *Naturalism and Normativity*, 89–99.

40. Putnam cites Tyler Burge's *Origins of Objectivity* (Oxford: Oxford University Press, 2010) in defense of the scientific legitimacy of realism about representation in the title essay of this volume.

The world cannot be completely described in the language game of theoretical physics, not because there are regions in which physics is false, but because, to use Aristotelian language, the world has many levels of forms, and there is no realistic possibility of reducing them all to the level of fundamental physics.[41]

The consequence of this is "conceptual pluralism," the necessity of using a plurality of mutually irreducible but not incompatible conceptual systems for dealing with the different levels of reality. It is important to note, however, that conceptual pluralism must not be confused with the different phenomenon of "cognitive equivalence."[42] The latter is linked to the cases, not uncommon in science, in which the same phenomena can be described with apparently contradictory conceptual schemes that can indeed be systematically translated into each other (such as when one describes space-time points as individuals or as mere limits).

10. A satisfying liberal naturalist view should assume that among the different levels of reality there is a relationship of supervenience. However, as Putnam writes in regard to human capacities (but these words could be applied to different cases),

> there is no one simple answer to the question of whether our agential capacities are locally supervenient (supervenient on just the relevant brain-states) or globally supervenient (supervenient on factors external to the brain, and even to the organism), because it depends on which agential capacities one is talking about, even if we restrict the issue to perceptual capacities.[43]

11. Finally, a notion that one should use with caution if one does not want to end up with the reconciliation problem is that of

---

41. Hilary Putnam, "From Quantum Mechanics to Ethics and Back Again," in *Philosophy in an Age of Science*, 51–71.

42. Sometimes Putnam instead of talking of "cognitive equivalence" talks of "conceptual relativity," but this term could be misleading since it can be interpreted as an opening to ontological relativity (which Putnam does not want to offer at all).

43. Hilary Putnam, "Reply to Stephen White," *European Journal of Analytic Philosophy* 4, no. 2 (2008): 29–32, quotation from p. 29.

causation. According to Putnam, causation is an intentional, context-relative notion—what the correct answer to the question "What caused the phenomenon x?" is depends on the specific interests of the inquirers. If I write a sonnet, what is the cause of that action of mine? My love for poetry? Some activations of my neurons? The specific cultural history of my society? The education I received? The physical arrangement of microparticles in my environment? All these potential explanations point to different potential causes; and each of these explanations can be correct (or incorrect) depending on what interests one has when one asks the question "Why?" Causation in fundamental physics is often simply not the relevant notion.

3. Normativity

Normativity and ethics are subjects discussed in Chapter 1, while Chapter 3 concerns the bearing of evolutionary theory on ethics, but neither normativity nor ethics are large topics in the other chapters of the present volume. However, Putnam has written extensively on them, and a word on those writings may help to clarify the discussion in those two chapters.[44] Recurrent themes in Putnam's past writings are:

1. That values grow out of human needs, and are historic products, but are not therefore arbitrary or merely culturally relative. (See Chapter 3.)
2. That neither epistemic values nor ethical values can be reduced to a single principle. (In particular, "seek successful prediction" and "try to falsify your theories" are completely insufficient by themselves.)[45]

44. Among those writings, in addition to two volumes, *The Collapse of the Fact / Value Dichotomy* (Cambridge, Mass.: Harvard University Press, 2002) and *Ethics without Ontology* (Cambridge, Mass.: Harvard University Press, 2004), particularly useful for readers approaching this side of Putnam's thought anew might be his essays on pragmatism and ethics, particularly "Pragmatism and Moral Objectivity" and (with Ruth Anna Putnam) "Dewey's *Logic*: Epistemology as Hypothesis," in *Words and Life*, ed. James Conant (Cambridge, Mass.: Harvard University Press, 1994), 151–181 and 198–220, respectively.

45. Putnam argued this in "The Philosophers of Science's Evasion of Values," collected in *The Collapse of the Fact / Value Dichotomy*.

3. That there is a sometimes useful *distinction* between factual judgments and value judgments, but philosophers have gone astray by elevating it to the status of a metaphysical *dichotomy*.[46]

4. That both factual judgments and value judgments require support by *reasons* (of both kinds). The notion of a reason does not require the kind of reduction that hard scientific naturalism seeks. (See Chapter 1.)

The aspect of Putnam's point of view that may be least familiar is his likening of epistemic values to aesthetic values. In his essay "The Philosophers of Science's Evasion of Values," Putnam recalls a conversation he had with Popper's friend Jacob Bronowski in which Bronowski said that he once told Popper, "You would not claim that scientists test every falsifiable theory if as many crazy theories crossed your desk as cross mine!"[47] Epistemic values such as *coherence, simplicity*, and even *elegance* play an essential role in deciding which theories to test. But all the familiar arguments for emotivism in ethics would, if they were right, condemn judgments of coherence and elegance to the wastebasket of mere subjectivity.

In order to appreciate this point, let us close by going back to a historical case discussed earlier, that of Galileo.

It is known that, when he opted for Copernican astronomy over Ptolemaic astronomy, Galileo did not have any purely "factual" support in his favor: only later did he refer to his astronomical observations (which, by the way, at that time did not offer a final confirmation of Copernicanism), and to the famously wrong theory that the tides depend on the rotation of the earth.

The real reason for which Galileo accepted Copernicanism was metaphysical, and it incorporated a strong aesthetic reason, namely, that the Copernican system was much simpler than the Ptolemaic one. ("*Simplex sigillum veri*," "Simplicity is the seal of truth," was a famous medieval adage that Galileo certainly accepted.) Accordingly, in his famous *Dialogue on the Two Main Systems of the World*, he wrote that, following Copernicus, he had become aware that the Ptolemaic system was

---

46. Putnam argues this in *The Collapse of the Fact / Value Dichotomy*, 135–145.

47. Putnam, "Philosophers of Science's Evasion," 142.

a monstrous chimera composed of mutually disproportionate members, incompatible as a whole. Thus however well the astronomer might be satisfied merely as a *calculator* [whose only role is to predict the future positions of planets], there was no satisfaction and peace for the astronomer as a *scientist* [the scientist-philosopher, who searches for the real laws of the universe]. And since he very well understood that although the appearances might be saved by means of assumptions essentially false in nature [false because disproportionate and adverse to geometrical simplicity], it would be very much better if he could derive them from true suppositions.[48]

And it is worth noticing that it was for the same metaphysical-aesthetic reason—the preference of geometrical simplicity over complexity—that later Galileo rejected Kepler's correct idea of the elliptical orbits of the planets.

The examples of the role that aesthetic factors play in science (and in mathematics) are innumerable. With this sort of example in mind, Putnam argues that values, including this sort of quasi-aesthetic evaluation, which obviously have a normative character, play a crucial role also in science.

However, an objection to this argument that one might certainly expect is that one has to distinguish the context of discovery from the context of justification; and that, in this way, one can separate what is justificatorily irrelevant (such as Galileo's aesthetic bias in favor of simplicity) from the real factual content of a scientific theory. But Putnam would dispute the claim that the reasons that *justify* accepting a theory only depend on the factual content of the theory. If considerations of a more holistic and even a "quasi-aesthetic" character, such as the simplicity of the theory, are the reasons that, *together with the observations*, lead us to accept certain theories and not even bother to test certain rivals, then if those reasons must be regarded as purely "subjective"—that is, as not reasons at all—our acceptance of the science we have must all be regarded as wholly subjective. And Putnam convincingly has claimed this should be seen as a *reductio* of skepticism about epistemic values.

---

48. Galileo Galilei, *Dialogo sopra i due massimi sistemi del mondo*, 1632; published in English as *Dialogue Concerning the Two Chief World Systems, Ptolemaic & Copernican*, trans. Stillman Drake (1953; Berkeley: University of California Press, 1967), 341 (emphasis added).

Nowadays philosophers tend to be specialized in very few and frequently very minor issues, which they scrutinize at the smallest degree. Hilary Putnam does not belong to this group. His way of doing philosophy rather resembles the way of operating of the thinkers of the classic tradition. He only deals with big questions, in all philosophical fields, and unceasingly tries to refine his answers to those questions and make them consistent and harmonious. The general framework of his philosophy is the attempt to reconcile the ordinary and the scientific views of the world, without prioritizing one over the other, in a naturalistic spirit respectful of the fundamental and irreducible role that normativity plays in our lives.

We should all be grateful to Putnam not only for the innumerable and invaluable contributions he has offered in many fields, but also because he represents a shining example of what philosophy has been in its most glorious moments and should always continue to be.[49]

49. I thank Massimo Dell'Utri, Andrea Lavazza, David Macarthur, Massimo Marraffa, Matteo Morganti, Barry Smith, and Stephen White for many useful exchanges on the issues dealt with in this introduction. A special thank goes to Hilary Putnam, with whom I have had the honor to discuss these issues for several years.

PART I

Liberal Naturalism
and Normativity

☙ 1

Naturalism, Realism, and Normativity

Naturalism

The terms "naturalism" and "realism" are useful (and even indispensable on occasion), but each of them has been applied to a wide range of different and even incompatible positions. I very much like the term "liberal naturalism," which I first encountered in an important collection of essays edited by Mario De Caro and David Macarthur entitled *Naturalism in Question*. In my essay in that collection,[1] I pointed out that while Boyd, Casper, and Trout's *The Philosophy of Science* admirably takes the trouble to tell us what the editors mean by "naturalism" (and their naturalism is certainly not "liberal"),[2] their definition is disjunctive, and thus offers us two possible meanings of "naturalism" rather than one. According to Boyd and colleagues, naturalism is "[t]he view that all phenomena are subject to natural laws, and / or [*sic*] that the methods of the natural sciences are applicable in every area of inquiry," and I argued that both disjuncts are extremely vague. In what sense does a "naturalist" have to believe that the "phenomenon" of Shakespeare's

---

1. Hilary Putnam, "The Content and Appeal of 'Naturalism,'" in *Naturalism in Question*, ed. Mario De Caro and David Macarthur (Cambridge, Mass.: Harvard University Press, 2004), 59–70.
2. Richard Boyd, Philip Casper, and J. D. Trout, eds., *The Philosophy of Science* (Cambridge, Mass.: MIT Press, 1991).

21

writing *Julius Caesar* was "subject to natural laws"? Is it enough to believe that writing that play didn't *violate* any natural laws? Surely that makes it too easy to be a "naturalist"! Or should one believe that in our "first-grade" conceptual system (W. V. Quine)[3]—or in "the absolute conception of the world" (Bernard Williams)[4]—there is no fact of the matter as to what a single sentence of that play *means*, but the production of those marks on paper was a physical process whose physical explanation exhausts what there is to be known about the play? Or must one rather try to "naturalize" questions about meaning, and so on? And what exactly does it mean to "apply" the supposed "methods of the natural sciences" to *Julius Caesar?* In fact, the sort of hard naturalism advocated by Boyd and Caspar's volume chooses to say nothing about such subjects as literary criticism, and even the "Cornell Moral Realists," a group of which Boyd is a leading member, regard talk of obligation ("ought") as belonging to the domain of the noncognitive. What makes them moral realists is the odd claim that "good" refers to a natural kind, on all four feet with biological kinds. Instead of seizing either horn of this dilemma, De Caro and Macarthur pointed to and celebrated the existence of a number of philosophical positions that are "naturalist" in the sense that John Dewey, the most famous naturalist philosopher of his period, was—namely, in the sense of rejecting all appeals to supernatural entities in philosophy while simultaneously rejecting the positivist demand that aesthetic and ethical concepts be reduced to the concepts of the natural sciences or expecting that they could, or eventually will be, so reduced. Nor do they accept the positivist view that history will eventually become a "science." In their introduction to *Naturalism in Question*, De Caro and Macarthur emphasized that the liberal naturalism they advocate doesn't regard normative utterances as somehow "second grade" or merely "expressive," but neither does it countenance a Platonic realm of normative facts independent of human practices and needs. At the same time, it does not countenance Moorean quasi-mystical faculties of moral intuition. All this I like very much.

3. See W. V. Quine, *Word and Object* (New York: Columbia University Press, 1960), and "Epistemology Naturalized," in *Ontological Relativity and Other Essays* (New York: Columbia University Press, 1969), 69–90.

4. Bernard Williams, *Descartes: the Project of Pure Enquiry* (Harmondsworth: Penguin, 1978).

I don't know whether Tyler Burge would ever employ the term "liberal naturalism," but I do know that his *Origins of Objectivity* is a great book.[5] It takes indispensability for good scientific explanations (the sciences in question being vision science and related parts of psychology, in particular) to be sufficient reason for accepting an unreduced notion of representation in psychology and philosophy of mind, and I agree; at the same time, what Burge writes about "naturalization projects in philosophy" is surely in the spirit of "liberal naturalism":

> Promoters of "naturalizing" projects are often driven, I think, by misconceptions of science. These misconceptions breed misconceptions of mind. The notion of representation—of reference or attribution that can be correct or incorrect and that helps type-individuate kinds of psychological states—is entrenched not only in commonsense explanation but in scientific explanation in psychology. There is nothing unnatural or supernatural about such explanation. Some of the relevant psychology is well-supported, mathematically rigorous, mature science. There is no basis, even a prima facie one, to the worry that psychological notions are invitations to mystery or miracle. Even if there were such basis, the role that these notions play in powerful empirical science would undermine it . . . I know of no good ground for thinking that . . . [psychologists'] explanatory claims must be twisted into the mold of biological or information-theoretic explanation, or any other explanation in the natural sciences, in order to be explanatorily successful.[6]

The reason I say that this is in the spirit of *liberal* naturalism is not just Burge's rejection of reductionism; some hard naturalists are quite proud of being "nonreductive materialists" or the like. But even when hard naturalists eschew the demand that reference and representation talk be reduced to physical vocabulary, they feel the need to *explain* reference and representation in terms of "causal relations."[7] Even if the

---

5. Tyler Burge, *Origins of Objectivity* (Oxford: Clarendon Press, 2010).
6. Burge, *Origins of Objectivity*, 296–297.
7. Richard Boyd, "What of Pragmatism with the World Here?" in *Reading Putnam*, ed. Maria Baghramian (Abingdon, United Kingdom: Routledge, 2013), 39–94.

explanations are, as I believe, pure hand-waving, the spirit, if not the details, is obviously reductionist.

However, liberal naturalism, as represented by De Caro and Macarthur's two volumes (the already mentioned *Naturalism in Question* and *Naturalism and Normativity*),[8] covers a wide range of positions, including ones I disagree with. For example, one contributor to *Naturalism in Question*, Huw Price, rejects the whole idea that reference is a relation between linguistic items and worldly objects,[9] an idea (he calls it "representationalism") that is an essential part of my own realism. Another contributor (and editor of the volume) advocates a version of Wittgensteinian "quietism,"[10] which I also reject.[11] Thus, although I am indeed a "liberal naturalist," that label does not say very much about my philosophy. To supplement it I need to say more—for example, I am a liberal naturalist, but I am also a realist in my metaphysics and a realist with respect to the normative. This essay will attempt to sketch the outlines of a liberal naturalist metaphysically realist and normatively realist position in philosophy.

Metaphysically Realist

Readers who know of my philosophy from Wikipedia may be surprised to find me saying that my position is "metaphysically realist." Had I not consistently attacked metaphysical realism from "Realism and Reason" (1978) on?[12] Well, not exactly. In that lecture and for a number of years afterward, I used "metaphysical realism" (sometimes with capital letters) as a term for a specific position whose main feature was the insistence that the world can be divided into (mind-independent) objects and properties in exactly one way. But the use of that term was a mistake on my part. It was a mistake because, although I repeatedly explained

8. Mario De Caro and David Macarthur, eds., *Naturalism and Normativity* (New York: Columbia University Press, 2010).

9. Huw Price, "Naturalism without Representationalism," in De Caro and Macarthur, *Naturalism in Question*, 71–105.

10. See David Macarthur, "Putnam, Pragmatism, and the Fate of Metaphysics," *European Journal of Analytic Philosophy* 4, no. 2 (2008): 33–46.

11. Hilary Putnam, "Reply to David Macarthur," *European Journal of Analytic Philosophy* 4, no. 2 (2008): 47–49.

12. Hilary Putnam, "Realism and Reason," in *Meaning and the Moral Sciences* (London: Routledge and Kegan Paul, 1978), 123–138.

what I meant by it, based on the natural understanding of the phrase "metaphysical realism," it refers to a broad family of positions and not just to the *one* position I used it to refer to. In effect I *was* saying that by refuting the one philosophical view I called by that name I was ipso facto refuting anything that deserved to be called metaphysical realism, and that was not the case.

In addition, in my Dewey Lectures,[13] which were the best known source for my post–"internal realist" views, I was still under the influence of Wittgensteinian quietism; although this is an aspect of Wittgenstein's thought that I grew increasingly unsympathetic to, it was not until my closing address to my eightieth birthday conference in Dublin that I was willing to say, in those words, that I am a metaphysical realist without capital letters, a realist in my metaphysics, but not a "metaphysical realist" in the technical sense I gave to that term in "Realism and Reason" and subsequent publications.[14] At the same time I was also willing to say,

> Let me say for the record that I utterly and totally reject all versions of the "end of philosophy" story, whether they come from Wittgensteinians, Rortians, Heideggerians, Derridians, or whoever. Philosophy was not a mistake; not in Parmenides's time, not in Plato's time, not in Aristotle's or Descartes's or Hume's or Kant's times, and not in our time. As Etienne Gilson put it, "philosophy always buries its undertakers."[15]

But what is it to be a metaphysical realist? In an elegant paper titled "Confessions of a Hard-Core, Unsophisticated Metaphysical Realist,"[16] Maudlin describes his reaction to first reading the lecture in which I first used the term "internal realism." In that lecture I had written:

13. Hilary Putnam, "Sense, Nonsense, and the Senses: An Inquiry into the Powers of the Human Mind," *Journal of Philosophy* 91 (1994): 445–517; reprinted in Hilary Putnam, *The Threefold Cord: Mind, Body and World* (New York: Columbia University Press, 1999), 3–70.

14. Hilary Putnam, "From Quantum Mechanics to Ethics and Back Again," in Baghramian, *Reading Putnam*, 19–36.

15. Putnam, "From Quantum Mechanics to Ethics and Back Again," 68.

16. Tim Maudlin, "Confessions of a Hardcore, Unsophisticated Metaphysical Realist," in *The Philosophy of Hilary Putnam*, ed. R. E. Auxier, D. R. Anderson, and L. A. Hahn (Chicago: Open Court, 2015), 487–501.

The most important consequence of metaphysical realism is that *truth* is supposed to be *radically nonepistemic—we* might be "brains in a vat" and so the theory that is "ideal" from the point of view of operational utility, inner beauty and elegance, plausibility, simplicity, "conservatism," etc. *might be false.* "Verified" (in any operational sense) does not imply "true," on the metaphysical realist picture, even in the ideal limit.

It is this feature that distinguishes metaphysical realism, as I am using the term, from the mere belief that there is an ideal theory (Peircean realism), or, more weakly, that an ideal theory is a regulative ideal presupposed by the notions "true" and "objective" as they have classically been understood. And it is this feature that I shall attack.[17]

And Maudlin's reaction:

We now have something quite concrete to discuss. The metaphysical realist thinks that an *operationally* ideal theory, a theory ideal *as far as we can tell*, might actually be false. This is a thesis that appears to be clear and concise. It is also a thesis that I take to be true and took to be true as a graduate student. So the most enduring impact "Realism and Reason" had on me, despite its intent, was to make me a confirmed metaphysical realist.[18]

The thesis that a theory "ideal as far as we can tell" might actually be false simply amounts to the claim that a statement that we are epistemically entitled to accept as part of our best theory of the world might be false, and there might be no way of verifying that it is false. And I agree with Maudlin that there are such statements.

Hence, if we understand metaphysical realism as he does, as simply making that claim, metaphysical realism is true. For example, there might be very strong reasons to believe that there are intelligent extraterrestrials, including radio signals or whatever, but the signals could be the product of quantum mechanical fluctuations of immensely low probability. And metaphysical realism in Maudlin's sense is part of my

17. Putnam, "Realism and Reason," 123–138. The passage quoted is at p. 125.
18. Maudlin, "Confessions," 485.

current view. Truth is not the same thing as warranted assertability under ideal conditions. "Realism and Reason" was wrong.

But a responsible metaphysical realist needs to say something about what truth is and not simply what it isn't, and what follows is an attempt to do that, to say *something* (of course, not everything) about what truth is.

Truth: Tarski's Contribution and Its Interpretation

In "The Concept of Truth in Formalized Languages,"[19] Tarski immeasurably advanced our grasp of the formal logic of the predicate "True sentence of L," where L is a formalized language, and by doing so he provided powerful new tools for mathematical logicians (something that is underappreciated by philosophers) as well as material for philosophers to assimilate and interpret. The tools for mathematical logicians that I refer to include techniques that were later adapted to formalize the statement that a set is definable over a given collection of sets with parameters from that collection and quantifiers ranging over that collection (tools that Gödel [1940] employed in the construction of the hierarchy of "constructible sets" that he used to prove the consistency of the Axiom of Choice and the Generalized Continuum Hypothesis[20]). These tools have been employed in many contexts ever since: the material for philosophers to assimilate and interpret includes the T-schema or truth schema in section 1 of "The Concept of Truth in Formalized Languages" (not to be confused with Convention T), Convention T, and the "truth definitions," as they have come to be called, that are required to meet that criterion of adequacy. (In both the German and the original Polish of "The Concept of Truth in Formalized Languages," "Convention T" is called a "criterion" and not a "convention." "Convention T" comes from the 1956 English translation, T being the first letter of the English word "true" and W being the first letter of the

---

19. The original publication was in Polish in 1933, and the German translation appeared in 1935. The 1956 English translation was reprinted as Alfred Tarski, "The Concept of Truth in Formalized Languages," in *Logic, Semantics, Metamathematics: Papers from 1923 to 1938*, ed. John Corcoran, trans. J. H. Woodger (Indianapolis: Hackett, 1983 [1956]), 152–278.

20. Kurt Gödel, *The Consistency of the Continuum Hypothesis*, Annals of Mathematics Studies 3 (Princeton, N.J.: Princeton University Press, 1940).

German word "*wahr.*") Although a minority of philosophers, including Popper, saw "The Concept of Truth in Formalized Languages" as putting forward a correspondence theory of truth, other philosophers have linked it to "deflationary" theories of truth, while the particular techniques Tarski employed led Hartry Field (correctly in my opinion) to see Tarski as finding an intimate link between *reference* (or, in Tarski's—and Field's—terminology, "denotation") and *truth*,[21] an insight that Field unfortunately linked to an unworkable "naturalization project" (to use Burge's term) and later abandoned completely. The next two sections elaborate on these remarks.

Tarski's Criterion of Adequacy

Following Tarski, let us pretend that we have a particular interpreted formal language in mind, and let us call it Bob. I choose an obvious proper name, Bob, and not *L*, because *L* looks like a *variable*—a variable for quantifying over formal languages—and it is essential to Tarski's approach that truth definitions are constructed *one language at a time*. Tarski (rightly) does not attempt to construct a definition of "true in L" *when L is a variable over all languages*, and doing so would immediately lead to paradoxes. We will assume that Bob has a finite number of primitive descriptive predicates and individual constants, and so on. To avoid any appearance of circularity or begging the question, we will also assume that none of these is interpreted as referring to semantic properties or entities, such as truth or reference or "correspondence" or facts or states of affairs. Let Meta-Bob be a second formal language that contains the whole vocabulary of Bob, one in which it is possible to quantify over inscriptions (sequences of symbols) in the language Bob. In addition, permit Meta-Bob to be set-theoretically more powerful than Bob in the ways needed for Tarski's purposes, but without having any primitive descriptive predicates or names other than those of Bob itself. A "truth predicate" for Bob is a formula FORM(x) of Meta-Bob with one free variable, say x. I avoid the custom of abbreviating the formula as "True-in-Bob" (or even worse, as "True-in-L") because doing so obscures the very issues I wish to raise. Of course, in

---

21. Hartry Field, "Tarsky's Theory of Truth," *Journal of Philosophy* 69, no. 13 (1972): 347–375.

ordinary language there is such a predicate as "true in Bob," with no hyphens, but that predicate involves the ordinary language notion of truth, which Tarski claimed is inconsistent. That is the reason why we need a formal replacement for it. "Defining truth in Bob," in Tarski's sense, means (1) finding a FORM(*x*) that is true of all and only those inscriptions *x* in Bob that are true in Bob and (2) reformulating this requirement in a way that does not involve using the everyday language word "true" or any related notion. Tarski's solution to this latter desideratum, defining "material adequacy" of a truth definition without using the word "true," is the famous Convention T, which we state by saying:

(T) FORM(*x*) is a materially adequate truth predicate for Bob just in case the result of replacing *s* by an arbitrary sentence of Bob and *s** by a structural-descriptive name of that sentence in:

$$s \Leftrightarrow \text{FORM}(s^*)$$

is a theorem of Meta-Bob.

Tarski's notion of a "structural-descriptive name" of an inscription is easiest to explain via an example: if *s* is "Snow is white," then the formal name *s** is "The letter capital *S* followed by the letter *n* followed by the letter *o* followed by the letter *w* followed by space followed by the letter *i* followed by the letter *s* followed by space followed by the letter *w* followed by the letter *h* followed by the letter *i* followed by the letter *t* followed by the letter *e*."[22]

Thus, pretending that "Snow is white" is a sentence of Bob: *Convention T requires that FORM(x) be defined in Meta-Bob in such a way that* "Snow is white" ⇔ FORM(the letter capital *S* followed by the letter *n* followed by the letter *o* followed by the letter *w* followed by space followed by the letter *i* followed by the letter *s* followed by space followed by the letter *w* followed by the letter *h* followed by the letter *i* followed by the letter *t* followed by the letter *e*) *is provable from Meta-Bob's axioms.*

Readers who have gone through life believing that Convention T is a Davidsonian T-sentence or that it is an instance of "disquotation" will be shocked to observe that "true" does not occur in Convention T

---

22. Tarski, "Concept of Truth," 57.

(although abbreviating FORM(x) as "True-in-Bob(x)" can make this hard to see, which is why I didn't do that)!

Field's Reconstruction of Tarski: The Link between Reference and Truth

In his deservedly often-cited "Tarski's Theory of Truth,"[23] Hartry Field argued that Tarski failed to reduce the notion of truth "to other non-semantical notions" but that what Tarski actually did was reduce the notion to other semantical notions.

This is an interesting reading, although I am not certain that Tarski had any such aim. What supports Field's reading is that, in "The Concept of Truth in Formalized Languages," Tarski begins by describing the ordinary language notion of truth, and that this is where Tarski puts forward the T-schema.[24] An instance of the latter is the famous *"Snow is white" is true if snow is white;* what perhaps counts against it is that at the end of that section (section l) Tarski seems to give up the project of clarifying the ordinary language notion of truth entirely:

> If these observations [concerning the inconsistency of the ordinary language notion—*HP*] are correct, *the very possibility of a consistent use of the expression "true sentence" which is in harmony with the laws of logic and the spirit of everyday language seems to be very questionable, and consequently the same doubt attaches to the very possibility of constructing a correct definition of this expression.*[25]

In any case, *one* of Tarski's purposes, which he achieved, was certainly to find a way to define in Meta-Bob a predicate that *has the same extension* as the ordinary language semantical predicate "true in Bob" (no matter which interpreted formalized language "Bob" might be); as I put it once, the predicate(s) FORM(x) we get by Tarski's method do not express the same *concept* as the semantical predicate "true in Bob."[26] In

---

23. Hartry Field, "Tarsky's Theory of Truth."

24. Schema (2) in Tarski, "Concept of Truth," 155.

25. Tarski, "Concept of Truth," 165 (emphasis in original).

26. Hilary Putnam, "A Comparison of Something with Something Else," *New Literary History* 17, no. 1 (1985): 61–79; reprinted in Hilary Putnam, *Words and Life,* ed. James Conant (Cambridge, Mass.: Harvard University Press, 1994), 330–350.

Fregean language, FORM(x) has the right *Bedeutung*, but not the right *Sinn*. But by giving two of his papers the titles "The *Concept* of Truth in Formalized Languages" and "The Semantical *Concept* of Truth" [emphasis added], Tarski certainly gave the impression that his formal results somehow do capture the *Sinn* of "true in Bob" (that is, that they capture the *concept* of truth) and not just the extension of that everyday language semantical predicate.

A Technical Section

To explain all this, I need to say something about how one defines FORM(x) following Tarski's recipe. Simplifying outrageously by pretending that all the predicates of Bob are monadic (the fact that this is in general not the case is the reason that all the mathematical ingenuity in Tarski's paper was required), the easiest way to do this is to imagine that we construct Meta-Bob in two stages. I shall also, less outrageously, simplify by assuming Bob contains no names, only predicates, and (since the universal quantifier can be defined in terms of the existential quantifier $[(x)F(x) \Leftrightarrow \neg(Ex) \neg F(x)]$), I shall assume the primitive notation of Bob has only the existential quantifier.

Stage 1. First, (if necessary) we add to the vocabulary of Bob enough apparatus to do logical syntax (but not semantics!), that is, logical means for quantifying over strings of symbols, such as the letter capital S followed by the letter n followed by the letter o followed by the letter w, and over finite sequences of such strings. We also ensure it is possible to define such syntactic predicates as "x (a string of symbols) is a wff (well-formed formula) of Bob" and "x (a string of wffs) is a proof in Bob," "x is a theorem of Bob," and so on.

Stage 2. We *temporarily* add to Meta-Bob a primitive predicate Ref(x, y), which we will read as "x (a wff of Bob with one free variable) refers to y." The interpretation of Ref should be clear from the following example: if x is "F(v)" and $\underline{a}$ is an entity in the range of the quantifiers of Bob, then [Ref($x, \underline{a}$) $\Leftrightarrow$ F($\underline{a}$)].

Next, we start to create an *inductive* definition of "Ref" by adding to the axioms (the axioms of Bob plus whatever axioms we need to do syntax and set theory in Meta-Bob) as follows: for each *atomic* predicate—say, "Glub(x)"—of Bob, we add as an axiom (y)[Ref("Glub" followed by "(" followed by x followed by ")," y) $\Leftrightarrow$ F(y)]. In words, "Glub(x)" refers to *y* if and only if Glub(*y*), and similarly for all the other atomic predicates of Bob. Note that there are only finitely many atomic predicates in what Tarski calls "formalized languages," and hence only finitely many of these axioms. These axioms are the *basis clauses* of the inductive definition.

Stage 3. We add further axioms recursively extending the definition of "Ref" to molecular formulas, for example, an axiom saying that if *x* is the result of writing the disjunction symbol "∨" between inscriptions *w* and *z*, then $\text{Ref}(x, y) \Leftrightarrow \text{Ref}(x, w) \vee \text{Ref}(x, z)$, and an axiom saying that if *x* is the result of writing the negation symbol "¬" before *w*, then $\text{Ref}(x, y) \Leftrightarrow \neg\text{Ref}(x, w)$.

And (important!) we add to the axioms the statement, duly formalized, that for all *w*, if *v* is a variable, and *w* is *z* preceded by an existential quantifier (E*v*), and *z* contains no free variables different from *v*, then $\{\text{Ref}(w,1) \Leftrightarrow (\text{E}x)\text{Ref}(z, x)\}$ & $\{(\text{Ref}(w, 0) \Leftrightarrow \neg(\text{E}x)(\text{Ref}(z, x)\}$. This amounts to adopting the convention that a *sentence* (a wff with no free variable) "refers to" 1 if it is true and to 0 if it isn't.

Note that even if Bob's primitive predicates were all monadic, Bob would in general still contain polyadic defined predicates, for example, "F(*x*) ∨ *y* = 0" and "F(*x*) & ¬F(*y*)"; therefore, we need a further clause in our inductive definition for existential quantification of a polyadic formula, but formulating such a clause requires more of Tarski's technique than we shall explain. Suffice it say that this technique involves constructing Ref as a relation between formulas and *sequences* (in fact, eventually constant infinite sequences) of objects.

Stage 4. Now comes the crucial stage. Given that "Ref" has been inductively defined, it is a straightforward application of techniques familiar to logicians from Frege on to turn the inductive definition of "Ref(*x*, *y*)" into an *explicit* definition of a two-place predicate, say, SAT(*y*, *x*) [read: "*y* satisfies *x*," employing Tarski's terminology][27] provided Meta-Bob has strong enough set theoretic axioms; if it doesn't, we just add them. And *voilà*, we have a predicate of Meta-Bob whose definition involves only the atomic predicates of Bob and (if necessary) the

---

27. Instead of speaking of a formula as referring to (a sequence of) objects, Tarski speaks of (the sequence of) objects as *satisfying* the formula; I have imitated Tarski's language here, which is why "Ref(*x*, *y*)" has suddenly become "SAT(*y*, *x*)." Note that "Ref(*x*, *y*)" gets dropped from the notation of Meta-Bob in the course of my "stages."

primitive predicates of our favorite set theory *but no nonlogical predicates that weren't already in Bob*—a predicate that *provably* satisfies all the clauses in the inductive definition of Ref![28]

Therefore, we can drop Ref from our list of primitive predicates, drop the axioms that contained it, and use "SAT(y, x)" instead of "Ref(x, y)," since we know that all the old axioms for Ref are theorems of Meta-Bob, once we simply replace "Ref(x, y)" with "SAT(y, x)." And again—*voilà!*—it can be verified that if we take FORM(x) to be "x is a wff with no free variables & SAT(1, x)," then for each sentence of Bob, the result of substituting it for s and its structural-descriptive name for "s*" in "FORM(s*) $\Leftrightarrow$ s" will be a theorem of Meta-Bob. Convention T is satisfied!

What Field Observed

What Field observed, and what I hoped to bring out clearly by breaking up the definition of SAT (Tarski's formal predicate for "satisfaction") into stages in the way I did, was that (1) the "truth predicate" [in the case of Bob, the predicate FORM(x)] is defined in terms of the "reference predicate" SAT, and (2) the construction can be said to *mimic* the process of defining truth in Bob in terms of reference in Bob (i.e., reference restricted to formulas of Bob); (3) reference in Bob (Field's "denotation") is defined—or rather SAT, a relation *coextensive* with the converse of reference in Bob is defined—by turning an inductive definition into an explicit definition by well-known means. Finally, (4) the basis clauses in the inductive definition "define" reference in the case of *atomic* (undefined) predicates or rather specify the *extension* of reference in the case of such predicates by a finite list of cases. From this, Field concluded that Tarski reduced reference to what Field called "primitive denotation" (denotation for atomic predicates) but that he failed to reduce "primitive denotation" to nonsemantical notions (which, on Field's reading of Tarski's article was Tarski's aim), but only *listed* the extensions of the primitive predicates. Thus, according to Field, what remains to be done after Tarski is to "naturalize" primitive denotation, that is, to define reference for atomic predicates in terms acceptable to

---

28. Note that inductive definition depends only on the logical and syntactical axioms we added, but not on any "semantical" axioms!

a materialist philosopher. A finite list of clauses such as "in Bob, 'w' followed by 'h' followed by 'i' followed by 't' followed be 'e' refers to all and only white objects" is not a reduction at all, let alone one acceptable to a "physicalist" like Field.

Philosophical Morals of the Above

(1) Apart from section l, which ends on a massively pessimistic note, there is no attempt in Tarski's "The Concept of Truth in Formalized Languages" to reduce any semantical notion to a nonsemantical notion (unless it be a failed attempt, which is what Field thought). What there is, is a definition of a predicate FORM(*x*) that is coextensive with "true in Bob," but one that defines a property the sentence "snow is white" has, for example, in a possible world in which snow is white and the word "white" means black! (This is so because nothing in the definition of FORM(*x*) refers to the use or meaning of expressions.) As a *conceptual analysis of "true,"* the predicate FORM(*x*) fails miserably.[29] People would not have had so much difficulty in grasping this undeniable fact if Tarski had titled his conception "The *Look No Semantics* Conception of Truth."[30] Of course, this is not to impugn the *mathematical* importance of the "material equivalence"—by which Tarski must mean the *coextensiveness*—of "true" (in the relevant language Bob) and the truth predicate [our FORM(*x*)] or the philosophical significance of Tarski's work, which can only be extracted if we are clear on what it did and what it did not accomplish.

(2) "Correspondence theory of truth" is the name traditionally given to theories of the form: "a statement [or thought or belief or proposition, etc., depending on the particular philosopher] is true if and only if the statement [or thought, etc.] corresponds to a fact [or to reality or to some appropriate piece of reality, depending again on the particular philosopher's metaphysical views]." The correspondence theory is discussed in section 1 of Tarski's article (where the T-schema [not Convention T!] is stated), but the section ends on a negative note about the whole project of clarifying the notion of truth in everyday language, as we noted

---

29. In 1953, Carnap suggested to me a way of meeting this objection. I describe Carnap's objection (which depended on defining Bob by Bob's "semantical rules") and show why it fails in Hilary Putnam, *Representation and Reality* (Cambridge, Mass.: MIT Press, 1988), 61–67.

30. I put it this way in "Comparison of Something with Something Else."

above. However, Convention T itself does not (as I have emphasized) contain the word "true." FORM(*x*) is a one-place predicate of Meta-Bob, and we have specified that Meta-Bob does not contain any words like "true" nor any words like "fact." Likewise, Convention T does not contain any words like "true" nor any words like "fact." Thus there is no way in which Meta-Bob, or Convention T, or the "truth predicate" FORM can even express the correspondence theory of truth.

(3) "Deflationary theory of truth" is the name given to the more recent, twentieth-century theory that *the notion of truth is wholly captured* by one or the other of the two following disquotation principles:

(*D*) To call a statement (or sometimes a "proposition," rarely a "sentence" as in Tarski's famous article) "true" is simply to affirm the statement.
  OR SOMETIMES,
(*D'*) The statement "*S is true*"[31] is equivalent to the statement *S*.

Since Convention T does not *mention* truth, as I have been emphasizing, it obviously does not state either *D* or *D'*. But it is plausible that it *presupposes D'* for the following reason: Tarski's reader is supposed to see that if all of the conditionals that are required to be theorems of Meta-Bob by Convention T *are* theorems—and *if we assume that the theorems of Meta-Bob are true, which cannot be taken for granted* because a mathematical theory may contain false statements without being inconsistent—then each sentence of the form

$$\text{FORM}(s^*) \Leftrightarrow s$$

is *true*—and, *using the T-Schema*

$$\text{true}(s^*) \Leftrightarrow s,$$

it follows that

$$\text{FORM}(s^*) \Leftrightarrow \text{true}(s^*).$$

Thus, it is *plausible* that the disquotation principle is presupposed by Tarski's claim that Convention T is a correct ("accurate," in the

---

31. A technical problem: in *D'* is *S* a variable over statements? Or is *D'* to be understood with some sort of systematic ambiguity? The literature discusses this problem extensively, and there are different proposals.

original Polish version) condition for the "material adequacy" of a formula like FORM(x) as a truth predicate for Bob. In any case, the idea of disquotation easily arises from a study of Tarski's great paper. But there is all the difference in the world between accepting a disquotation principle and accepting the claim that such a principle captures completely what one has to know about truth. The latter is the thesis of deflationism. I conclude that Tarski is not committed to *that* thesis any more than he is committed to the correspondence theory of truth.

(4) Just as it is plausible to see a disquotation principle as presupposed by Convention T, even if Tarski did not state one, it is plausible to see the fact that the *extension of "true in Bob" is determined by the extension of "denotes in Bob"* as driving the entire strategy of defining the desired truth predicate [FORM(x)] inductively in terms of a predicate [in our simplified version of Tarski, above, $SAT(y, x)$] that is constructed to have precisely the extension of the everyday language predicate "*x* refers *to y* in Bob."

In sum, and this is something I regard as of great importance, *Tarski's formal methods intuitively draw on and presuppose not just* one *property of truth, the T-schema, or disquotation, but on that property and the further property that the extension of "true" depends on the extension of "refers." The concepts of truth and of reference are intimately related, and his entire procedure exploits the relation, as Field saw in 1972.*

Realism Is Incompatible with Deflationism

If one says "Asteroids [or daisies or marsupials] exist," but one's account of what it is to *understand* these speech sounds (or if one writes it instead of saying it out loud, if one's account of what it is to understand such a string of symbols) does not mention any connection whatsoever between those "vocables" (or those "strings") and asteroids or daisies or marsupials or objects and properties in terms of which such entities can be described, then I, for one, fail to see how what one says can be understood in a realist way. This is a point I debated with Michael Devitt[32] as well as with Rorty,[33] and I will not repeat all that here. What follows is

---

32. See Hilary Putnam, "Comment on Michael Devitt," in Baghramian, *Reading Putnam*, 121–126.

33. See Hilary Putnam, "Richard Rorty on Reality and Justification," in *Rorty and His Critics*, ed. Robert Brandom (Oxford: Blackwell, 2000), 81–87.

addressed to a reader who "gets it" and agrees. Of course, a *nonrealist* can be a deflationist and simply refuse to understand sentences about such things in a realist way. For a logical positivist to know the meaning of a sentence is just to know its method of verification, and the method of verification is to be described in terms of tests *we* can perform.

Moreover, saying that certain sentences are *causally connected* to asteroids (or daisies or marsupials) isn't enough to capture the way in which truth-apt assertions about real objects relate to the world. If I say that there are marsupials in Australia, I intend my utterance to be related to marsupials and not to anything else that the event of my making that utterance may have been caused by, for example, textbooks or zoos. In short, when I say it, I am *referring* to marsupials, and that fact is not captured by pointing out that my saying it was *causally connected* to marsupials.

If this is often underappreciated by deflationists, it seems to me that missing it comes from missing the point with which I closed the previous section and will repeat here:

Tarski's formal methods intuitively draw on and presuppose not just one *property of truth, the T-schema, or disquotation, but on that property and the further property that the extension of "true" depends on the extension of "refers" (and on the possible extensions of "refers," if the logical vocabulary includes modal operators.[34] Tarski did not consider such languages.) The concepts of truth and of reference are intimately interrelated.*

If deflationists regularly fail to mention the interdependence of truth and reference, they do, however, recognize the need for some account of meaning or at least of the sameness of meaning. After all, I can speak of true sentences in a language that is not properly contained in my own language. The sentence " 'Schnee ist weiss' is true if and only if Schnee ist weiss" is not a well-formed sentence in either English or German. The standard form of disquotation in this case (a generalization of

---

34. If a modal primitive is added to the language, say the symbol ◊, then the appropriate clause will read: $\underline{a}$ satisfies ◊F just in case ◊($\underline{a}$ satisfies F). Here is a word example: take F(x) to be (Ey)(x loves y). Interpret ◊ as physical possibility (or, alternatively, sociological possibility), and take $\underline{a}$ to be Alice. Then "$\underline{a}$ satisfies ◊F" says that Alice satisfies "it is possible x loves somebody," "◊($\underline{a}$ satisfies F)" says that it is possible that Alice satisfies "x loves somebody," and these two formulas have the same truth condition, namely, that in some possible world there is a person whom Alice loves. In mathematical jargon, "satisfies" commutes with ◊. [In my view, "in some possible world there is" means that it is possible that there is a world in which there is; modal logic does not presuppose the actual existence of possible worlds.]

Tarski's T-schema) is to say that if I am using English (or a formalized version thereof) as a metalanguage (for a part of German that is free of semantical words and includes the sentence "Schnee ist weiss"), then the appropriate T-sentence is:

"Schnee ist weiss" is true in German if snow is white.

And more generally, for any sentence s in the part of German in question,

(T) "s" is true in German if . . .

where the three dots are to be replaced by the translation of the sentence s in English.

That the notion of translation is needed for disquotation and therefore needed by deflationists (since their thesis *is* that grasp of disquotation is all that is needed for an understanding of truth) is widely recognized. But what I have not seen discussed by deflationists, let alone taken seriously, is the thought that *translating sentences presupposes knowing what their descriptive constituents* refer *to*. It is an illusion that disquotation does not presuppose the relation of reference.

The idea that one can speak of translation as if it didn't involve reference can't, of course, just stem from verificationism, as it did in Carnap, although Horwich, a leading deflationist, once suggested that sameness of meaning is just sameness of "use" and coupled this with an explicitly verificationist account of "use." He wrote, "The communal disposition to use a word in a certain way should not be regarded as simply the disposition to treat certain sentences as definitely and permanently acceptable and others not. In addition, there are dispositions to sanction various levels of confidence [*cashed out as "betting behavior"*] in the truth of certain sentences—where the appropriate degrees of belief are *a function of observable circumstances*."[35] Degrees of confirmation were also identified with betting behavior by Carnap.

---

35. Paul Horwich, "Wittgenstein and Kripke on the Nature of Meaning," *Mind and Language* 2 (Summer 1990): 105–121 (emphasis added).

Field (even after his conversion to deflationism) is no verificationist. But given that Field was a student of Quine's (as well as of myself), I suspect that Quine's account of "radical translation" in *Word and Object* may well have influenced him, and in the next section I shall say why I think Quine's account of radical translation was mistaken (something Burge does in detail in chapter 7 of *Origins of Objectivity*).

Quine's Unrealistic Account of Linguistic Development and Translation

In Quine's view, originally spelled out in *Word and Object* and developed and sometimes modified subsequently (in ways that do not affect the criticisms that follow), the translator who has no prior knowledge of the semantics of the language she is trying to figure out and children who are learning their first language have nothing to go on except sounds that their informants (parents, in the case of the child) are disposed to produce in response to stimulations of their nerve endings (their "speech dispositions," a concept Quine takes from Skinner's behaviorist psychology, as chapter 1 of *Word and Object* makes clear). To describe one of those dispositions as, in Quine's famous example, "a disposition to say 'gavagai' when the speaker sees a rabbit," *as opposed to* "a disposition to say 'gavagai' when the speaker sees a collection of undetached rabbit parts" is regarded as an arbitrary imposition. The child, according to Quine's developmental account,[36] does not discriminate rabbits as opposed to undetached rabbit parts, or "rabbithood-exemplified," in any determinate way, and the linguist's assumption that her "jungle language" informant does so is likewise unwarranted.

It is easy to miss the fact that a very substantial position on the psychology of perception, child development, and language learning is presupposed by this Quinean account, one that supports Quine's whole indeterminacy thesis. As Burge points out, in Quine's picture the sciences of linguistics and psychology float free of connections with biological accounts of the relations between the basic needs and activities

---

36. W. V. Quine, "Speaking of Objects," *Proceedings and Addresses of the American Philosophical Association* 31 (1958): 5–22; reprinted in W. V. Quine, *Ontological Relativity and Other Essays* (New York: Columbia University Press, 1969), 1–25.

of animals and the ecological facts about their environments.[37] That picture also ignores psychological explanations of perception, which rely on biological accounts and feedback into them. No biological account describes the environment as containing undetached rabbit parts, and undetached rabbit parts do not figure in any scientific explanation in perceptual psychology either. When I say this, I am not turning my back on "liberal naturalism" and opting for "scientific naturalism"; I am rather opting for a *liberal naturalist understanding of what natural-scientific explanations are*, one that takes seriously what the natural sciences actually do, and does not require them to conform to "physicalist" scruples (by avoiding notions like representation). Although Quine may have abandoned logical positivism, his insistence in *Word and Object* that the account of "speech dispositions" begin with proximal stimuli ("nerve endings") and his view that children cannot be said to perceive objects until they have learned the apparatus of quantification are reminiscent of the positivist picture, in which a "constructional system" is used to interpret bare sense data. There *is* a difference between linguistic reference, which presupposes complex cognitive capacities, and primitive perceptual representation, but the idea that organisms cannot discriminate objects prior to acquiring those cognitive and linguistic capacities is misguided. Linguistic reference grows out of perceptual representation, as Burge rightly argues, and if we can accept that, we need not be frightened into denying that truth of linguistic representations is a form of *accurate representation*. Moreover, if we see reference as growing out of perceptual transactions between organisms and things in their environments, we also won't be tempted to deny that reference *is* a relation between words and things, as Sellars at times did. Deflationism about reference typically goes with deflationism about truth. If saying that representation is a relation between organisms (and states of organisms and, derivatively, bits of language) and real things, properties, and events is "representationalism," then representationalism is no sin!

Normativity in Ethics

When philosophers teach ethics courses, they naturally emphasize the places at which the major theories and thinkers disagree. Less often do

---

37. Burge, *Origins of Objectivity*, 211–212.

they try to see how insights from different schools of thought can be combined. Yet it is especially important to do that in ethics because when the subject matter is *how to live*, as John Dewey emphasized in his sections of Dewey and Tufts's monumental *Ethics*,[38] no one school has a monopoly on insight. Utilitarianism is inadequate as an account of our ethical lives, but it does identify a question that all too often needs be put to someone who proposes a significant rule of action, law, or policy: "Would it contribute to the satisfaction of more people's desires or interests than the alternatives?" At the same time, pragmatists such as Dewey point out that desires and interests may be partial and selfish and that even when they are not, they may be based on bad reasoning or bad information. Desires and interests are not simply *givens* whose satisfaction needs to be maximized (as too many economists have assumed); they need to be subjected to intelligent and informed criticism.[39] And Kantians have long pointed out that what satisfies the desires and interests of even a substantial majority may be wrong because it tramples on the rights of a minority.

Although, I don't agree with Scanlon's claim that morality can be *founded* on the single principle that "an act is wrong if its performance under the circumstances would be disallowed by any set of principles for the general regulation of behavior that no one could reasonably reject as a basis for informed, unforced general agreement,"[40] I do see that principle as a laudable attempt to state what is right in Kant's categorical imperative in a naturalistic spirit—that is, to state it in a way that does not depend on Kant's untenable belief that respect for the moral law has a "supersensible" source (as contrasted to our "inclinations" that have a natural source). Like Dewey,[41] I see the categorical

---

38. John Dewey, *Ethics*, vol. 5: *1908*, in *The Middle Works, 1899–1924*, ed. Jo Ann Boydston (Carbondale: Southern Illinois University Press, 1978), 283–284.

39. See Hilary Putnam, "Dewey's Central Insight," in *John Dewey's Educational Philosophy in International Perspective: A New Democracy for the Twenty-First Century*, ed. L. A. Hickman and Giuseppe Spadafora (Carbondale: Southern Illinois University Press, 2009), 7–21.

40. I criticize that idea in "Capabilities and Two Ethical Theories," collected in Hilary Putnam, *Philosophy in an Age of Science: Physics, Mathematics, and Skepticism*, ed. by Mario De Caro and David Macarthur (Cambridge, Mass.: Harvard University Press, 2012), 299–311. The quotation from Scanlon is from *What We Owe to Each Other* (Cambridge, Mass.: Harvard University Press, 1998).

41. Dewey, *Ethics*, 283–284.

imperative (as well as Scanlon's principle, just quoted) as "a method for realizing the full meaning of a proposed course of action,"[42] but not as the *foundation* on which morality rests. Morality rests on a complex and evolving set of human needs and interests, but those needs and interests are neither biological givens nor the product of mere contingency. As long as free inquiry and discussion survive, they will continue to be forced to meet the test of rational scrutiny, to answer the demand for good reasons.

What makes Scanlon's naturalism clearly a liberal naturalism is the willingness to use the notion of a *reason* without any accompanying "naturalization project," and I am delighted that he chose to follow *What We Owe to Each Other* with a set of Locke Lectures entitled *Being Realistic about Reasons* devoted to the legitimacy and importance of doing just that.

In Closing

Part of what I have been saying might be summarized thus: the fact that something—perceptual representation or reference or truth or intentionality or reasons—can't be "naturalized" in the way that "physicalists" demand doesn't make those things "non-natural" or "queer" or suspiciously close to "supernatural." It is true that the notion of a reason, for example, is not the subject matter of a special science, but that notion is presupposed by all science as well as by fields like history and politics and criticism (including philosophical criticism) that are not sciences, because in all of them one has to decide what there is *reason* to consider, and "elegance" figures in the *reasons* scientists give for testing certain theories at all. They are not scientific notions, but the activity of science presupposes a *reasonable* command of them.[43]

---

42. Concerning the Categorical Imperative, Dewey wrote, "As a method (though not of course the only one) of realizing the *full meaning* of a proposed course of action, nothing could be better than asking ourselves how we should like to be committed forever to its principle: how we should like to have others committed to it, and to treat us according to it? . . . In short, by generalizing a purpose, we make its *general* character evident" (*Ethics*, 283–284).

43. See Hilary Putnam, "The Philosophers of Science's Evasion of Values," in *The Collapse of the Fact-Value Dichotomy* (Cambridge, Mass.: Harvard University Press, 2002), 135–145.

Science depends on what is not fully scientific at every point. And both pragmatists and Wittgensteinians have rightly criticized the bad habit of turning what are sometimes useful distinctions into untenable dualisms, and that includes the dichotomy between normative and descriptive language (a dichotomy that our thick ethical concepts—including such ancient concepts as *brave* and *wise*—leap over without the slightest sign of embarrassment) and also includes the dichotomy between science and nonscience itself. One can learn from pragmatists and Wittgensteinians and philosophers of so many other kinds without becoming a card-carrying member of any philosophical sect. And that is something I have always tried to do in my philosophical life.

2

On Bernard Williams's "Philosophy as a Humanistic Discipline"

$\mathcal{I}_N$ "Philosophy as a Humanistic Discipline,"[1] Bernard Williams has misunderstood my criticisms of his position, and thus ends up talking past me. Because I hope we can soon have an interchange of views that is not marred by misunderstandings and mutual misinterpretations, I want to say where I think I have been misunderstood and what my criticism actually was.

I shall quote and discuss several passages in William's lecture. Williams writes,

> In the course of Putnam's book (which contains a chapter called "Bernard Williams and the Absolute Conception of the World"), I myself am identified as someone who "views physics as giving us the ultimate metaphysical truth." Now I have never held any such

1. Bernard Williams, "Philosophy as a Humanistic Discipline," *Philosophy* 75 (2000): 477–496. My criticisms of Williams, to some of which he replies in this lecture, were contained in "Objectivity and the Science / Ethics Dichotomy," collected in my *Realism with a Human Face*, ed. James Conant (Cambridge, Mass.: Harvard University Press, 1990), 163–178; "Bernard Williams and the Absolute Conception of the World," a chapter in my *Renewing Philosophy* (Cambridge, Mass.: Harvard University Press, 1992), 80–107; and "Pragmatism and Relativism: Universal Values and Traditional Ways of Life," collected in *Words and Life*, ed. James Conant (Cambridge, Mass.: Harvard University Press, 1994), 182–197. [Unfortunately, Bernard Williams's demise in 2003 put an unanticipated end to our debates. Note added on July 15, 2015.]

views, and I agree with Putnam in rejecting it. However, I have entertained the idea that science might describe the world "as it is in itself," that is to say, give a representation of it which is to the largest possible extent independent of the local perspectives or idiosyncrasies of enquirers, a representation of the world, as I put it, "as it is anyway."[2]

Since I did not mean by "the ultimate metaphysical truth" any more than "a description of the world as it is anyway," there is already a misunderstanding at work here. The reason I spoke of physics in the passage Williams quotes, and not more vaguely of "science" as Williams does here, is that Williams himself has elsewhere said explicitly that the notion of an "absolute conception" does not "look too pale" because we have a conception of "what an adequate physics might look like."[3] I did make—and will go on making, until and unless Williams himself corrects me—one further assumption: I take Williams's position to be that the description of the world in terms of its nonperspectival properties is a complete description of all of the world. It isn't, that is to say, that an exhaustive description of the world in terms of all the "absolute" properties would only describe a part of the world, and there is another part, the "perspectival part," that would still remain to be described. This means that if a semantical statement, for example, "John referred to object X," describes a "perspectival fact"—say, the fact that in such-and-such a perspective, John referred to object X—then that whole fact, including the perspective and John and the object X and the relation between them—must somehow appear in the "absolute conception." And the absolute description is envisaged as being given in terms of the fundamental magnitudes of physics! Thus, it seemed to me that Williams does need to somehow reduce semantical facts to purely physical facts if he is not to become an outright denier of the reality of the semantical (an "eliminationist," in the jargon of contemporary analytic philosophy).[4] And in his book *Descartes: The Project of Pure Enquiry*

2. Williams, "Philosophy as a Humanistic Discipline," 481.

3. Bernard Williams, *Descartes: The Project of Pure Enquiry* (Harmondsworth, United Kingdom: Penguin, 1978), 247.

4. In current parlance, an "eliminationist" (Paul Churchland is the paradigm case) holds that propositional attitudes (e.g., belief) and semantic relations (e.g., reference) don't exist, and that the idea that they do is a superstition (Churchland has compared it to belief in

he did suggest, if I do not misread him, that eliminationism with respect to the semantical is probably the right line to take. For he wrote,

> If the various sorts of considerations [Quinian and Davidsonian
> considerations—*HP*] which have been summarily sketched here
> are correct, then we have to give up not just dualism but the belief
> in the determinacy of the mental. These considerations converge
> on the conclusion that there are no fully determinate contents of
> the world which are its psychological contents.[5]

Indeterminacy of psychological contents (in the sense of Quine and
Davidson) is indeterminacy of the semantical. And that indeterminacy,
if their arguments are accepted, must be far reaching indeed. (Quine
says, for example, that there is no fact of the matter as to whether
"Tabitha" refers to his cat Tabitha or to "the whole cosmos minus the
cat."[6])

It is true that Davidson, while giving full credit to Quine for the arguments that allegedly establish "indeterminacy," says that the extent
of indeterminacy is much reduced in his theory by his willingness to
make "a more far reaching application of the principle of charity" than
Quine.[7] (Perhaps this is the reason that Williams wrote "no fully determinate contents" and not simply "no determinate contents.") But
charity is a maxim of interpretation—that is, of translation into the in-
terpreter's home language—and it cannot bestow any additional deter-
minacy on the home language itself. It isn't as if one could really argue
that reference is partially, even if not "fully," determinate, except in the

---

witches, or in phlogiston). Compare "Activation Vectors vs. Propositional Attitudes: How
the Brain Represents Reality," in Churchland's *On the Contrary: Critical Essays, 1987–1997*
(Cambridge, Mass.: MIT Press, 1998). [In my view, Quine's claim that reference is indeterminate to the extent that there is no fact of the matter as to which object "Tabitha" refers to
is just eliminationism under another name.] I criticize the cited essay of Churchland's in
"Truth, Activation Vectors, and Possession Conditions for Concepts," *Philosophy and Phenomenological Research* 52, no. 2 (1992): 431–447. Note that eliminationism is very different
from reductionism.

5. Williams, *Descartes*, 300.

6. W. V. Quine, *The Pursuit of Truth* (Cambridge, Mass.: Harvard University Press,
1990), 33.

7. Donald Davidson, *Inquiries into Truth and Interpretation* (Oxford: Clarendon Press,
1984), 228.

sense (which even Rorty could agree with) of "determinate relative to a translation scheme"). That the vocabulary of physics (or a perfected future physics) is rich enough to give a complete description of the world is the view I (perhaps misleadingly) described by saying that Williams views physics as giving us the ultimate metaphysical truth. Indeed, the view that any single vocabulary could suffice to give a complete description of the world does seem to me a metaphysical fantasy.[8] But if the word "metaphysical" is what is leading to misunderstandings, I am willing to omit it.

That it did lead to misunderstandings is evident, I think, when Williams writes,

> [Putnam] supposes that the idea of an absolute conception of the world must ultimately be motivated by the contradictory and incoherent aim of describing the world without describing it: as he puts it, we cannot divide language into two parts, a part that describes the world "as it is anyway" and a part that describes our conceptual contribution . . . My idea was not that you could conceptualize the world without concepts.[9]

I never thought that this was Williams's idea; I have far too much respect for Williams's intelligence to charge him with such an obvious blunder. Nor did the assertion he quotes ("we cannot divide language into two parts, a part that describes the world 'as it is anyway' and a part that describes our conceptual contribution") accuse him of making that blunder. To think, as I said Williams thinks, that there is a part of language that describes the world "as it is anyway" is to accuse him of thinking that there are concepts that do this, and not to accuse him of thinking that we can describe the world "as it is anyway" without using concepts (whatever describing without using concepts might mean). Our disagreement is over whether it makes sense to think that the concepts of physics do this (assuming, as I said I will continue to assume until Williams corrects me, that the description of the world in terms of its "absolute" properties is supposed to be a description of all of the world.)

8. See my "From Quantum Mechanics to Ethics and Back Again," in *Reading Putnam*, ed. Maria Baghramian (Abingdon, United Kingdom: Routledge, 2013), 19–36, esp. 28–30.

9. Williams, "Philosophy as a Humanistic Discipline," 482.

Putnam's basic argument against the idea of the absolute conception is that semantic relations are normative, and hence could not figure in any purely scientific conception. But describing the world involves deploying terms that have semantic relations to it; hence, it seems, Putnam's conclusion that the absolute conception is supposed to describe the world without describing it.[10]

I have already said that there was no such "Putnam's conclusion." Also, my basic argument was not that semantic relations are normative (although there is a sense in which they are), "and hence could not figure in any purely scientific conception," but that Williams himself denies that semantic relations are determinate (I have already quoted him on this point). But if semantic relations are "perspectival" in the sense of holding only relative to some scheme of interpretation or other, and if [as Quine claims] there is no fact of the matter as to whether any scheme of interpretation that correctly predicts the stimulus-meanings of whole sentences is more right than any other [or, in Davidson's case, whether any collection of reference-assignments that comes out right on the truth-conditions of whole sentences is more right than any other], then "absoluteness"—a notion which Williams employs semantical terms to define—is also "perspectival" in the sense of holding only relative to our choice of one scheme of interpretation [that satisfies the constraint] or another. I shall spell this point out in more detail in a moment. But, broadly speaking, my argument was that unless "the absolute conception of the world" is more than our projection, it cannot do the metaphysical work (of supporting a sense in which scientific truth is less "perspectival" than, say, semantical truth) that Williams wants it to do. Williams, I claimed, needs an absolute notion of "absoluteness." But his denial that semantic relations could figure in any purely scientific conception—not mine—leaves Williams with only a perspectival notion of absoluteness, not an absolute one. As I put it in the chapter to which he refers, "Is Williams saying that it is just our local perspective that there is an absolute conception? Even Rorty might be able to agree with that."[11]

A few words more on Williams's claim that "Putnam's basic argument against the idea of the absolute conception is that semantic rela-

---

10. Williams, "Philosophy as a Humanistic Discipline," 482–483.
11. Putnam, *Renewing Philosophy*, 101.

tions are normative, and hence could not figure in any purely scientific conception."

I myself have never affirmed or denied that there could be a "scientific conception" of semantic relations. As I have explained elsewhere,[12] I think the terms "science" and "scientific" are much too vague for that question to make sense. But I take it that what Williams means by the phrase "purely scientific conception" here is "absolute conception," or, perhaps, conception that is at least a good sketch of what an absolute conception might be. (He says, and I have already quoted this, that we already have a notion of what an "adequate physics" might be, and that this fleshes out our understanding of what an "absolute conception" could be; he has also said that "the world itself has only primary qualities.")[13] Thus it seems clear that Williams himself provides all the premises I needed to argue that, on his own view, semantic relations do not figure at all in the absolute conception. Indeed, in the lecture to which I am replying he wrote, "I take it as obvious that any attempt to reduce semantic relations to concepts of physics is doomed." So I do not see why references to my view that "semantic relations are normative," and the expression "Let us grant for the sake of the argument the principle, which is certainly disputable, that if semantic relations are normative, an account of them cannot figure in the absolute conception," come into Williams's discussion at all. Given what Williams says about the absolute conception (e.g., that it contains only primary qualities—and, presumably, what is definable in terms of primary qualities using the apparatus of mathematical physics), and what he says about semantic relations, it follows from Williams's premises—not just from mine—that "an account of them cannot figure in the absolute conception." And given his characterization of the absolute conception, it is not hard to see that he is right. What would an account of a semantical relation in the language of mathematical physics (or in terms of "primary qualities") be?

It is, of course, true that I believe that semantic relations are normative, not in the sense of believing that semantical statements are value judgments, which would be absurd, but in the sense (and this far I agree

12. Compare with my "The Idea of Science," *Midwest Studies in Philosophy* 15 (1990): 57–64; collected in my *Words and Life*, 481–491.

13. Williams, *Descartes*, 247.

with Davidson) that there is no criterion for the correctness of statements to the effect that words have either the same meaning or the same reference above and beyond reasonable interpretative practice. Judgments of reference and meaning, I have claimed, essentially involve judgments of reasonableness; and the idea of reducing judgments of reasonableness to exact science (in the sense in which mathematical physics is an exact science) are nothing but scientistic fantasies.[14] Certainly this is controversial, but it also is something on which, unless I misunderstand him completely, Williams and I agree.

And a word to explain my statement that Williams employs semantical terms to define "absoluteness." Williams's basic thought experiment is the following: imagine that there are various tribes of intelligent extraterrestrials who (independently of us, and without even knowing of our existence) investigate the world scientifically. What they would converge in believing—or better, what they would converge in believing not for accidental reasons, but because it is the way things in fact are independently of what we think or believe—is the absolute conception. [This is, roughly, Williams's definition of "absolute conception."][15] Now "A and B converge in believing C" means that, from a certain point on, A and B both believe C. But if there is a fact of the matter as to what the "psychological contents" (e.g., the beliefs) of A and B are only relative to a scheme of interpretation, then there is a fact of the matter as to whether A and B converge in believing C (or anything else, for that matter) only relative to a scheme of interpretation. "Converge" is a semantical term.

I now turn to a different issue—quite possibly the real issue between us. Williams writes,

So why does Putnam assume, as he obviously does, that if there were to be an absolute conception of the world, philosophy would have to be part of it? I doubt that he was simply thrown by the

---

14. I have argued this in a number of places, most recently in the *Threefold Cord: Mind, Body and World* (New York: Columbia University Press, 1999), 119–125, and in "Aristotle's Mind and the Contemporary Mind," in Demetra Sfendoni-Mentzou, Jagdish Hattiangadi, and D. M. Johnston, eds., *Aristotle and Contemporary Science* (New York: Peter Lang, 2000), 7–28.

15. Compare Bernard Williams's *Ethics and the Limits of Philosophy* (London: Routledge, 1985), 136.

Hegelian implications of the word "absolute," with their implication that if there is absolute knowledge, then philosophy possesses it. What perhaps he does think is the conjunction of two things: first that philosophy is as good as it gets, and is in no way inferior to science, and, second, that if there were an absolute conception of the world, a representation of it which was maximally independent of perspective, that would be better than more perspectival or locally conditioned representations of the world. Now the first of these assumption is, as it were, half true; although philosophy is worse than natural science at some things, such as discovering the nature of the galaxies (or, if I was right about the absolute conception, representing the world as it is in itself), it is far better than natural science at other things, for instance making sense of what we are trying to do in our intellectual activities. But the second assumption I have ascribed to Putnam, that if there were an absolute conception, it would somehow be better than more perspectival representations—that is simply false. Even if it were possible to give an account of the world that was minimally perspectival, it would not be particularly serviceable to us for many of our purposes, such as making sense of our intellectual or other activities, or indeed in getting on with most of those activities. For those purposes—in particular, in seeking to understand ourselves—we need concepts and explanations which are rooted in out more local practices, our culture and our history, and these cannot be replaced by concepts which we might share with very different investigators of the world.[16]

To take the second of the two assumptions that Williams ascribes to me first, I don't think I ever assumed that "if there were an absolute conception of the world, a representation of it which was maximally independent of perspective, that would be better than more perspectival or locally conditioned representations of the world." And as for the

---

16. Williams, "Philosophy as a Humanistic Discipline," 483–484. Williams continues there: "The slippery word 'we' here means not the inclusive 'we' which brings together as a purely abstract gathering any beings with whom human beings might conceivably communicate about the nature of the world. It means a contrastive 'we,' that is to say, humans as contrasted with other possible beings; and in the case of many human practices, it may of course mean groupings smaller than humanity as a whole."

supposed first assumption, "that philosophy is as good as it gets, and is in no way inferior to science"—that is at best misleadingly put. But let me explain.

The two sorts of judgments that were chiefly at issue in "Bernard Williams and the Absolute Conception of the World" were (1) semantical judgments, and (2) ethical judgments. My claim that Williams himself needs an absolute conception of absoluteness, not a perspectival one, refers to semantical judgments.[17] I take it that when he speaks of "philosophy" in the long passage that I quoted, he is counting both sorts of judgments as part of "philosophy." Confining attention here to the former sort, the question becomes: why, if I was not making the two assumptions attributed to me, did I assume semantical statements must be "absolute" if Williams's view is to work?

I think I already answered this above, but it may make matters clearer if I now discuss the assumption that I am supposed to make "that philosophy is as good as it gets, and is in no way inferior to science." Consider a statement that might be part of the absolute conception, namely, that the sun is approximately 93 million miles from the earth. (Of course, it couldn't be referred to as "the sun" and "the earth" in the absolute conception; but the same problem arises with any example I might give—and it is a problem for Williams, not for me, I believe.[18]) And consider the semantical statement (which I take to be part of what Williams here calls "philosophy") that when I just asked you to consider that statement, I was using "the earth" and "the sun" to refer to a planet and the star around which it revolves, respectively. What I believe is that the semantical statement states a fact—the fact that the words "the sun" and "the earth" bear a semantical relation to two things that are not marks and noises and do not consist of marks and noises—which is just as much an objective fact as the fact that the sun is approximately 93 million miles from the earth.

I am unable to make coherent sense of Williams's notion of a "perspectival" truth, but since he seems to depend on Quine and Davidson

17. I discuss what Williams says about ethics in *Ethics without Ontology* (Cambridge, Mass.: Harvard University Press, 2004), 122–129.

18. Having gone Davidsonian, Williams cannot avail himself of the solution that "the earth" and "the sun" are rigid designators and not descriptions in these judgments!

for his view that "psychological contents" (and hence meaning and reference) are not "absolute," let us see how this statement fares on their respective philosophical views. In Quine's view, to say that "the earth" refers to a certain planet is "parochial" in the sense that (1) the term "the earth" can be mapped on infinitely many different things via what Quine calls "proxy functions," and (2) each of the resulting mappings is as entitled to be regarded as "the" relation of reference as any other. Of course, each of the infinitely many resulting models of my language is such that (in the corresponding model of my metalanguage) the sentence " 'the earth' refers to the earth" is true; but that doesn't mean that there is a fact of the matter as to which object the term "the earth" in the above statement refers to (just as there is no fact of the matter as to which object "Tabitha" refers to, even though " 'Tabitha' refers to Tabitha" remains true no matter what proxy function we choose). It is only relative to a "translation scheme" that I am talking about the earth at all. And in Davidson's account of reference, the same thing happens, as I have already noted, notwithstanding his claim that his greater willingness to appeal to charity "reduces" indeterminacy.[19]

There is an important difference between Quine and Davidson (but I do not see how Williams will be able to take advantage of it). Davidson does think that whole sentences have determinate truth conditions, and truth, for Davidson, is not simply disquotational (as it is for Quine). It is not that Davidson defines "true"; famously, he holds that it is a simple and clear idea that needs no definition. But in his view there is a connection between my sentence "The earth is 93 million miles from the sun" and the world external to language, one that is captured precisely by the truth condition for my sentence. And to be a thinker at all, according to Davidson, I have to have such notions as "holds true" and "is true"; otherwise, I cannot even form concepts. So Davidson's view implies that all those extraterrestrial investigators that Williams hypothesizes in his thought experiment must have the notion of truth; that there is a difference between a false sentence and a true one is something they must recognize from the word "go." So "true" would seem to belong to the absolute conception—unless the reason they converge

---

19. Davidson, *Essays on Truth and Interpretation* (Oxford: Clarendon Press, 1984), 221–240.

on this belief isn't that there is "anyway" a difference between a false sentence and a true one. But I hope that will not be Williams's way out (the seas of language would be too high for me to sail, in that case). In sum, it isn't a question of "philosophy" (semantics, in this case) being better or worse than physics; it is simply the case, I am arguing, that if physics is to be "absolute" in Williams's sense, then our talk about physical entities had better refer—had better objectively refer. And so at least one semantical notion—"refer," or if you believe Davidson, "true"—had better be "absolute." For Quine's version of perspectivalism with respect to the semantical utterly guts Quine's so-called robust realism of any content that Richard Rorty would have any reason to object to.[20]

Isn't this an objection to Davidson as much as to Williams? In a way it is. For, given Davidson's insistence that experience has only a causal and no justificatory role with respect to our beliefs, I do not think Davidson really does have a satisfactory answer to McDowell's charge that it is unintelligible, in Davidson's picture, how sentences do have determinate truth conditions.[21] But here I have only been concerned to argue that if Davidson has an answer, that answer depends on a kind of realism with respect to the semantical concept of truth that seems incompatible with Williams's identification of the "absolute" with the physics of "primary qualities."

I said that I discuss Williams on ethics in another place. But just to avoid misunderstandings, let me say this much here: of course there could be beings whose lives were such that our ethics was simply inapplicable to them. Very likely, they couldn't even find our ethical notions intelligible. But I don't believe (1) that ethical notions are, in general, descriptions (so the dichotomy that seems to be implicit in Williams's discussions—"absolute" description of objects in terms of their primary qualities or just a "perspective" on such objects—seems to me to leave out of account a huge range of judgments that are objective but not descriptions (not even "perspectival" ones), including all purely mathematical judgments); and (2) the fact that not every creature might need

---

20. I argue this in detail in "A Comparison of Something with Something Else," collected in *Realism with a Human Face*, 330–350.

21. John McDowell, *Mind and World* (Cambridge, Mass.: Harvard University Press, 1994), 129–161.

a certain concept doesn't, I would argue, imply that judgments involving that concept are only true in the "social world" of the creatures who do need that concept. But these are views that I have defended elsewhere.[22]

22. Although I disagree with some of Wittgenstein's views about mathematics, that mathematics is not a *description* (e.g., of intangible and necessarily existing "mathematical objects") is something I have long agreed with. See my "Mathematics without Foundations," collected in my *Mathematics, Matter and Method*, vol. 1 of *Philosophical Papers* (Cambridge: Cambridge University Press, 1979), 43–59, and my "On Wittgenstein's Philosophy of Mathematics," *Proceedings of the Aristotelian Society, Supplementary Volumes* 70 (1996): 243–264. I criticize the inference from the fact that a particular ethical concept is peculiar to a certain society and reflects that society's needs and interests to the conclusion that what is said with the aid of that concept is only true "in that social world" in "Pragmatism and Relativism: Universal Values and Traditional Ways of Life," in *Words and Life*, 189–196.

3

What Evolutionary Theory
Doesn't Tell Us about Ethics

$\mathcal{P}$ERHAPS, there has to be a skeptic at every academic conference. I fear that today, it is my turn to play that not altogether enviable role, for I shall defend the view that the answer to the question to which the conference for which the present chapter was written was devoted, namely "to what extent *can* we understand the roots and complexity of ethical judgments from a Darwinian perspective?" is "Not very much." But first, a couple of caveats.

If the reference to "moral sentiment" in the title of the book from which this chapter derives includes minimally conceptualized emotions that are relevant to ethics,[1] that is, certain emotions that have not yet become entangled with concepts that have a complex cultural role and a complex cultural history—emotions such as spontaneous sympathy—then it is indeed plausible that evolutionary theory can tell us something about them. It is also quite plausible that the origin of altruistic behaviors is something that evolutionary theory can shed light on. But one thing I would like to do today is to show you how far short explanations of altruistic behavior and of sympathy (as manifested in, for example, groups of apes) fall of dealing with what

1. Hilary Putnam, Susan Neimann, and Jeffey Schloss, eds., *Understanding Moral Sentiments from a Darwinian Perspective: An Exploration of the Roots and Complexity of Ethical Judgment* (New Brunswick, N.J.: Transaction, 2014).

we have come to call *ethics*. (Of course, I do not deny that sympathy and altruistic behaviors, even if they do not *amount to* ethics all by themselves, are among the *preconditions* for the complex institution that we call ethics. Indeed, they are probably among the preconditions for the complex institution that we call *science*, and for the complex institution that we call *government*—perhaps for all complex human institutions.)

I speak of "what we have come to call *ethics*,"[2] because my claim is that ethics is something with a long cultural history. Ethics has developed and changed throughout recorded history (and doubtless had a prehistory that is much longer than recorded history). I know, of course, that stressing the role that culture plays in producing what we call "ethics" is often considered tantamount to endorsing "moral relativism" or even "nihilism"; that is, it is considered to entail that there is no objective rightness or wrongness to ethical judgments, but that, I believe, is a mistake. That ethics has a cultural and not only an evolutionary history, that it underwent a long process of development, and that it wasn't something that was "fixed in our genes" from the beginning does not by itself imply anything about either the rationality or the objectivity of ethical judgments.

To illustrate what I mean by the "cultural history" of ethics, I will offer a much-too-brief account of a few moments in the development of Western ethics; ideally, one would wish to consider also the history of Chinese ethics over the same period of time, the history of Indian ethics, and so on. (In *The Idea of Justice*,[3] Amartya Sen draws on the history of Indian ethics at a number of places.) At any rate, the term "ethics" in the West assumes something like its present meaning with Aristotle's lectures, particularly the ones written up by his students and preserved for us as the *Nicomachean Ethics*. Although Aristotelian ethics is still relevant today and one of the leading approaches among Anglophone ethicists, called "virtue ethics," acknowledges Aristotle as its forefather, there are many ways in which this concept of ethics is very different from post-Enlightenment ethics.

---

2. I shall not distinguish, as some theorists do, between "ethics" and "morals"; indeed, "*moralis*" functioned for Latin ethicists, such as Cicero who introduced it, as simply the *translation* of the Greek "*ethika*."

3. Amartya Sen, *The Idea of Justice* (Cambridge, Mass.: Harvard University Press, 2009).

Aristotelian ethics is considered to be a form of "virtue ethics" because the central concern is to identify "virtues," that is, traits that we should wish citizens of a political community (in Aristotle's time, a Greek *polis*) to possess, both because those traits are good for the community and because they are seen as admirable in themselves, not to formulate "rules" or "maxims" of conduct. It is noteworthy that "altruism" is *not* explicitly listed as one of the virtues, although public-spiritedness (which is not exactly the same thing by any means) is highly valued. Indeed, insofar as the Greeks saw something we might see as "altruism" as a virtue, they certainly did not conceive of it in the way in which, for example, Marc Hauser seems to conceive of it in the primate experiments he describes in *Moral Minds*,[4] that is, in the Kantian-cum-Rawlsian way, according to which the "altruistic" person (or animal) is disposed to act cooperatively and beneficially toward others, regardless of their social ranks. It would be an understatement to say that there is very little said in Aristotelian thought about showing "altruism" toward one's *slaves*. (We do, of course, find the usual slave-holders' paternalistic claim that those who are slaves by nature are better off being slaves; and perhaps, Hauser would consider this an expression of altruism.) On the other hand, both theoretical intelligence and practical intelligence (*sophrosyne*) are important virtues for Greek thought. Note that, while we do not consider theoretical intelligence a *moral* virtue at all, it certainly is one for both Plato and Aristotle. It is considered a part of the highest form of human flourishing, and human flourishing is a central topic of Greek ethics. By "sophrosyne" is meant the sort of discriminating intelligence that enables one not simply to follow rules "mechanically," but to discern what is appropriate to a particular situation. It is not surprising that in societies that frequently found themselves at war, and where all the males were expected to defend the *polis* in armed combat when necessary, the "manly" virtue of *courage* (carefully distinguished by Plato and Aristotle from foolhardiness, or mere fearlessness) was regarded as a central virtue. *Moderation* was also a central virtue, *prudence* was a central virtue, and for Aristotle and Plato and the Greek and Roman moralists that came

---

4. Marc Hauser, *Moral Minds: How Nature Designed Our Universal Sense of Right and Wrong* (New York: Ecco, 2006). I prescind from the problems that surfaced about Professor Hauser's research.

after them, knowing what *the good life* consists in, particularly knowing that the highest goods in life are definitely *not* the accumulation of wealth, fame, or sensual pleasure, were *the* central topics.

Fast-forwarding more than two millennia and coming to the Enlightenment, we find that *equality* has become a central topic.[5] The great historical changes that culminated in the American and French Revolutions were influenced by the idea of government as a "social contract" into which all the citizens enter, and after those revolutions, it eventually became the dominant model in the West (and powerfully influenced such leaders as Sun Yat-sen and Mahatma Gandhi in the East as well). It is true, of course, that as late as World War I, many of the leading states of Europe were still monarchies, albeit "constitutional monarchies"; nonetheless, the idea that a just government rests on the consent of the governed has become the dominant moral-political idea in the West and, at least at the level of lip service, in the world.

If we look more closely at the process by which democratic and egalitarian values acquired their present centrality, we can also see that changes in epistemology, many of them connected with changes in our understanding of how the natural sciences should proceed, played a large role in changing our conceptions of ethics.

What I have in mind is this: according to Aristotle—and Aristotle was the most influential philosopher of science for almost two millennia—science reveals necessary truths about the world. Aristotle indeed valued observation, and he even spoke of "induction." But, in the end, observation and induction are to lead us to necessary truths, and necessary truths, once properly perceived, are supposed to be "apodictic," unrevisable. This idea was, of course, challenged by empiricists from the seventeenth century on. In our own time, the overthrow of the idea of apodictic truth was part of the overthrow of the analytic–synthetic dichotomy, and more broadly of the a priori–a posteriori dichotomy, that Quine deserves so much credit for.

Why do I mention equality, democracy, and the a priori–a posteriori dichotomy virtually in the same breath? The reason is this: as early as Aristotle and Plato, the question of the equality or inequality of men

---

5. In this connection, see my Spinoza Lectures, "Enlightenment and Pragmatism," collected in my *Ethics without Ontology* (Cambridge, Mass.: Harvard University Press, 2004), 89–129.

and women, particularly the question whether women should be the *political* equals of men, was one about which there was disagreement. In his *Republic*, Plato famously argued[6] that women should be eligible to be "Guardians," that is, members of the ruling elite of his ideal state. Aristotle, however, "justified" the prejudices of his time (and his "justification" was widely accepted—by men, of course—for more than two thousand years) by arguing that women should not be eligible because they lacked the higher form of intelligence, intellectual *nous*. Today, such a claim would be regarded as an empirical claim and as a claim that has been falsified. But in Aristotle's time and after, it was accepted (by men!) as something more or less self-evident. Originally, this "justification" was accepted (by those men who saw the need for a justification) largely on Aristotle's authority, and eventually it came to be regarded as one of those self-evident truths that reason simply comes to perceive after appropriate examination of the phenomena. And once a supposed truth about nature had achieved that status in ancient and medieval science, it was viewed as unnecessary and inappropriate to look for "evidence" for or against.

If the whole history of ethics were simply a history of different "codes" of conduct supported by claims of the "superiority" or "inferiority" of different groups of people, or the "superiority or "inferiority" of different ways of life, *that were not themselves subject to rational challenge*, then it could indeed be argued that the fact that ethical codes are cultural products supports "ethical relativism," or even what Alex Rosenberg has called "nihilism," but that argument goes too fast. For with the Enlightenment came not only the valorization of equality but also the valorization of the new post-Galilean science. And with the valorization of modern science came the idea that claims about nature, including claims about human nature, are empirical claims that can be challenged and investigated.

It is true that so-called "racial science" exerted a baneful influence well into the last century, and in the eyes of the German Nazis provided a "justification" for the Holocaust; but today we do know that the claims of "racial science" were both empirically false and profoundly unscientific in their supposed methodology. Generalizing this case, we see that the *presuppositions upon which a supposedly ethical form of behavior*

6. See also *Eurthyphro*; see my discussion in *Ethics without Ontology*, 89–92.

are based can themselves frequently be rationally criticized, and this is enough to show that the "nihilistic" picture of ethics as just a matter of "conditioning" by one's culture, "conditioning" to value behaviors that are rationally arbitrary, is a naive oversimplification. We are, of course, brought up in cultures, and we acquire beliefs from our cultures, but it is possible to ask whether those beliefs are reasonable or unreasonable. For example, the idea that the highest type of human being is a brave male warrior, and that society should therefore be led by brave male warriors—the idea that the standard of human value should be bravery in battle—was one that had already come to seem unreasonable by the time of Plato and Aristotle (which is obviously not to say that they didn't value bravery in battle).

Of course, a "nihilist" may retort, "Sure, but what is 'reasonable' and 'unreasonable' is itself just a matter of conditioning." But if judgments of the reasonable and unreasonable are themselves outside of the domain of rational criticism, then science itself must lie outside the domain of rational criticism. For science is not just a matter of checking "predictions," as the positivists seemed to think; it is also a matter of deciding which hypotheses are worth the time and expense of experimental testing, as the great pragmatist C. S. Peirce already emphasized, and such decisions, as Walsh and I have argued in a number of papers,[7] presuppose *epistemic values*. Indeed, even when a theory is tested experimentally, the decision as to which experiments to trust and which to regard as dubious requires judgments of "coherence" and "plausibility," which resemble aesthetic judgments. (This is particularly true of evolutionary theories, by the way, which are always open to the suspicion of being just-so stories.) If all values are regarded as matters of *arbitrary* conditioning, then science itself should be regarded "nihilistically" as well.

I don't mean to suggest that virtue ethics and social contract theory exhaust all the different sorts of ethical concerns we have; obviously they don't. Rather, my picture is this: ethics, as we know it, rests on a certain number of human interests. Some of those interests, for example, the interest in a stable *polis*, large or small, are virtually universal among human communities, and perhaps evolutionary psychology can

---

7. These papers are collected in Hilary Putnam and Vivian Walsh, *The End of Value-Free Economy* (Abingdon, United Kingdom: Routledge, 2014).

tell something about them. Others, however, came to the fore only after the old claims of the innate superiority of one "race" over another, or one gender over another, or warriors over nonwarriors crumbled in the face of *reasonable criticism.* In short, I believe that there are learning processes in history, and that the rise of ethical systems that value equality and not inequality and that see just governments as resting upon the consent of the governed rather than on the divine right of kings (or the innate superiority of philosophers) represents progress. If there is evolution here, it is cultural evolution, and cultural evolution, as has often been remarked, is "Lamarckian"; in cultural history, there *is* an "inheritance," that is to say a transmission, of acquired characteristics, and those characteristics are not themselves written into our genes.

As I pointed out above, certain of the interests that became central to ethics in the West did so as the result of enormous political transformations, transformations that are still continuing or striving to continue in many parts of the world (for example, as I write these words, in Iran), as the demand for the rule of law and the idea of the "consent of the governed" become fundamental and acquire the aspiration to universality.

The interest that my colleague and good friend Thomas Scanlon sees as constitutive of ethics, the interest in being guided by a set of rules that are accepted by all with an interest in a just society, and that no one with that interest can reasonably object to, I see not as *the* foundation of ethics but as something that has *come to be* one of the basic interests of ethics. But there are others. I do believe that Scanlon has well described how one sort of ethical claim can have motivating force in any community that shares one of the basic interests of morality. But I also believe that morality has a number of basic interests, including respect for the humanity in the Other, equality of moral rights and responsibilities, compassion for suffering, and concern to promote human well-being, and not only the desire to be governed by principles for which one can give one another reasons, although that too is one of them. Even though these interests sometimes conflict, I believe that, on the whole and over time, promoting any one of them will require promoting the others. Precisely for this reason, a philosopher who succumbs to the temptation to see ethics as standing on a single "foundation" can always write a book "showing" that all of ethics "derives" from that interest—indeed many such books have already been written.[8] But I believe this temptation should be resisted.

To sum up, then: I am suggesting that the history of ethics is what I just called "Lamarckian" and not "Darwinian." It is the history of the evolution of a set of distinctive interests that themselves presuppose certain historical developments; in particular, they more and more presuppose the development of democratic societies. I do not agree that these interests are arbitrary; I don't believe that the interest in democracy is an "arbitrary" interest; on the contrary, I agree with de Tocqueville that even if "the great democratic revolution" that occurred in his time was "a new thing" it also represented "the most continuous, ancient and permanent tendency known in history."[9] But if Tocqueville is right, and the aspiration to democracy is a very old one, the realization of that aspiration, even to the imperfect extent that it has been realized today, is a very recent phenomenon as historical time goes. Certainly, there were those who aspired to see the equality of men and women and the equality of all races and an end to theocracy, nonconstitutional monarchy, and all forms of dictatorship in the very distant past, but it required new *means of criticism*, scientific and philosophical criticism, to overthrow the arguments for inequality that dominated for so long. In short, we have in ethics a vast *complex* of institutions and a vast *complex* of concerns, and one doesn't even begin to scratch the surface of that complex if one confines oneself to talking about "altruism."

Before closing, however, I need to say something about the "Chomskian" view proposed by Marc Hauser in *Moral Minds*. According to that view, our species has an "innate moral grammar," and all the historical developments that I have described would be just so many different realizations of that universal moral grammar. According to Hauser, the grammar itself can be accounted for by evolutionary psychology. There are at least two major difficulties with this theory, in my view.

---

8. In *Ethics without Ontology*, I said of the ethicists who succumb to this temptation that "it is as if they wanted to see ethics as a noble statue standing at the top of a single pillar" [Nelson's Column, perhaps], and I added that "I see ethics as a table with many legs, which wobbles a lot [because the floor is not even] but is very hard to turn over" (28).

9. Alexis de Tocqueville, *Democracy in America*, trans. George Lawrence (Chicago: Encyclopedia Britannica, 1990), 1.

The first, and most serious, is that "universal grammar, in Chomsky's sense, has to provide for *all possible concepts*. (Chomsky likens the "language organ" to a switch box, and he tells us that when the "switches" in a child's brain are appropriately set, "the child has command of a particular language and knows the facts of the language, that a particular expression has a particular meaning and so forth.")[10] Now, if all possible concepts were definable from a reasonably small number of concepts that might have been selected for by evolution—say, observation concepts—then this might be compatible with evolutionary psychology. But the picture of all our concepts as reducible to observation concepts is precisely what Quine demolished (and Chomsky himself certainly wants no part of this positivist picture). Even if Hauser only wants all *moral* concepts to be reducible to some determinate number, any attempt to specify such a reduction basis will be refutable by showing that the proposed definitions of the innumerable different moral concepts that different cultures actually have in terms of the alleged "basic" ones are riddled with counterexamples. (That proposed "analyses" of concepts have counterexamples is something "analytic philosophers" have become very good at showing, which is why the very term "analytic" philosophy has become somewhat of a misnomer, as Jerry Fodor has pointed out.)

A second problem, perhaps less serious in the eyes of those who, like Steven Pinker and possibly Hauser, hold on to the idea that concepts are innate, is that Chomsky himself does *not* think that evolutionary explanations of the existence of the "language organ" work; he famously thinks it is simply serendipitous that we have the language organ we have.[11] The whole idea of innate language is, needless to say, highly controversial, and I continue to represent the negative pole of the controversy. But evolutionary psychology already labors under the unfair accusation of being a mere collection of just-so stories. It must not burden itself with the science-fiction idea of a "language organ" with a code for all possible concepts.

10. Noam Chomsky, *Language and the Problems of Knowledge* (Cambridge, Mass.: MIT Press, 1988), 62–63.

11. However, if, as Chomsky claims in *Language and the Problems of Knowledge*, all possible "particular meanings" are definable in terms of the positions of a finite number of "switches" in the "language organ" (62–63), then it would seem as if something like the explicit definability of all concepts from *some* fairly limited basic vocabulary is still presupposed by Chomsky's picture.

PART II

Realism and Ontology

4

Sosa on Internal Realism and Conceptual Relativity

$\mathcal{E}$RNEST SOSA's 1993 paper, "Putnam's Pragmatic Realism,"[1] is one of the most important of the many papers that were published analyzing and criticizing the "internal realism" that I defended in books and papers published between 1976 and 1989.[2] Not only is the argumentation outstanding, as is the case in all of Ernest Sosa's work, but the scope of the discussion is extraordinarily comprehensive.

1. Ernest Sosa, "Putnam's Pragmatic Realism," *Journal of Philosophy* 90 (1993): 605–626.
2. My "internal realism" was first announced in "Realism and Reason," my presidential address to the Eastern Division of the American Philosophical Association (Boston, Mass., December 29, 1976), reprinted in my *Meaning and the Moral Sciences* (London: Routledge and Kegan Paul, 1978), 123–138; the position was further elaborated and developed in *Reason, Truth and History* (Cambridge: Cambridge University Press, 1981), in the papers collected as *Realism and Reason*, vol. 3 of *Philosophical Papers* (Cambridge: Cambridge University Press, 1983), and in *The Many Faces of Realism* (LaSalle, Ill.: Open Court, 1987), and the concluding chapter of *Representation and Reality* (Cambridge, Mass.: MIT Press, 1988). I first renounced the identification of truth with "idealized rational acceptability," which had been a central element of that position (although I retained—and still retain—another element that I called "conceptual relativity"), in my reply to Simon Blackburn at the Gifford Conference on my philosophy at the University of St. Andrews (November 1990); the proceedings, including that reply, are published as *Reading Putnam*, ed. P. Clarke and R. Hale (Oxford: Basil Blackwell, 1993), and I repeated that renunciation in more detail in my reply to David Anderson in the issue of *Philosophical Topics* 20, no. 1 (1992) devoted to my philosophy. The position that I sketched in the reply to Anderson was later developed as my Dewey Lectures, "Sense, Nonsense and the Senses," *Journal of Philosophy* 91 (1994): 445–517, collected as part I of *The Threefold Cord* (New York: Columbia University Press, 1999).

If I did not reply to the paper at the time, the reason is that I had only relatively recently given up some of the views that Sosa criticized, and was still in the process of working out my present position. But I welcome the opportunity that I very much value to explain just which of Sosa's criticisms I accept and which I believe that I can meet. I look forward very much to learning his response!

The Model-Theoretic Argument

Sosa sets the stage for his discussion of my "internal realism" with a quotation from a paper of Donald Davidson's.[3] By internal realism I had in mind not just that the truth of sentences or utterances is relative to a language. That much, Davidson observed, was "familiar and trivially correct." But, he continued, "Putnam seems to have more in mind—for example that a sentence of yours and a sentence of mine may contradict each other, and yet each be true 'for the speaker.'" It is hard to think in what language this position can be coherently, much less persuasively, expressed."[4] Sosa opens his paper by asking, "What arguments might lead to such a view?"[5] and picks four that, as he says, "stand out." "First, the "model-theoretic' argument; second, the argument from the nonobjectivity of reference and of the sort of causation involved in contemporary accounts of reference; third, the argument from the unlikelihood of scientific convergence on a finished science that provides an objective and absolute conception of reality; and, finally, the argument from the nonabsoluteness of objecthood and of existence."[6]

Before I discuss what Sosa has to say about these arguments, permit me to object strongly to Davidson's report of my view. The place where

3. Donald Davidson, "The Structure and Content of Truth," *Journal of Philosophy* 87 (1990): 279–328.

4. What is strange about this paper of Davidson's is that I had heard Davidson present these arguments (at a conference at the Universidad Autonoma de Mexico) several years earlier and replied to them not only on the spot but also in print in "Truth and Convention: On Davidson's Refutation of Conceptual Relativism," *Dialectica* 41 (1987): 69–77; collected as "Truth and Convention," in my *Realism with a Human Face*, ed. James Conant (Cambridge, Mass.: Harvard University Press, 1990), 96–104. Davidson's paper ignored my rebuttal entirely.

5. Sosa, "Putnam's Pragmatic Realism," 606.

6. Sosa, "Putnam's Pragmatic Realism," 606.

I stated the view Davidson was attacking (the view I called "conceptual relativity") was my first Carus Lecture,[7] and *nothing like* the assertion that "a sentence of yours and a sentence of mine may contradict each other, and yet each be true 'for the speaker'" occurs in that lecture. (In fact, neither the notion of *contradiction* nor the notion *true for the speaker* occurs.) What does occur is an example: the example of a world in which the number of objects will be said to be three if one disallows mereological sums as objects and seven if one allows them, and a discussion in which I claimed that it is absurd to suppose that there is some kind of metaphysical fact of the matter as to whether "mereological sums really exist." We can extend our language so that we speak of such things, and in the sense of "exist" and "object" we thereby create, it will be true that "there are such objects as mereological sums," or we can refuse to extend our language in that way; and both procedures are legitimate. I thereby drew the conclusion that *the logical primitives themselves, and in particular the notions of object and existence, have a multitude of different uses rather than one absolute "meaning."* What this implies is that the sentence "There are seven objects (in the relevant world)" (spoken by a "Polish logician" who has introduced mereological sums into his language) and the sentence "There are three objects (in the relevant world)" (spoken by my fictitious "Carnap") do *not* "contradict" each other. Moreover, as I explained in the follow-up paper "Truth and Convention," it does not help to say that the difference in the use of "object" in the two languages is a "difference in meaning" either—especially if the criterion for sameness / difference of meaning is supposed to be "translation practice." But I shall return to this issue below.

In contrast, the model-theoretic argument was *not* an argument for conceptual relativity, but rather an argument for the identification of truth with "idealized rational acceptability."[8] In his essay, Sosa decided to "set the controversy [provoked by that argument] aside, as one with little prospect of any new progress or insight beyond what is already contained in the literature about it," and "to discuss instead, and in turn,

---

7. These were published as *The Many Faces of Realism.* "Conceptual relativity" is explained on pp. 16–21.

8. My internal realist notion of truth coincided with the notion that Crispin Wright calls "superassertibility" in his *Truth and Objectivity* (Cambridge, Mass.: Harvard University Press, 1992) (although that is not how *he* interprets me!), if we prescind from possible differences over the notion of "assertibility."

the other three *arguments* that sustain Putnam's pragmatic realism."[9] Since Sosa does not discuss the model-theoretic argument, I shall refrain from discussing it as well.[10]

The "Second Argument"

The second of the four arguments attributed to me by Sosa he describes as "the argument from the nonobjectivity of reference and of the sort of causation involved in contemporary accounts of reference."[11] He gives what he calls "a thumbnail sketch" of this argument (which he attributes to my "Why There Isn't a Ready-Made World")[12] as follows:[13]

1. Truth depends on, and is constituted by, reference (at least in part).
2. Reference depends on, and is constituted by, causation (at least partly).
3. Causation is radically perspectival.
4. Reference is radically perspectival (from 2, 3).
5. Truth is radically perspectival (from 1, 4).
6. Reality is "internal" to one's perspective (from 5).

As I will now explain, I do not recognize this argument in my writing. Nevertheless, what Sosa says in this section of his paper,[14] and indeed in each of the sections that follow, is important to consider carefully.

Before I consider what Sosa says about the argument he attributes to me, I wish to say briefly what *I* thought I was doing in the papers in which he perceives this argument. The philosophers I was debating against subscribe to the kind of scientism that Bernard Williams defended in *Descartes: The Project of Pure Enquiry* and later in *Ethics and the Limits of Philosophy*. That means that they thought the description of the world as it is in itself, mind-independently (Williams calls it

9. Note that Sosa here uses "pragmatic realism" as synonymous with "internal realism." I would today describe myself happily as a pragmatic realist, but *not* as an "internal realist."

10. My reasons for giving up "internal realism" are given in detail in "Sense, Nonsense and the Senses."

11. Putnam, "Sense, Nonsense and the Senses," 606.

12. In Putnam, *Realism and Reason*, 205–228.

13. Putnam, "Sense, Nonsense and the Senses," 607.

14. Sosa, "Putnam's Pragmatic Realism," 607–608.

"the absolute conception") could be given in the language of a perfected natural science, indeed, in physicalistic terms. In strikingly similar language, in fact, both Michael Devitt and Clark Glymour asserted that reference is some kind of "causal connection." And they conceived of "causal connection" as something that holds between (mind-independent) physical events mind-independently. In short, they held that *the semantical (or, as I prefer to say, the "intentional") can be reduced to the nonsemantical.*

In the context of this debate, it was natural that I should attack this reductionist claim. In "Why There Isn't a Ready-Made World," however, I envisaged only two possible positions: either my own "internal realism," with its "verificationist semantics," or a materialist version of metaphysical realism (a dichotomy I blush at today). In Sosa's reconstruction of that essay, however, point 3 reads "Causation is radically perspectival" and what follows from 3, together with 2, is "Reference is radically perspectival." But I did *not* argue in that paper that the context-and-interest relativity of "the cause" leads to a context-and-interest relativity of "refers."[15] ("Internal realism," which I did argue for, does not automatically imply a relativity of "refers.") What I did argue is that "the cause" means, roughly, "that part of the total cause that may reasonably, given the interests appropriate to the context, be *regarded as* the bringer about as opposed to a background condition," and hence that concept "the cause" involves something *intentional.*

Thus, from my point of view, Sosa's point 4 should have read: "Reference is *intentional,*" his 5 should have read "Truth is *intentional*" and his 6 should not have been there at all.

One philosopher who saw that that is what I was arguing and who was deeply concerned to rebut my arguments is Jerry Fodor, who wrote:

> I have helped myself to the notion of . . . one event being the cause
> of another. I have therefore to claim that whatever the right

15. It might be thought, after all, that all the interest-relativity is already allowed for in the fact that reference is relative to a context, and that there will be no possibility of *different* answers to "What does word *W* refer to?" once the context *in which* W *was used* has been specified. Actually, I do not think this is the case: I think that the answer to this question may depend on *who is asking and for what reason* and not only on the context of the user of the word *W* in question. But this is something I did not argue in the paper Sosa refers to.

unpacking of [this concept] may be, it doesn't smuggle in intentional / semantic notions.[16]

That was precisely what my argument was designed to show: that "the
cause" *does* "smuggle in intentional / semantic notions," and hence the *only*
way that materialist metaphysical realists have suggested for avoiding
the model-theoretic argument doesn't work.

Given *his* reading of my argument, however, I find it natural that Sosa
writes:

Perhaps it is true that our concepts of reference and truth are
ineliminably perspectival. Even so it still would not follow that
reality itself could not be largely as it is independently of us and
our thought, in the sense that plenty of reality could not have
existed propertied and interrelated very extensively just as it is in
fact propertied and interrelated even if we had never existed to
have any thoughts, and even if no other finite thinkers had existed
to take our place. What is more, our perspectival references and
truths may be seen to derive necessarily from absolute and unper-
spectival reality.[17]

But I never claimed that "truth is perspectival," as far as I can see,
although how we express it is certainly dependent on perspective.
Moreover, no antirealist (including my former self) denies that,
for example, the moon exists "independently" of our perceptions
and thoughts in the sense of having existed *before* there were perceptions and thoughts. Its existence was not *caused* by perceptions
and thoughts.[18] To pretend that advocates of antirealist (or "verificationist") semantics deny the *causal* independence of the moon or
the solar system from human thoughts and perceptions is to misde-
scribe their position.

---

16. Jerry Fodor, *Psychosemantics* (Cambridge, Mass.: MIT Press, 1988), 126.

17. Sosa, "Putnam's Pragmatic Realism," 608.

18. Sosa, "Putnam's Pragmatic Realism," 609. In *Realism with a Human Face*—a work
Sosa cites in his essay—I write, "It is a part of [our image of the world] itself that the world
is not the product of our will—or our dispositions to talk in certain ways either" (29). Compare Sosa's own distinction between existing *relative* to a conceptual scheme and existing *in
virtue* of that conceptual scheme ("Putnam's Pragmatic Realism," 621).

Sosa continues his analysis and criticism of my arguments from the "nonobjectivity of reference" [Sosa's terminology, not mine][19] in a section titled "II. Objectivity, Absoluteness and the Many Faces of Realism."[20] Here again he repeats the charge of fallacy, this time in connection with the criticisms I made many years later of Bernard Williams's position:

> What the metaphysical realist is committed to holding is that there is an in-itself reality independent of our minds and even of our existence, and that we can talk about such reality and its constituents by virtue of correspondence relations between our language (and / or our minds) on the one hand, and things-in-themselves and their intrinsic properties (including their relations) on the other. This does not commit the metaphysical realist to holding that reference itself (or correspondence, or causal explanation) is among the objective properties constitutive of in-itself reality.[21]

What Sosa claimed is that I overlooked the possibility that there could be an "in itself" reality [in Williams's sense] *even if* reference, truth, correspondence, and so on, are all "perspectival" in the sense of being relative to interests (and other features of the contexts in which we think and speak). However, Williams's position is that the description of the world in terms of its *nonperspectival* properties is a *complete* description. As I explain in Chapter 2, that means that if it is a fact that some speaker referred to object X from such-and-such a perspective, then that *whole* fact, including the perspective and the object X and the relation between the speaker and X, must *somehow* appear in the "absolute conception," and so Williams *does* need to somehow reduce facts that involve intentionality to pure physical facts if he is not to become a sheer eliminationist with respect to the intentional. I think it is because

19. I do not myself see why the fact that something is interest-relative need mean that it is *nonobjective*. As Richard Boyd (surely no "antirealist"!) once remarked, reference can be interest-relative, but that fact that a word refers to X given certain interests is perfectly objective.

20. Sosa, "Putnam's Pragmatic Realism," 608–614.

21. Sosa cites my "Objectivity and the Science / Ethics Distinction" (Putnam, *Realism with a Human Face*, 174) as the locus of the alleged fallacy. Note that this was published in 1990, and written *after* I had given up "internal realism." Its purpose was to defend the objectivity of ethics, not to argue that "reality is perspectival," however *that* might be understood.

Sosa himself does not feel the appeal of the idea of reducing the intentional to the nonintentional (nor the appeal of denying its existence altogether) that my physicalist opponents are so attracted to that he (charitably) misdescribes Williams's views.

One sees such a charitable misdescription when Sosa writes,

> There is nevertheless an argument open to Williams's view if the latter includes commitment to "objectivism," which is defined by Putnam . . . as *the view that what really has a place in objective reality is only what is included in the ontology and the ideology of "finished science," only what the absolute conception recognizes.*[22]

Sosa immediately adds "It is not at all clear that Williams himself would accept objectivism." In fact, not only is it *clear* that Williams accepts objectivism, but he wrote a whole book the gravamen of which is that objectivism is the lasting element of truth in Descartes philosophy![23]

"Finished Science"

As Sosa points out, in my criticism of Bernard Williams's views I argued that

> there is no evidence at all for the claim . . . that science converges to a *single* theory. We simply do not have the evidence to justify speculation as to whether or not science is "destined' to converge to some one definite theoretical picture . . . Mathematics and physics, as well as ethics and history and politics, show our conceptual choices; the world is not going to impose a single language upon us, no matter what we choose to talk about.[24]

(As examples of questions on which we cannot expect science to dictate a single answer I listed whether stones are identical with mere-

22. Sosa, "Putnam's Pragmatic Realism," 610. Here Sosa is quoting from *The Many Faces of Realism*, p. 4 (emphasis added).

23. Bernard Williams, *Descartes: The Project of Pure Enquiry* (Harmondsworth, United Kingdom: Penguin, 1978). See Chapter 2 in this collection for a description of Williams's agreements with it.

24. Sosa, "Putnam's Pragmatic Realism," 613.

ological sums of particle-time-slices and whether points are individuals or limits.) In his essay, Sosa reconstructs this argument as follows:[25]

a. There is no real possibility of a finished science.
b. Things-in-themselves are by definition the things in the ontology of a finished science, and intrinsic properties are by definition those in the ideology of finished science.[26]
c. Hence, there is no possibility that that there are things-in-themselves with intrinsic, objective properties.

I do have to concede that I argued badly.

What I *should* have said was that the question "Do mereological sums exist?" is not a *scientific* question at all, and not that science isn't going to "converge" to an answer. "Science" couldn't care less whether we quantify over mereological sums or not, or whether we take points to be individuals or (as Whitehead and Russell did) to be limits, or, to shift to a mathematical example, whether we take sets as primitive (and identify functions with sets of ordered pairs), or we take functions and numbers as primitive (and identify sets with "characteristic functions," as is customary in recursion theory), or take functions and numbers *and* sets as *all* primitive. Even if science "converges" it isn't going to converge to *one single "ontology" and "ideology."* (But that doesn't mean there aren't other senses in which it may well converge.)

I was mistaken to write as if "one definite theoretical picture" required one single ontology and one single ideology (i.e., as if theories did not have a number of alternative versions—a point that I myself stressed in other writings). I believe that this mistake accounts for Sosa's attribution of "a" to me. But "b" is a proposition (indeed, the most important one) that *Bernard Williams* argues for. I absolutely do not see why Sosa thinks that I agree with it. I have argued against "things-in-themselves" in various places, but always, I believe, in the context of some debate, and then the term was to be understood as the particular

---

25. Sosa, "Putnam's Pragmatic Realism," 612–614.

26. Sosa also reads the following "definition" of *subjective* into my writings (p. 612): "ϕ is a subjective property $= Df \nearrow$ is postulated by a particular language or conceptual scheme." This would commit me to the view that all the properties we ever talk about are "subjective"!

opponent (who might not be a realist at all) understood it. What I reject is not the idea of *mind-independent things* (in the sense of things causally independent of the mind), but (1) the idea that there is one single metaphysically privileged use of "thing" (or "object," or "entity"), and (2) the idea that there is a fact of the matter as to such questions as "Is a table identical with the mereological sum of its time-slices?" But I would not express this by saying "There are no things in themselves," because I don't think any of the metaphysical uses of the notion I have seen to date are *intelligible.*

The situation is similar with respect to "intrinsic properties." I would not define them in terms of Williams's concept of finished science (or rather, asymptotically approachable finished science). Actually, I would say that when people talk about "intrinsic properties" they generally suppose them to be essential properties in the Aristotelian sense (properties without which something would not be the thing that it is), and also supposes them to be interest-independent. And I don't think that there is a definite set of properties possessed by, say, *dogs* that are *the* "intrinsic properties" of dogs *interest-independently.* What is "essential" to being a dog from the point of view of a molecular biologist is not what is "essential" from the point of view of an evolutionary biologist, nor what is "essential" from the point of view of someone who is interested in dogs as *pets.* (I argue this in detail in "Aristotle after Wittgenstein").[27]

So I throw the ball back to Sosa in the following sense: I say, "Ernie, you want to read me as *defining* these metaphysical notions ('thing-in-itself,' 'intrinsic property'), in fact defining them the way Bernard Williams did, and then asserting 'there are no things-in-themselves with intrinsic properties.' But I don't think these notions are intelligible (as used by metaphysicians), nor do I think that all the different (unfortunate) ways they have been used are captured by Williams's definition. *I* don't want to either assert or deny the thesis that 'there are things-in-themselves with intrinsic properties.' So do we have any remaining disagreement about this issue?" If the answer is "yes," I suspect the remaining disagreement(s) will come up in what I shall say now about *conceptual relativity.*

27. Collected in Hilary Putnam, *Words and Life,* ed. James Conant (Cambridge, Mass.: Harvard University Press, 1994), 62–81.

Conceptual Relativity

As Sosa describes, in *The Many Faces of Realism*, I used the following example (I quote Sosa's presentation of the example, which is quite accurate):[28]

> Suppose a world with just three individuals $x1$, $x2$, $x3$. Such a world is held by some "mereologists" to have in it a total of seven things or entities or objects, namely, $x1$, $x2$, $x3$, $x1 + x2$, $x1 + x3$, $x2 + x3$, $x1 + x2 + x3$. Antimereologists by contrast prefer the more austere ontology that recognizes only the three individuals as objects that *really* exist in that world. Talk of the existence of $x1 + x2$ and its ilk is just convenient abbreviation of a more complex discourse that refers to nothing but individuals. Thus, suppose $x1$ is wholly red and $x2$ is wholly black. And consider
>
> 1. There is an object that is partly red and partly black.
> 2. There is an object that is red and an object that is black.
>
> For the antimereologist, statement 1 is not true, if we assume that $x3$ is also wholly red or wholly black; it is at best a convenient way of abbreviating the likes of 2.

Sosa goes on to quote my response (which, as he correctly points out, was in agreement with Carnap's views on similar questions), namely, that "the question is one of the choice of a language. On some days it may be more convenient to use [antimereological] language: . . . on other days it may be convenient to use [mereological] language."[29]

Explaining this answer, Sosa writes:[30]

> Take the question,
>   How many objects with a volume of at least 6 cubic centimeters are there in this container?

28. Sosa, "Putnam's Pragmatic Realism," 614.

29. The quotation is from my "Truth and Convention: On Davidson's Refutation of Conceptual Relativism," in *Dialectica* 41 (1987): 69–77; quotation from p. 75.

30. Sosa, "Putnam's Pragmatic Realism," 614–615.

This question can have no absolute answer on the Carnap-Putnam view, even in a case where the container contains a vacuum except for three marbles each with a volume of 6 cubic centimeters. The antimereologist may say

3. There are three objects in the box.

But the mereologist will reply

4. There are at least seven objects in the box.

The Carnap-Putnam line is now this: *which statement we accept—3 or 4—is a matter of linguistic convenience.* The language of mereology has criteria of existence and identity according to which sums of individuals are objects. The language of antimereology rejects such criteria, and may even claim that by its criteria only individuals are objects.

Sosa begins the first of his criticisms with the following words: "There is a valuable insight here, I believe, but I am puzzled by the linguistic wrapping in which it is offered."[31]

After saying "I am puzzled by the linguistic wrapping," Sosa continues,

> After all, none of 1–4 mentions any language, or any piece of language, nor does any of them say we shall or shall not or should or should not use any language or bit of language. So I do not see how our decision actually to use or not to use any or all of the sentences 1–4 can settle the question of whether what these sentences *say* is true or false.

My reply to this objection is that what settles the question whether what these sentences say is true or false is not merely our decision to use (assert?) any or all of them, but our adoption of what Sosa himself called "the criteria of existence and identity" of mereology or "the criteria of

---

31. Sosa, "Putnam's Pragmatic Realism," 615. However, there is one (possibly quite consequential) change I would make in the above explanation of "the Carnap-Putnam line": in the last sentence, I would change the last clause to read "and may even claim that by its criteria *there are no such objects* as the 'sums' $x1 + x2$, $x1 + x3$, $x2 + x3$, $x1 + x2 + x3$."

existence and identity" of antimereology, *together with certain empirical facts.* The way that works is as follows: if the Eiffel Tower does not exist (and that, I agree with Sosa, is not a question with respect to which there is any "conceptual relativity") or if the Statue of Liberty does not exist (ditto), then *the mereological sum of the Eiffel Tower and the Statue of Liberty* also does not exist (no matter which of the criteria we adopt). But if they do both exist, then *if we adopt the mereological criteria of existence and identity, then we have adopted conventions of language that make it trivially correct to say that the mereological sum of the Eiffel Tower and the Statue of Liberty exist.* The example itself was meant to illustrate precisely how there can be a choice between different uses of "exist," on some of which it is true to say that mereological sums exist, while on others it is false.

["But Hilary, how can you talk of *conventions* after Quine?" I can imagine my old friend Burton Dreben (and not only Burton Dreben) exclaiming. The answer here, as I explained long ago,[32] is that while I find the notion of convention indispensable, I do not explain it in terms of the Carnapian notion of "analyticity." What is and what is not a matter of convention is something on which we may change our minds, and empirical facts may turn out to be relevant. But I do not agree with Quine that the notion is simply to be discarded.]

Perhaps anticipating some such response, Sosa immediately suggests that a linguistic formulation of the doctrine of conceptual relativity would render it trivial. He writes:

Here for a start is a possibility [i.e., a possible interpretation]:

LR1. In order to say *anything* you must adopt a language. So you must "adopt a meaning" even for so basic a term as "object." And you might have adopted another. Thus you might adopt Carnap-language (CL) or you might adopt Polish-logician language (PL). What you say, i.e., the utterances you make, the sentences you affirm, are not true or false absolutely, but are true or false only relative to a given language. Thus, if you say "There are three objects in this box" your utterance or sentence may be true understood as a statement of CL while it is false understood as a statement in PL.[33]

32. See Hilary Putnam, "Convention, a Theme in Philosophy," in *Realism and Reason*, vol. 3 of *Philosophical Papers* (Cambridge: Cambridge University Press, 1983), 170–183.

33. Sosa, "Putnam's Pragmatic Realism," 615.

But under this interpretation linguistic relativity seems trivially true. Who could deny that inscriptions of shapes and emissions of sounds are not true or false independently of their meaning, independently of all relativization to language or idiolect?

My reply to this consists of three points:

1. The speaker of, say, PL does not do anything that would ordinarily be called giving (or "adopting") a meaning to the word "object" (if this is not clear, substitute "entity"). When he says that there are such objects (or such entities) as mereological sums, he counts, at least for linguistic purposes, as simply using "object" ("entity") in the normal (Anglo-American) way. So the trivial linguistic truth that the truth-value of our utterances depends on the meanings we give to their words (or that our linguistic community has already given them) is *not* the same as the thesis of conceptual relativity that I affirmed above, unless "meaning" is already being given a special philosophical interpretation.

2. To see that it is *not* trivially true that if we adopt CL we *thereby* make "There are seven objects in the box Sosa described [the one with 3 marbles in a vacuum]" true, consider the question from the standpoint of a *metaphysical realist* who does not believe in the existence of mereological sums. (I called him "Professor Antipode" in *The Many Faces of Realism*.) Obviously Professor Antipode will say something like this: "I don't mind your saying that when you use the word 'object' you mean to include mereological sums as objects. But that doesn't make 'Mereological sums exist' true, any more than saying 'When I use the word "object" I mean to include leprechauns' makes 'Leprechauns exist' true."

3. On the other hand, according to my own unmetaphysical sort of realism, adopting the conventions of PL does make it true to say (in PL) "Mereological sums exist," and adopting the conventions of (CL) makes it true to say "Only three objects exist" [in the relevant world], and *a fortiori* that mereological sums do not exist. Whether I am right in this claim or not is not an instance of trivial linguistic conventionality, as Professor Antipode's argument shows.

Sosa's "Nonlinguistic" Restatement

After expressing dissatisfaction in this way with "the linguistic turn taken by Carnap and now Putnam,"[34] Sosa moves to a more positive assessment, writing, "Nevertheless, it still seems to me that there is a valuable insight in Putnam's now repeated appeal to the contrast between the Carnapian conceptual scheme and that of the Polish logician. But, given our recent reflections, I would like to put the insight without appeal to language or to any linguistic relativity."

The insight, as expressed at the close of Sosa's essay,[35] is that by extending my reasoning, we reach a set of options in contemporary ontology that present us with "a rather troubling trilemma."

To comment on these words, I need to explain Sosa's trilemma, which he presents with the aid of an example:

> I am supposing a snowball to be constituted by a certain piece of snow as constituent matter and the shape of (approximate) roundness as constituent form. That particular snowball exists at that time because of the roundness of that particular piece of snow. More, if at that time that piece of snow were to lose its roundness, then at that time that snowball would go out of existence.
>
> Compare now with our ordinary concept of a snowball, the concept of a snowdiscall, defined as an entity constituted by a piece of snow as matter and as form any shape between being round and being discshaped. At any given time, therefore, any piece of snow that constitutes a snowball constitutes a snowdiscall, but a piece of snow might constitute a snowdiscall without then constituting a snowball. For every round piece of snow is also in shape between being discshaped and round (inclusive), but a discshaped piece of snow is of course not round.
>
> Any snowball SB must hence be constituted by a piece of snow PS which also then constitutes a snowdiscall SD. Now, SB is distinct (a different entity) from PS, since PS would survive squashing and SB would not. By similar reasoning, SD is also distinct from PS. And, again by similar reasoning, SB must also

---

34. Sosa, "Putnam's Pragmatic Realism," 619.
35. Sosa, "Putnam's Pragmatic Realism," 626.

be distinct from SD, since enough partial flattening of PS will destroy SB but not SD. Now, there are infinitely many shapes S1, S2 . . . between roundness and flatness of a piece of snow, and for each i, having a shape between flatness and Si would give the form of a distinctive kind of entity to be compared with snowballs and discballs. Whenever a piece of snow constitutes a snowball, therefore, it constitutes infinitely many entities all sharing its place with it.

Under a broadly Aristotelian conception, therefore, the barest flutter of the smallest leaf hence creates and destroys infinitely many things, and ordinary reality suffers a sort of "explosion."[36]

The first of the three responses to this threat of ontological "explosion" that constitutes the "trilemma" Sosa himself calls "conceptual relativity," and he explains it as follows:

> Perhaps snowballs do exist relative to all actual conceptual schemes ever, but not relative to all conceivable conceptual schemes. Just as we are not willing to countenance the existence of snowdiscalls, just so another culture might have been unwilling to countenance snowballs. We do not countenance snowdiscalls because our conceptual scheme does not give to the snowdiscall form (being in shape between round and disc-shaped) the status required for it to be a proper constitutive form of a separate sort of entity—at least not with snow as underlying stuff.[37]

And Sosa points out that:

> That would block the explosion of reality, but the price is conceptual relativity. Supervenient, constituted entities do not just exist or not in themselves, free of any dependence on or relativity to conceptual scheme. What thus exists relative to one conceptual scheme may not do so relative to another. In order for such a sort of entity to exist relative to a conceptual scheme, that

---

36. Sosa, "Putnam's Pragmatic Realism," 620.
37. Sosa, "Putnam's Pragmatic Realism," 620–621.

conceptual scheme must recognize its constituent form as an appropriate way for a separate sort of entity to be constituted.[38]

Sosa now considers a possible objection to this first response, which he promptly rebuts:[39] mustn't we think of *the existence of the framers and users of the conceptual scheme as also relative to that conceptual scheme?* "Are we then not caught in a vicious circle?" And he replies that "existence *relative* to a conceptual scheme is *not* equivalent to existence *in virtue* of that conceptual scheme. Relative to scheme C the framers of C exist *in virtue* of their constitutive matter and form, and in virtue of how these satisfy certain criteria for existence and perdurance of such subjects (among whom happen to be the framers themselves). There is hence no vicious circularity." And he sums up this first response (conceptual relativity) thus:

> The picture is then roughly this. Each of us acquires and develops a view of things that includes criteria of existence and perdurance for categories of objects. When we consider whether an object of a certain sort exists, the specification of the sort will include the relevant criteria of existence and perdurance. And when we correctly recognize that an object of that sort does exist, our claim is elliptical for ". . . exists relative to *this* our conceptual scheme."[40]

Comment: Both Ernest Sosa and Jennifer Case have noted that all the examples I gave (and, I might add, that Sosa now gives) of "conceptual relativity" involve what Sosa called "recondite entities" (he added "of controversial status," but I have explained above why I don't think that is always the case). And Case went on to make an important suggestion:

> Reading Davidson's discussion of conceptual schemes as contravening Putnam's agenda requires overlooking the difference between natural languages and languages like Carnap's and the Polish Logician's. For lack of a better term, let me call languages of the

---

38. Sosa, "Putnam's Pragmatic Realism," 621.
39. Sosa, "Putnam's Pragmatic Realism," 621.
40. Sosa, "Putnam's Pragmatic Realism," 621.

latter variety "optional languages." If having a conceptual scheme is to be associated with having a language, it should be associated with having an optional language. Modifying a remark of Davidson's, we may say that where conceptual schemes differ, so do *optional* languages.

It is not necessarily the case that where conceptual schemes differ so do *natural* languages. Someone who has a single natural language may have multiple optional languages and, therefore, multiple conceptual schemes.[41]

If one looks at the matter this way, as I think we should, then one will not say that "we" (or "our culture") *do not countenance* snowdiscalls or mereological sums. Our culture allows us to do different things in different contexts, including introducing, if we want, an optional language in which we quantify over snowdiscalls—and "snowdiscalls" are, after all, no more unusual than, say, "the mereological sum of my nose and the Eiffel Tower."

Second, I don't think it is happy to say that "mereological sums exist *relative to* the Polish Logician's language" (or "snowdiscalls exist *relative to* the SD scheme"). If we use PL, in some context and for some appropriate reason, then we should simply say, "There is an object that is the mereological sum of my nose and the Eiffel Tower," or "The mereological sum of my nose and the Eiffel Tower exists." We do not have to relativize existence *to* PL *in* PL. What we have to do is make clear which optional language we are speaking.

"But then what you count as the same sentence in English may have different truth-conditions in different contexts!" That is the case anyway! ("Tomatoes are vegetables" has different truth-conditions in the mouth of a grocer and the mouth of a botanist, for example, and none is disturbed by this.)

Third, I do not see why Sosa thinks he has "put the insight without appeal to language or to any linguistic relativity." Talk of criteria of existence and perdurance is *metalinguistic* talk on the face of it. (Perhaps Sosa read me as advocating that we must always restate existence claims in the formal mode, as Carnap did. But this was not the aspect

41. Jennifer Case, "On the Very Idea of a Conceptual Scheme," *Southern Journal of Philosophy* 35, no. 1 (1997): 1–18; quotation from p. 11.

of Carnap's view that I endorsed. What I endorsed was his tolerant attitude to a plurality of—to use Jennifer Case's term—optional languages, with different so-called ontologies.)

Fourth, as already mentioned, I think that—very importantly—conceptual relativity should be our approach not only to questions of existence and perdurance, but to many questions having to do with cross-category identification (such as "Are points mere limits?," or "Are functions sets of ordered pairs?").[42]

Living with the Explosion

A second approach to the problem illustrated by the snowdiscall example is what Sosa calls "try[ing] to live with the explosion." This is his term[43] for just saying that *all* the objects in *all* the alternative conceptual schemes (what I would now, taking Case's suggestion, call all the alternative optional languages) are genuine elements of reality. There are, we will say if we take this line, snowballs *and* snowdiscalls *and* whose knows what else besides? ("Possible worlds?")

As Sosa points out, however,

If we allow the satisfaction by any sequence S of any form F of the appropriate polyadicity and logical form to count as a criterion of existence for a corresponding sort of object, then reality right in front of us, before us, and all around us is unimaginably richer and more bizarre than we have ever imagined. And any way we shall still face the problem of giving some explanation of why we focus so narrowly on the objects we do attend to, whose criteria of existence and perdurance we do recognize, to the exclusion of the plethora of other objects all around and even in the very same place.[44]

Comment: "Trying to live with the explosion" is tremendously costly for additional reasons having to do with the problem of *criteria of*

---

42. A possible fifth point: as I say in a passage that Sosa quotes, I think yet another approach to the kind of problem he raises with the snowdiscalls example is *sortal identity*. I know that both Kripke and Quine shudder, but isn't just this sort of example a good reason to reconsider the shudders?

43. Sosa, "Putnam's Pragmatic Realism," 621

44. Sosa, "Putnam's Pragmatic Realism," 622.

cross-category identity that I mentioned a moment ago. Consider the fact that I have mentioned a couple of times in this essay that in recursion theory and hierarchy theory (one of the branches of mathematics I wrote quite a few articles in) we regularly take numbers as individuals, and functions of numbers, functions of functions, functions of functions . . . (as in type theory, but extended through the transfinite) as primitive. We do not take sets to be still additional entities, but "identify them" with characteristic functions. In another branch of mathematics (set theory), we regularly take sets as primitive, and identify functions with sets of ordered pairs. I have never met a philosopher *or* a mathematician who thinks there is a "fact of the matter" as to which is right! Yet they can't *both* be right.[45] According to "conceptual relativity," there is only the question of a choice of an "optional language" here. But if we go for the "exploding reality" approach, what do we do? Do we say there is a (possibly unknowable) "fact of the matter" as to whether sets are characteristic functions or functions are sets of ordered pairs? That, I must admit, seems crazy to me![46]

Nor does the problem arise only in pure mathematics. Typically, when we find a way of "interpreting" one version of a physical (or geometrical) theory in another, the different alternative "translations" are incompatible if taken at face value. For example, even if we decide that points are limits, there are just as many ways of formalizing the notion of a "limit" as there are of formalizing the notion of a "set." Yet surely the adoption of one or another way is a choice of a linguistic option, and not a metaphysical claim.

The Last Option: Eliminativism

The third of the three options that constitutes Sosa's trilemma is "eliminativism":

> A third option is a disappearance or elimination theory that refuses to countenance supervenient, constituted objects. But then

45. Assuming the Axiom of Foundation, anyway.

46. [Davidson and Quine have at times suggested a move that would come to this: asserting that there are sets$_1$ and functions$_1$ and sets$_2$ and functions$_2$ and that sets$_1$ are (characteristic) functions$_1$ while functions$_2$ are sets$_2$ of ordered pairs (which are . . . ?). Any takers for that one?!]

most if not all ordinary reality will be lost. Perhaps we shall allow ourselves to continue to use its forms of speech ". . . but only as a convenient abbreviation." But in using those forms of speech, in speaking of snowballs, chains, boxes, trees, hills, or even people, we shall *not* believe ourselves to be seriously representing reality and its contents. "As a convenience": to *whom* and for what *ends?* "As an abbreviation": of *what?*[47]

Sosa recognizes that "with alternatives so grim, we are encouraged to return to our relativistic reflections." But now he raises an additional worry—and a deep one:

Our conceptual scheme encompasses criteria of existence and perdurance for the sorts of objects that it recognizes. Shall we say now that a sort of object O exists (has existed, exists now, or will exist) relative to a scheme C at t if and only if, at t, C recognizes O by allowing the corresponding criteria? But surely there are sorts of objects that our present conceptual scheme does not recognize, such as artifacts yet uninvented and particles yet undiscovered, to take only two obvious examples . . . What is it for there to be such objects? Is it just the in-itself satisfaction of constitutive forms by constitutive matters? That yields the explosion of reality.[48]

Part (but only a part!) of the answer to this worry is that we should not think of ourselves has having *one* conceptual scheme. We have a language within which we can already introduce an indefinite number of conceptual schemes or optional languages (and as that language develops, there will be the possibility of still more). But we must not think of all the optional ontologies as if they might be simply *pooled:* that leads right back to "the explosion of reality" (with the consequences noted a moment ago). Yet reality does force us to recognize that we need, for example, at least *one* optional language in which we can describe (for example) quantum reality. That there are a number of such optional

47. Sosa, "Putnam's Pragmatic Realism," 622.
48. Sosa, "Putnam's Pragmatic Realism," 623.

languages (and ways of "translating" back and forth between them) is well known.[49]

To take Sosa's two very different examples separately: we already have in ordinary language the broad (and indispensable) category *artifact*. So we can *now* say that *there are kinds of artifacts that will probably be invented that we do not now have names for*. Saying that does not, of course, permit us to answer such questions as *What is the exact cardinal number of uninvented artifacts?*, even "in principle," but that is a bad question anyway if conceptual relativity is right—bad because there will doubtless be more than one (optional) way of counting artifacts. The question does not become sensible by relativizing it to something called "our" conceptual system because, as I am emphasizing, we use and need to use *many*.

The problem of undiscovered sorts of particles submits to a similar treatment. But what if Sosa were simply to ask "What of *presently indescribable but yet to be discovered sorts of physical entities?*" With respect to this I would say that to say that there are such is to say that reality is not exhausted by what we can talk about in any precise way, and certainly not by our relatively precise optional languages of present-day science. As I said in my Dewey Lectures, we renegotiate—and are forced to renegotiate—our notion of reality as our language and our life develop.

Sosa closes this penultimate part of his discussion by repeating his three options, *eliminativism, absolutism* (the "explosion of reality"), and *conceptual relativism*, and writes, "Right now I cannot decide which of these is least disastrous. But is there any other option?"

Conclusion

I cannot resist quoting Sosa's closing paragraph, which I very much appreciate, in full:

---

49. Such "translations"—the technical term for them is "relative interpretations"—do not, however, necessarily preserve what Quine has caused philosophers to call the "ontology" of a theory, nor are they certifiable as correct by *linguists* on the basis of what Davidson refers to as "translation practice." Rather, they are accepted because they *preserve explanations* under passage from one version of a theory to another. For a detailed discussion, see Putnam, "Truth and Convention"; and Putnam, "Equivalence," in *Realism and Reason*, 26–45.

Of the four Putnamiam arguments for pragmatic realism—the model-theoretic argument; the argument from the perspectival character of causation, reference and truth; the argument from agnosticism regarding scientific convergence upon a finished science; and the argument for conceptual relativity—this fourth and last of them seems to me far the most powerful and persuasive. It raises a threefold issue—the choice between eliminativism, absolutism, and relativism—still wide open on the philosophical agenda, and a most exciting issue before us today.[50]

Thank you, Ernie!

50. Sosa, "Putnam's Pragmatic Realism," 626.

5

Richard Boyd on Scientific Realism

$\mathcal{I}$ AGREE WITH MANY of the things Richard Boyd says.[1] What's more I've agreed with them for a long time, but Boyd misses this because he reads me in a systematically wrong way. Boyd was so upset by the things I wrote in my "internal realist" period that he has been projecting those views onto my publications ever since, and he shouldn't do that. But even in that period, as I explained in "From Quantum Mechanics to Ethics and Back Again,"[2] I mistakenly believed that scientific realism, in Boyd's sense,[3] was *compatible* with my "verificationist semantics."[4] I have long believed two principles that I learned from Boyd, namely that *theories in the mature sciences are typi-*

1. This paper is a reply to Richard Boyd, "What of Pragmatism with the World Here?," in *Reading Putnam*, ed. Maria Baghramian (Abingdon, United Kingdom: Routledge, 2013), 39–94.

2. This is chapter 2 of my *Philosophy in an Age of Science: Physics, Mathematics, and Skepticism*, ed. Mario De Caro and David Macarthur (Cambridge, Mass.: Harvard University Press, 2012), 51–71.

3. I described and supported Boyd's version of scientific realism in *Meaning and the Moral Sciences* (London: Routledge and Kegan Paul, 1978), 20–22.

4. I identified "internal realism" with the thesis that truth is "idealized rational acceptability" in *Reason, Truth and History* (Cambridge: Cambridge University Press, 1981). I used the term "verificationist semantics" in "Computational Psychology and Interpretation Theory," in my *Realism and Reason*, vol. 3 of *Philosophical Papers* (Cambridge: Cambridge University Press, 1983), 139–154.

cally approximately true, and *terms in the mature sciences typically refer*, and I am unrepentant in that respect.[5] However, I also think that those principles are not enough to refute the idea that the "right" semantics is verificationist semantics (whether of Dummett's kind, or of the kind I advocated in *Reason, Truth and History*), because antirealists may claim that it is possible to *reinterpret the whole language*, including all scientific hypotheses expressible in it, and if these two principles represent a scientific hypothesis, in a very liberal sense of "scientific" (as we both claimed), then antirealists should claim that they can reinterpret them too. And that was what I tried to do in my lecture titled "Realism and Reason"[6] and subsequently: accept scientific realism, *but reinterpret it to make it compatible with verificationist semantics*. I have always been a scientific realist, in Boyd's sense, in spite of the misunderstanding, which is very widespread, that I renounced scientific realism—that's just wrong. And I've never accepted Nelson Goodman's idea that we "make" the world.

Moreover, I even repented, in my Dewey Lectures,[7] of saying that "the mind and the world together make up the mind and the world."[8] And I've written a lot about Pragmatism, and in every single paper I say that I don't think that the pragmatist theories of truth—*any* of the pragmatist theories of truth—Peirce's, James's or Dewey's—were right. (Fortunately, Dewey never really *depended* on the pragmatist theory of truth. He mentions it in *one* footnote in the *Logic*,[9] but what he is otherwise concerned with is *warranted assertibility*, and that means that, fortunately, his belief that Peirce got the definition of truth right actually

---

5. I explain why I am unrepentant in "On Not Writing Off Scientific Realism," in my *Philosophy in an Age of Science*, 91–108.

6. "Realism and Reason," *Proceedings and Addresses of the American Philosophical Association* 50 (1977): 483–498; reprinted in *Meaning and the Moral Sciences*, 123–140. This is where I first used the term "internal realism."

7. Hilary Putnam, "Sense, Nonsense, and the Senses: An Inquiry into the Powers of the Human Mind," *Journal of Philosophy* 91 (1994): 445–517; reprinted in *The Threefold Cord: Mind, Body and World* (New York: Columbia University Press, 1999), 3–70.

8. Hilary Putnam, *Reason, Truth and History* (Cambridge: Cambridge University Press, 1981), xi.

9. The footnote in question reads, "The best definition of *truth* from the logical standpoint which is known to me is that by Peirce: 'The opinion which is fated to be ultimately agreed to by all who investigate is what we mean by the truth, and the object represented in this opinion is the real'." John Dewey, *Logic: The Theory of Inquiry* (New York: Henry Holt, 1938), 343n.

plays no real role in anything Dewey does. But in any case one can learn from a philosopher without believing everything he says, or even believing everything he regards as tremendously important. John McDowell and I both believe we can learn a great deal from Kant, but that doesn't mean we don't reject certain ideas from the first *Critique* that Kant would have regarded as absolutely essential to his whole vision. It had better be the case that we can learn from dead philosophers, 'cause we're all gonna be dead!)

Now, with respect to *Ethics without Ontology:* I did not mean to reject the idea of metaphysics with a small "m." Sometimes I describe what I do as metaphysics, but I know that very often, because of who my teachers were,[10] and perhaps because of the bad influence of a certain side of Wittgenstein, I do use the word "metaphysics" as a pejorative. But I am very well aware that I have metaphysical views. And the point of *Ethics without Ontology was not* that one shouldn't have a metaphysical view—a *naturalist* metaphysical view—of the nature of ethical judgment and ethical practices. In fact, in *Ethics without Ontology* I tried to present one, namely, I suggested that ethics rests on a certain set of human interests. I compared ethics to a table on many legs, and I said such a table wobbles a lot because the ground isn't even, but it is very hard to overturn. And I had something to say about what those interests are. Like Stanley Cavell,[11] I think that ethics isn't the only way, but it is far preferable to other ways of settling conflicts. It's not the only way of settling conflicts, Cavell says, but the other ways are often inaccessible or brutal. And I don't think that it should be a constraint on the semantics of ethical terms that anyone who repudiates ethics or rejects ethics is *irrational.* A lot of bad arguments for noncognitivism assume that cognitivists think that something like that *is* a constraint on the semantics of ethical terms. They think that a cognitivist must make a certain traditional philosophical Platonist view come out right. But that isn't what I think.

But let me return to the subject of ontology, and to my dissatisfaction with Quine's criterion of ontological commitment, and the implicit

10. Here I am thinking primarily of W. V. Quine and Hans Reichenbach.

11. See my "The Fact / Value Dichotomy and Its Critics," in *Philosophy in an Age of Science*, 283–298, for a discussion of the view of Cavell's to which I referred.

assumption that goes with it, the assumption that "exist" is univocal.[12] I wish to draw a distinction here that is foreign to Quine's way of thinking: the distinction between saying that an expression has different *truth conditions* in two or more different circumstances, and the difference between saying it has "different meanings" in the sense that is connected with translation practice (call it, "the usual linguistic sense").[13] In the latter sense, it is (roughly) true that "exist" has a constant meaning. I say that because, with Charles Travis, I think that a word may have the same meaning in different contexts even though the truth-evaluable content of what you say by using that word may vary with the context. ("There is a lot of coffee on the table" may used to say either that there is coffee to drink, or that coffee has been spilled on the table; these uses go with different truth conditions, but it is not the case that the words have meanings other than those given in a good dictionary, and those meanings are the same in the two cases). The truth-evaluable content of what we say using the word "exist" varies a great deal, and in some contexts it is perfectly right to say that mereological sums exist, and in other contexts it is right to say there aren't really such things as mereological sums, that's "just one way of talking," and we can say what we want to say without it, for example, by talking about sets. I'm sure Carnap would have said it's a matter of convention whether or not we say that there are such things as mereological sums, and my gut feeling is that that's got to be right. The view that somehow there is a deep problem as to whether mereological sums "really exist" seems absurd. I know that Gideon Rosen thinks that the problem is so hard that we'll never know whether there are really mereological sums or not. That seems to me crazy! And I would assume that Dick Boyd

---

12. There are deep tensions in Quine's thinking: for example, between thinking of "exist" as univocal, and admitting that it admits of both "objectual" and "nonobjectual" interpretations. Moreover, even when Quine clearly thinks of "exist" as univocal, he equivocates (or, perhaps, he is torn) between thinking of the univocality of "exist" as something trivial (what better standard of univocality do we have, he asks in effect, than how something looks when properly "regimented"?) and thinking of it as involving a substantive claim, the claim that being committed to the existence of abstract entities (when quantification over them cannot be explained away as "nonobjectual") is doing something he calls "positing" intangible objects, objects whose existence has to be inferred from the contribution that positing their existence makes to the success of prediction, particularly in physics.

13. For more on these two senses, see my *Ethics without Ontology* (Cambridge, Mass.: Harvard University Press, 2004).

probably shares my intuition here. But it's this idea that there's just one correct way of using "exist" *and* that way determines a unique answer to the question "are mereological sums included in the furniture of the universe or not?" that I reject. That's the sort of "ontology" that I wrote an obituary for.[14]

Thus, I am not the internal realist that Boyd thinks I still am, although there are certainly deep issues about which we disagree. Some of them go beyond the scope of this comment,[15] but I will say something about whether truth is "correspondence." I agree with Boyd that true empirical statements correspond to states of affairs that actually obtain. But I would not say that I have a "correspondence theory of truth." In *The Threefold Cord: Mind, Body, and World*, I defended what I described as Fregean *disquotation* (not, please note, Fregean *deflation*). I believe that the disquotational property of "true" is an extremely important one, as Frege and Tarski both realized, whatever the differences between their theories, but neither thought that the disquotation property is all there is to say about truth, which is the characteristic thesis of what is called "deflation."[16] I think one problem with speaking of truth as defined in terms of a correspondence theory of truth is, first, that it is misleading. I believe that, in addition to the disquotation property, it is a property of the notion of truth that to call a statement of any kind—not only an empirical statement, but also a mathematical statement, a statement of logic (e.g., *such-and-such a schema is valid*), an ethical statement, and so on—true is to say that it has the sort of correctness appropriate to the kind of statement it is. When we speak of "states of affairs" what we normally think of are empirical states of af-

14. Chapter 4 of *Ethics without Ontology* is titled " 'Ontology': An Obituary."

15. Examples of our disagreements: I believe that all the familiar moral predicates—"oughts" as well as "good"—are truth-apt, while Boyd believes that "good" is the name of a "natural kind," but oughts are noncognitive; I believe that value judgments and descriptive judgments are entangled, in the sense of presupposing one another, while Boyd rejects this claim; Boyd styles himself a "materialist," and I think that his claim (in "What of Pragmatism with the World Here?," 63) that "reference is a real relation holding because of relevant causal interactions between language users and the features of the world to which they refer" either amounts to nothing more than a supervenience claim, in which case it does nothing to show that reference is "physicalistically" acceptable, or else simply assumes that the "relevant causal interactions" are describable at the level of *physics*, which is what needs to be shown. [Note added July 4, 2015.]

16. Paul Horwich's *Truth* (Oxford: Oxford University Press, 1990) is an excellent account and vigorous defence of the "deflationist" position.

fairs, ways the universe can be.[17] And correspondence to such a state of affairs—one that actually obtains—is the standard of correctness for empirical statements. Here Boyd and I agree, I believe. When we confine attention to empirical statements, *both* correspondence and disquotation are features of truth. But even this statement is misleading.

It is misleading because said just like that it could be read as implying that there is one and the same kind of correspondence at stake no matter what the empirical statement is, and no matter what the occasion of its utterance may be. But that is not the case. "This piece of beef weighs one pound" may "correspond to reality" by the standard of correspondence appropriate to a butcher shop, but be extremely wrong by the standard of laboratory science. And the kind and degree of correspondence changes again when the statement is "John is very neurotic," or . . . The difficulty in giving a picture of our notion of truth (I doubt we can give anything that deserves the title of a "theory") is to do justice simultaneously both to the *unity* of the notion and to the *plurality* of the correctness-conditions that go with it and give it content.

Moreover, when it comes to mathematical statements and logical statements I am not sure I want to speak of their correctness conditions as "correspondence," but I don't have time to unpack this remark here.[18] Suffice it to say that if one must speak of correspondence, then let us recognize that *what sort of thing* (in what Sellars once called "the widest possible sense of thing") a statement has to correspond to in order to count as "true" varies from language game to language game. Nevertheless, the concept of truth does exhibit certain constant features; the disquotation schema describes one.

I would also say that "true" is a logical word like "and," "or," or "not." That is why it can apply to every kind of sentence, without being incompatible with the fact that different sorts of sentences have different sorts of truth-conditions. I can say a tautology is true without being forced to regard the tautology as "describing" something or "corresponding to a state of affairs," or inventing a "vacuous state of affairs" for tautologies to correspond to. Just as one can conjoin a descriptive sentence and an evaluation with an "and" or an "if-then," one can say

17. On the indispensability of such talk, see my "From Quantum Mechanics to Ethics and Back Again," in Baghramian, *Reading Putnam*, 19–36.

18. See chapter 3 of *Ethics without Ontology* for an explanation of why I say this.

that a descriptive sentence and an evaluation are both "true" without implying that they have the same sort of truth-conditions. And, by the way, my rejection of the fact / value *dichotomy* doesn't mean that there's no use for a *distinction* between descriptions and evaluations. A metaphysical dichotomy and a distinction are not the same thing. But if I say, for example, "If you'd practiced the piano an hour every day for the last year, you would have played better," I am putting an "if___ then ___" between an empirical statement and a judgment of aesthetic merit. And that's perfectly fine.

In closing, what I've said doesn't necessarily preclude correspondence-talk. But I fear that "correspond" tends to suggest that truth depends on a relation (moreover, one and the same relation) between whole statements and something (reality? parts of reality? what sort of parts?), no matter what sort of statement we are calling "true." So I would prefer to say that *descriptive* statements (note the restriction!) are connected to the world via the reference of the names and predicates that they contain, and *reference* is a relation to things (and sets of things, and sets of ordered pairs of things, etc.) in the world. This is a difficult metaphysical issue, but I don't think it bears on whether one is a realist in Boyd's sense or not a realist in his sense.

PART III

Realism and Verificationism

6

Hans Reichenbach

REALIST *AND* VERIFICATIONIST

$\mathcal{I}$N *Meaning and the Moral Sciences*,[1] I remarked that "it is *not* clear that [Reichenbach's] form of verificationism (the "probability theory of meaning") is incompatible with realism." (However, I added that I thought it was wrong on other grounds.[2]) And after rehearsing the reasons why the identification of meaningfulness with "conclusive verifiability in principle" (accepted by the Vienna Circle at one point)[3] *is* incompatible with realism, I went on to ask,

Why should it be impossible from a realist point of view that (1) every meaningful sentence have some weight or other in some ob-

1. Hilary Putnam, "Reference and Understanding," in *Meaning and the Moral Sciences* (London: Routledge and Kegan Paul, 1978), 97–119. The remark I quote occurs on p. 112.

2. The grounds in question were that Reichenbach's "probability theory of meaning," as he explained it, ignores two central principles of the "externalist" semantics I advocated in "The Meaning of 'Meaning'" and subsequently, namely, the linguistic division of labor and the fact that paradigms external to the speaker often serve to fix reference. In the case of the word *gold*, for example, speakers rely on experts (whose criteria the average speaker doesn't know), and the experts rely on ongoing scientific investigation of the metal. I wrote that "there is nothing in the meaning to enable us *individually* to assign a 'weight' to 'such and such is gold' in many circumstances—contrary to the "probability theory of meaning" (Putnam, "Reference and Understanding," 113).

3. In "Testability and Meaning," Part I, *Philosophy of Science* 3 (1936): 422, Carnap wrote that this identification was "exhibited in the earliest publications of our *Vienna Circle*; it is still held by the more conservative wing of this Circle."

servable situation, and (2) every *difference* in meaning be reflected in some difference in weight in some observable situation? (These are, in my formulation, the two principles of Reichenbach's "probability theory of meaning.") At least it should be an open question for the realist whether this is so or not, and not something that realism rules out.[4]

What I want to argue here (and did not argue at that time) is that this observation is essential to understanding the structure and content of Reichenbach's only work in pure epistemology, *Experience and Prediction*.[5] That is, not only is it the case that one might *suppose* that realism and Reichenbach's form of verificationism are compatible, but that was, so to speak, the *point* of *Experience and Prediction*. What Reichenbach was trying to do in the whole book was *simultaneously* to be a particular sort of realist (a materialist, in particular) *and* preserve a weak form of the verifiability theory of meaning—weak, but not *too* weak to exclude metaphysics. This is not to say that Reichenbach did not feel some discomfort; after all, his friend (with whom he co-founded *Erkenntnis*) Rudolf Carnap (and the other members of the Vienna Circle as well)[6] had characterized the realism / idealism issue as a pseudo-issue, and Reichenbach defers to this view to the extent of claiming that the issue is just a question of a choice of a linguistic framework. But I wish to claim that the arguments Reichenbach gave only make sense if we realize that his realism was much more robust than these disclaimers suggest.

To argue this properly would require a much longer paper than this one. What I shall do here is point to places in Reichenbach's argumentation at which his realism is most evident, and also briefly discuss the claim just alluded to, that the issue is one of choosing a "language."

4. Putnam, "Reference and Understanding," 113 (emphasis in original).

5. Hans Reichenbach, *Experience and Prediction* (Chicago: University of Chicago Press, 1938).

6. Reichenbach, it should be noted was not a Vienna Circler; he led his own group, the "Berliner Gesellschaft für empirische Philosophie," in Berlin. Its most famous members, besides Reichenbach himself, were C. G. Hempel and Olaf Helmer. *Erkenntnis*, founded in 1930, was the official journal of *both* the Wiener Kreis and the Berliner Gesellschaft. In 1933, a few days after Hitler took power, Reichenbach fled Europe. *Experience and Prediction*, which appeared in 1938, was written in Istanbul, which provided positions for dozens of refugee professors from Nazi Germany.

I also want to consider another aspect of Reichenbach's thought, one not, as far as I know, mentioned in his writings. When I was Reichenbach's student he repeatedly expressed the view that in "Testability and Meaning"[7] and thereafter Carnap had "converged" to a position close to or perhaps identical with (my memory is not clear here) Reichenbach's own position. I want to briefly consider this idea, and argue that while there is a superficial appearance of convergence, Carnap's way of thinking is really very far from what I have described as Reichenbach's realism, even after "Testability and Meaning," and, in fact, to the end of Carnap's life.

Background: The Probability Theory of Meaning

I have already mentioned the two principles of "the probability theory of meaning." Here they are in Reichenbach's words): (1) a proposition[8] has meaning if it is possible to determine a weight, that is, a degree of probability, for the proposition;[9] and (2) every *difference* in meaning is reflected in some difference in weight in some observable situation.[10] It is necessary to add that at this time neither Reichenbach nor Carnap considered any other possible meaning for "probability" than relative frequency, and that Carnap questioned whether it was possible to assign numerical degrees of probability (in this sense) to hypotheses.[11]

---

7. Rudolf Carnap, "Testability and Meaning," *Philosophy of Science* 3 (1936): 420–471, and 4 (1937): 2–38.

8. Reichenbach's term for a sentence. "The words 'sentence' and 'statement' are also in use. But this distinction being of little importance and rather vague, we shall make no distinction between 'propositions' and 'sentences' and 'statements'" (*Experience and Prediction*, 21n).

9. Reichenbach neglects to say "on the basis of some possible observation," but the formulation of the second principle makes it clear that this is what he means.

10. Reichenbach, *Experience and Prediction*, 54.

11. At least we know that as late as "Testability and Meaning" (1936–1937) Carnap could write (speaking of Reichenbach's probability theory of meaning), "It presupposes the thesis that the degree of confirmation of a hypothesis can be interpreted as the degree of probability *in the strict sense which this concept has in the calculus of probability, i.e., as the limit of relative frequency.* Reichenbach holds this thesis" (427). Of course, Carnap was later to develop his theory that "degree of confirmation" is itself a quantitative notion and a possible interpretation of "probability" *different* from "the limit of the relative frequency." But in "Testability and Meaning" he wrote (also on p. 427), "It seems to me that at present it is not yet clear whether the concept of degree of confirmation can be defined satisfactorily as a quantitative concept, i.e. a magnitude having numerical values" (emphasis added).

(The "chief difficulty," Carnap wrote—citing Popper as the origin of this criticism—"lies in how we are to determine for a given hypothesis the series of 'related' hypotheses to which the concept of frequency is to apply.")[12]

Reichenbach, as we shall see, viewed scientific hypotheses in a very different way from that in which they are most often viewed (although his view has some affinity to "bootstrapping" views about scientific confirmation, such as those proposed by Clark Glymour). His belief that we can assign a numerical probability to, say, the existence of electrons was based on the idea that electrons are by no means mere "constructs," added to the language of physics for the sake of predictive efficacy. Electrons are *things*, much as billiard balls are things, and we *infer* their existence. Moreover, the very inferences by which we infer their existence permit us to assign a probability to that existence. It is obvious that this is (intuitively at least) a realistic conception, in stark contrast to that of the Vienna Circle.

There are many other symptoms of Reichenbach's attraction to realism, indeed to an almost naive materialism, in the opening chapter (titled "Meaning") of *Experience and Prediction*. Not only does Reichenbach emphasize that linguistic symbols are "physical things" (although this plays no role whatsoever in the probability theory of meaning), but, oddly, he adopts what sounds like a naive correspondence account of reference, writing:

> Let us formulate our first answer [to the question, "What is . . . meaning"] as follows: *Meaning is a function which symbols acquire by putting into a certain correspondence with facts.*"[13]

And again,

> If "north" means a certain relation of a line to the North Pole of the earth, the symbol "north" will occur in connection with the symbols "London" and "Edinburgh," as for example, in the sentence, "Edinburgh is north of London," because the objects London and Edinburgh are in the relation to the North Pole cor-

---

12. Carnap, "Testability and Meaning," 427.
13. Reichenbach, *Experience and Prediction*, 17 (emphasis in original).

responding to the word "north." So the carbon patch "north" before your eyes has a meaning because it occurs in relation to other carbon patches in such a way that there is a correspondence to physical objects such as towns and the North Pole. Meaning is just this function of the carbon patch acquired by this connection.[14]

This pair of sentences in *Experience and Prediction*, contrary to what one might expect, is not the beginning of a sustained discussion of how one gets from putting symbols in correspondence with "facts" or "objects" to the definition of the concept "truth-value of a sentence." (There is no hint of Tarskian semantics in *Experience and Prediction*.) In fact, although we have just been told that meaning depends on a "correspondence," Reichenbach moves at once to other topics (that meaning is a property of a proposition as a whole, that it is related to the direction of actions, and then to the discussion of the "truth theory of meaning" [i.e., the Viennese theory that meaningfulness requires the possibility of "verification"] and to his own "probability theory of meaning"). *"Correspondence" is never mentioned again.* So what are these assertions doing here?

I submit that they represent *declarations of faith*. Reichenbach is telling us that he subscribes to an intuitive realist picture of meaning as correspondence. He has already told us that epistemology deals with "rational reconstruction"[15] (Reichenbach takes the term from Carnap's "rationale Nachkonstruktion" in the *Aufbau*). The subsequent discussion, which does not mention correspondence, is I believe, precisely Reichenbach's *rational reconstruction* of the notion of meaning; but the initial declarations I have quoted show that it is not offered as a repudiation of realism, but intended to make these realist intuitions more precise.

Reichenbach's Cubical World Argument

The most interesting but also the most difficult chapter of *Experience and Prediction* is titled "Impressions and the External World." The difficulties begin with the title. Although Reichenbach adopts the strategy of speaking of "impressions" in this chapter, and makes the traditional

14. Reichenbach, *Experience and Prediction*, 17.
15. Reichenbach, *Experience and Prediction*, 5.

assumption that impressions are what we "directly observe," he opens the very next chapter, "An Inquiry Concerning Impressions," by attacking that whole way of thinking.

> The foregoing chapter was based on the presupposition that impressions are observable facts. We introduced them because we found that physical observations, even of the most concrete type, can never be maintained with certainty; so we tried to reduce them to more elementary facts. It may be doubtful, we said, that there is a table before me; but I cannot doubt that at least I have the impression of a table. Thus impressions came to be the very archetype of observable facts.
>
> This train of thought is of convincing power and there are not many philosophers who have been able to resist it. As for myself, I believed it for a long time until I discovered at last some of its weak points.[16] Although there is something correct in these reflections, it seems to me now that there is something in them which is essentially false.[17]

Reichenbach immediately goes on to declare, "I cannot admit that impressions have the character of observable facts. What I observe are things, not impressions."[18] To be sure, Reichenbach does not doubt the existence of impressions. "I believe that there are impressions; but I

---

16. One of those "weak points," in Reichenbach's view, is the assumption that no proposition could be known with probability unless some basic propositions were known with certainty. In a remarkable paper titled "Are Phenomenal Reports Absolutely Certain?" *Philosophical Review* 61 (1952): 147–159, delivered at a symposium with C. I. Lewis and Nelson Goodman, Reichenbach returns to this question late in his life and argues devastatingly against Lewis's defense of this assumption. Compare my "Reichenbach and the Myth of the Given," in my *Words and Life*, ed. James Conant (Cambridge, Mass.: Harvard University Press, 1994), 115–130.

17. Reichenbach, *Experience and Prediction*, 163. The only one of the "exceptional" philosophers who have been able to resist the idea that impressions are observable facts cited by Reichenbach is Richard Avenarius. This is interesting because we know that it was reading Avenarius that first inspired James to turn to his own version of direct realism. D. C. Lamberth, *Metaphysics, Experience and Religion in William James' Thought* (Cambridge: Cambridge University Press, 1997) provides a detailed account of the development of James's metaphysics.

18. Reichenbach, *Experience and Prediction*, 164.

have never *sensed* them. When I consider this question in an unprejudiced manner, I find that I *infer* the existence of my impressions."

What is happening in chapter 2 of *Experience and Prediction*, then, is not really an account of how we infer the existence of things from impressions; if Reichenbach's view (in chapter 3) is correct, *there is no such problem*. Rather, it is an account of how we infer the existence (and behavior) of unobserved things from the existence and behavior of observed things. What Reichenbach assumes for the purposes of chapter 2 is that if "things" only existed when observed by me and had only the properties that they appear (to me) to possess, then these "things" would be, to all intents and purposes, just as "phenomenal" as the empiricist impressions; this justifies, he thinks, (temporarily) *identifying* the traditional problem of justifying "the inference from impressions to the external world" with the problem of justifying the inference from observed things to unobserved things.

He argues vigorously against what he calls the "positivist" view (Reichenbach never accepted the label as applied to himself) that talk about unobserved objects is just highly derived talk about one's own impressions and / or about observed objects. Instead, he likens it to inferring the existence of birds we cannot see, but whose shadows are visible to us on the ceiling of the cage. To make the inference more complicated, he imagines a setup in which the human race is confined to an enormous cubical room with translucent walls. There are birds outside the cube and a mirror that causes the images of the birds to be reflected onto a sidewall of the cube so that each bird produces two "shadows," one on the ceiling and one on the side wall. To make sure that it is physically impossible for human beings to directly verify the existence of the birds, Reichenbach also stipulates that there is a "system of repulsive forces" that makes any near approach to the walls "impossible for men."[19] And he asks, "Will these men discover that there are things outside their cube different from the shadow-figures?"[20]

The answer he gives is that

after some time, however, I think there will come a Copernicus. He will direct telescopes to the walls and discover that the dark

19. Reichenbach, *Experience and Prediction*, 117.
20. Reichenbach, *Experience and Prediction*, 116.

spots have the shape of animals, and what is more important still, that there are corresponding pairs of black dots, consisting of one dot on the ceiling and one dot on the side wall, which show a very similar shape.[21]

Reichenbach goes on to describe how Copernicus will

> surprise mankind by the exposition of a very suggestive theory. He will maintain that the strange correspondence between the two shades of one pair cannot be a matter of chance but that these two shades are nothing but effects caused by one individual thing situated outside the cube within free space. He calls these things "birds" and he says that there are animals flying outside the cube, different from the shadow figures, having an existence of their own, and that the black spots are nothing but shadows.[22]

Reichenbach now imagines a positivist, who insists that the "birds" are just logical constructions; in fact they can be identified with pairs of black spots.[23] And he insists that a physicist would *reject* this positivist interpretation.

> The physicist, however, would not accept this . . . theory . . . It is not because he wants to combine with the term "causal connection" some metaphysical feelings, such as "influence from one thing to another" or "transubstantiation of the cause into the effect" . . . Freed from all associated representations, his inference has this form: Whenever there were corresponding shadow-figures like the spots on the screen [in the case of similar phenomena observable *within* the cubical world], there was, in addition, a third body with an independent existence; it is therefore highly probable that there is also such a third body in the case in question. It is this probability inference which furnishes a different weight [probability] for the projective complex and the reducible complex.[24]

21. Reichenbach, *Experience and Prediction*, 116–117.
22. Reichenbach, *Experience and Prediction*, 118.
23. Reichenbach, *Experience and Prediction*, 119.
24. Reichenbach, *Experience and Prediction*, 123.

In this last quotation, two technical terms appear: "projective complex" and "reducible complex." A "projective complex" is an item to whose existence we infer with probability on the basis of similar cases in the past; a "reducible complex" is something whose existence is guaranteed by the existence of the evidence because it is a mere logical construct out of that evidence. Reichenbach is arguing that, on the (early Vienna Circle) view he is attacking, the existence of the "birds" [unobserved objects] is *certain*, because they *are* nothing more than logical constructs out of the observables (pairs of shadow-figures); on the view he regards as correct, their existence has a probability less than one, and is thus not logically equivalent to the existence of the logical constructs. On Reichenbach's "probability theory of meaning," the two propositions which the "positivists" regarded as equivalent in meaning are quite distinct assertions.

"Illata" versus "Abstracta"

Two quite opposed reactions are possible to this argument. On the one hand, a traditional epistemologist might say that the argument simply begs the question. Reichenbach's inference presupposes that *there are places outside the cubical world at which unobserved objects can be situated*. Is this not precisely begging the question of "the existence of unobserved objects"? [This is Reichenbach's "stand-in" for the question of the existence of objects other than our sense impressions.]

Reichenbach's answer to this objection is stated in what he himself acknowledges to be Carnapian language, which leaves him open to the suspicion (which he himself shared) that the difference between Reichenbach and "the positivist" is just the difference between the Carnap of, say, "Testability and Meaning," and the earlier positions of the Vienna Circle. (This is the second possible reaction.) What Reichenbach says in answer to the first reaction is that the decision to postulate places we do not observe and to allow inductive speculation about the behavior of (possible) objects at such places is a matter of "the difference of two languages." I shall discuss this claim in a later section, as well as the question of whether, indeed, there is an identity of view between the Reichenbach of *Experience and Prediction* and the Carnap of "Testability and Meaning." But certainly, as far as the status of statements about objects we do not observe but *could* (physically possibly) have observed, what Carnap writes in "Testabililty and Meaning" is in full agreement with Reichenbach's position. Discussing "the following sentence discussed by [C. I.] Lewis and Schlick: 'If all minds (or: all living beings)[25] should disappear from the universe, the stars would still go on in their courses'," Carnap writes:

> Both Lewis and Schlick assert that this sentence is not verifiable. This is true if "verifiable" is interpreted as "completely confirmable." But the sentence is confirmable and even testable, though incompletely . . . The sentence in question is meaningful from the point of view of empiricism, i.e., it has to be admitted in an empiricist language, provided generalized sentences are admitted at all and complete confirmability is not required.[26]

The "partial confirmation" Carnap speaks of here is just the confirmation (during our lifetimes) of "the laws C of celestial mechanics."[27]

In his lectures at the University of California–Los Angeles, Reichenbach used to employ the following example: suppose I see a tree-shaped shadow in front of me on the ground. Whether I turn around and look at the tree or not, I infer that there is a tree behind me, because I have confirmed—in situations in which I *was* in a position to see the place in question—that whenever there is a tree-shaped shadow on the ground, then (almost always, if we allow for a small number of cases where the shadow is cast by something else), in the place at which the base of the tree-shaped shadow is located, there is also a real tree. The statement that there is an unobserved tree behind me is simply a deduction (or an induction, if the generalization is statistical) from a generalization which is itself *inductively* confirmed. Concerning this view, I wrote in *Meaning and the Moral Sciences:*

> What seems right to me about this is that if we had no inductive logic *at all*—if we had only pattern recognition and deductive logic—there would be no basis for ascribing to us any *concept* of an "unobserved object." Our linguistic behavior would fit the account

---

25. The parenthetical remark is Carnap's.
26. Carnap, "Testability and Meaning," Part II, *Philosophy of Science* 4, (1937): 37–38.
27. Carnap, "Testability and Meaning," Part II, 37.

"tree" means "observed tree"—and, more generally, "object" means "observed object." In this sense our inductive logic is *part of* our concept of an unobserved object, and hence of an object at all.[28]

But Reichenbach does not only speak of the inference from observed objects (birds, trees) to unobserved objects. As already remarked, he regards the inference to *unobservable* objects (e.g., "electricity, radio waves, atoms") as of exactly the same nature.[29] Such theoretical entities, he claims, are *illata* (inferred entities),[30] not *abstracta* (logical constructions). With respect to this claim I want to make two remarks, one historical and one purely philosophical.

The historical claim is that the agreement between Carnap and Reichenbach regarding the status of sentences about *unobserved* objects decidedly did *not* extend to agreement about the status of *unobservable* objects, such as the "electricity and radio waves" Reichenbach mentions. The predicates we need to even speak about such objects are only "partially interpreted," Carnap insisted to the end of his life; talk about them is highly derived talk about observables (and, strange to say, *sets* of observables, sets of sets of observables, etc.). Although these "theoretical constructs," as Carnap's followers continued to call them,[31] were no longer claimed to be individually definable in "observational vocabulary," the theory of contemporary science *as a whole* was held to be expressible in a language with no primitive vocabulary except "observation terms."[32] This is precisely the attitude that Reichenbach rejected.

28. Putnam, *Meaning and the Moral Sciences*, 112.

29. I use "unobservable" here as the logical empiricists themselves did. In *The Threefold Cord: Mind, Body and World* (New York: Columbia University Press, 1999), 43–70, I criticize the idea that things we observe only with the aid of scientific instruments are "unobservable" in any epistemologically significant sense. But the view I defend there is not compatible with Reichenbach's view that all scientific knowledge comes from (1) unaided human perception and (2) what he was prepared to allow as "inductive logic." (On the problems with the latter, see "Reichenbach and the Limits of Vindication," in my *Words and Life* (Cambridge, Mass.: Harvard University Press, 1994), 131–148.

30. Reichenbach, in *Experience and Prediction*, writes, "We use the participle *illatum* of the Latin *infero*, to denote this kind of thing" (212).

31. This term appears repeatedly in the volumes of *Minnesota Studies in the Philosophy of Science* edited by Carnap's ally Herbert Feigl during Carnap's lifetime.

32. For references, and also for a criticism of this view, see Hilary Putnam, "What Theories Are Not," in *Mathematics, Matter and Method*, vol. 1 of *Philosophical Papers* (Cambridge: Cambridge University Press, 1975), 215–227.

The philosophical remark (a critical one) is that Reichenbach's view is, however, almost certainly incompatible with his own doctrines respecting inductive logic. For Reichenbach, induction is simply the projection of an observed relative frequency, and induction in this sense is the *only* legitimate method of nondemonstrative inference.[33] Even if we accept (as I think we should) *some* inferences to the existence and behavior of physical things too small to see or touch as of essentially the same character as the inference to the existence of the birds outside the cubical world, what Reichenbach ignores is the problem of inferences that are not to the existence of little *things* at all, but to the existence of fields (modifications of space itself), and of novel magnitudes of all kinds. (It is striking that when he discusses his doctrine of "illata" he writes that "modern physics has shown that electrons, positrons, protons, neutrons, and photons are the basic elements out of which all things are built up *in the form of reducible complexes*."[34] Here he entirely ignores the *predicates* involved, and thinks only of the objects!) In *The Philosophy of Space and Time*, Reichenbach allows himself to pretend that there are arbitrarily small "clocks" and "measuring rod[s]"; however useful and legitimate such a device may be in explaining relativity theory, we cannot seriously suppose that an inference to the existence of such a magnitude as electricity and to the differential equations that it obeys are simply "inductive" inferences (in Reichenbach's limited sense) to the behavior of arbitrarily small measuring instruments!

The problem will appear strange to most philosophers since we are used to thinking, with Mill, that something called the "hypothetico-deductive method" is an essential part of the apparatus of "induction," and that it is by confirming the *predictions* of theories about electricity that we confirm the existence and behavior of electricity. But Reichenbach *rejected* the hypothetico-deductive method, or, rather, he had a Bayesian attitude toward it: the method is legitimate only when sanctioned by Bayes's Theorem, which requires a knowledge of the *prior probabilities* of the alternative hypotheses. But the difficulty is in seeing how Reichenbach's inductive method can assign any probability at all to hypotheses about such "illata."

---

33. See part V of *Experience and Prediction*, "Probability and Induction."
34. Reichenbach, *Experience and Prediction*, 215 (emphasis added).

The reason that Reichenbach held such a restrictive view of induction has to do, strangely, with a *rationalist* strain in his thinking: he believed that he had found a *deductive vindication of induction*, and that this limited sort of induction was the *only* method for which such a deductive vindication could be given.[35]

Just "the Difference between Two Languages"?

In §16 of *Experience and Prediction*, "An Egocentric Language," Reichenbach formulates the difference between positivism and realism as a matter of choice between an "egocentric language" (in which things exist only when observed to exist by the subject, and have all and only the properties they appear—to that same subject—to have), and "usual language" which allows inferences to unobserved objects. (A similar distinction occurs in "Testability and Meaning," although not under these labels.) At the beginning of the next section, §17, "Positivism and Realism as a Problem of Language," he writes, "The difference of the positivistic and the realistic conception of the world has taken a different turn; this difference has been formulated as the difference of two languages." And he immediately adds, "This form of consideration, *which has been applied particularly by Carnap*, seems to be a means appropriate to the problem in question, and we shall make use of it for illustration of our results."[36]

What a reader of Carnap would expect at this point is some such argument as the following: the more liberal language ("usual language") allows the formulation of statements from which we can deduce or induce many useful predictions which are not permitted by the restrictions of the older positivism (because the statements cannot be formulated in "egocentric language"). In short, the statements science makes about, for example, objects too small to see, or events before there were sentient beings, are part of a system that leads to valuable predictions about what we observe here and now, predictions each scientist could in principle test for herself. But Reichenbach offers a remarkably different argument:

---

35. See part V of *Experience and Prediction*, "Probability and Induction."
36. Reichenbach, *Experience and Prediction*, 145 (emphasis added).

The insufficiency of a positivist language in which talk of events after my death is construed as a device for predicting my experiences while I am alive is revealed as soon as we try to use it for the rational reconstruction of the thought processes underlying actions concerned with events after our death, such as expressed in the example of [purchasing] life insurance policies.[37]

I contend that this argument makes a deep point, and one quite unlike anything to be found in Carnap's writing. What Reichenbach is telling us is that if I view my whole language as just a device for predicting what experiences *I myself* will have—if even statements about my family, and about what will happen to them after I die, are no more than gears in a prediction machine, a machine whose whole purpose is to predict what I will experience here and now—then that view will violate the deepest intuitions we have about *what we are doing* when we utter sentences about others and about events after (and before) our own lives. One might add (although Reichenbach unfortunately did not) that even if I deny that such statements are *translatable* into an "egocentric language," if the only account I have of what it is to *understand* a "realist" language is that it consists in being able to use it to predict *one's own* sensory stimulations, the view remains just as unsatisfactory. As I have myself put this further moral:

> *Moral: to preserve our commonsense realist convictions it is not enough to preserve some set of "realist" sentences; the interpretation you give those sentences, or, more broadly, your account of what understanding them consists in, is also important![38]*

I do not claim that Reichenbach drew this further moral. Indeed, I have argued elsewhere that he failed to see that in consistency his ar-

---

37. Reichenbach, *Experience and Prediction*, 150. In "Logical Positivism and Intentionality," in *Words and Life*, 90–93, I argue that Reichenbach fails to realize that this defense of realist language is, in fact, incompatible with the defense he offers of the claim that all that is at stake is a choice of a language. It assumes, in particular, that my *understanding* of the language doesn't consist merely in my ability to assign weights to sentences on the basis of my own experiences, but recognizes that some account of reference is needed.

38. Hilary Putnam, "Richard Rorty on Reality and Justification," in *Rorty and His Critics*, ed. Robert Brandom (Oxford: Blackwell, 2000), 81–87 (emphasis in original).

gument required him to give a nonpositivist account of *understanding.*[39] But the intuition behind Reichenbach's little argument about "the life insurance policies" is, I think, quite clear.

Conclusion

In closing, it is appropriate to ask, when all is said and done, just what did Reichenbach understand by his contrast of "the positivistic and realistic conceptions of the world"? I take it, that at least this much is safe to say: (1) A realistic conception of the world did not, in Reichenbach's eyes, presuppose a theory of truth. His realism was, in the main, a *rejection* of a picture that he saw as inadequate to our scientific lives and, in the re- markable paragraph I just quoted, to our humanity as well, not a proposal for a metaphysical foundation of some kind. (2) Reichenbach did not, however, *think through* the question of whether what he retained from positivism was fully adequate to his "realistic conception of the world."

39. Putnam, "Richard Rorty on Reality and Justification."

7

Between Scylla and Charybdis

DOES DUMMETT HAVE A WAY THROUGH?

𝓛IKE QUINE'S ESSAYS, starting with "On What There Is" and "Two Dogmas of Empiricism," and like Donald Davidson's essays, starting with "Meaning and Truth," and like Kripke's lectures published as *Naming and Necessity*, Michael Dummett's essays and books blazed entirely new paths in philosophy of language, construed not narrowly, but as absolutely central to the whole of metaphysics and epistemology. In all three of these cases, the reverberations still continue to be felt, and they will be going on being felt for a long time to come. In my own case, it was hearing Dummett's William James Lectures delivered in 1976 at my own university that exerted a profound influence.[1] Even if my own orbit has carried me some distance away from the point of closest approach to Michael Dummett's philosophical planet, I continue to feel his gravitational attraction, and I feel tremendously enriched by our interactions, personal as well as philosophical.

The Problem Dummett Sees with Realistic Semantics

The difficulty Dummett sees with realistic semantics is summed up in his famous "manifestation argument," to the effect that if we *did* have

1. Michael Dummett, *The Logical Basis of Metaphysics*, The William James Lectures 1976 (Cambridge, Mass.: Harvard University Press, 1991).

a conception of "realist" truth, truth as fully independent of all possibility of verification, then there would be no way in which we could "manifest" our conception in our behavior, and hence no way in which we could teach our realist conception of truth to others, determine which others really *have* this concept of truth, and so on.[2] But one all-important remark: although Dummett has concentrated for many years on arguing that there are (apparently insuperable) difficulties with realism, there is a sense in which the "antirealism" or "justificationism" that Dummett regularly treats as the alternative to realism is not precisely *advocated* by Dummett. Instead, Dummett (admirably, in my view) sees himself as *exploring* a philosophical issue, or exploring a philosophical dialectic (with, to be sure, a predilection to one side of the debate). As he himself puts it in the preface to *Truth and the Past*,[3] "I do not think anyone should interpret everything that a philosopher writes as if it was just one chapter in a book he is writing throughout his life. On the contrary, for me every article and essay is a separate attempt to arrive at the truth, to be judged on its own."

If the "antirealist" position Dummett proposes as the alternative to realist semantics remains in this way "work in progress," the manifestation argument against realism has remained a constant in the many years Dummett has been making his "separate attempts to arrive at the truth" in this area.[4] A pithy statement of the manifestation argument occurs, in fact, in an essay titled "Truth: Deniers and Defenders" that he added to the lectures that make up the body of *Truth and the Past*. Dummett writes,

2. Michael Dummett, "What Is a Theory of Meaning, I," collected in his *Seas of Language* (Oxford: Clarendon Press, 1993), 97–138.

3. Michael Dummett, *Truth and the Past* (New York: Columbia University Press, 2004).

4. However, I don't wish to give the impression that it was the manifestation argument that was responsible for what I described as a close approach of our philosophical orbits around the time of Dummett's William James Lectures (and for a number of years subsequently). If anything it was because of a different argument, my model theoretic argument against metaphysical realism, that I was prepared to accept the claim that "we have no means" for acquiring the realist notion of truth. The model theoretic argument is set out in a lecture titled "Realism and Reason" to the American Philosophical Association reprinted as the last chapter of my *Meaning and the Moral Sciences* (London: Routledge and Kegan Paul, 1978), and at more length in my *Reason, Truth and History* (Cambridge: Cambridge University Press, 1981). I explain what I think is wrong with it in *The Threefold Cord: Mind, Body and World* (New York: Columbia University Press, 1999).

What prompts [justificationist] theories of truth is a thought similar to that of Rorty in concluding that justification is the goal of inquiry: namely that when we acquire the practice of using language, what we learn is what is taken to justify assertions of different types. We learn what is accepted as entitling us to make those assertions; we learn also whether what justifies us in doing so is conclusive or whether it is defeasible, that is, capable of being overthrown by subsequent counterevidence. We do *not* learn what it is for those assertions to be true independently of any means we have for establishing their truth. How could we? If we are not in a position either to assert or to deny a given proposition, we cannot be shown what nevertheless makes it true or false. So, according to a theory of this kind, to grasp the meaning of a statement is to know what would justify asserting it or denying it.[5]

Redefining "Realism"

What I hope to do in this essay is to make clear how it was that I came to see what I regard as insuperable difficulties with antirealism. In this way, I hope to open yet another page in the dialogue that Michael Dummett and I have been having for forty years.

The term "realism" occurs quite often in my essays prior to 1975.[6] In those essays, it means one thing and one thing only: the rejection of logical positivism, operationalism, and related positions. As I explained in one of those essays, "A Philosopher Looks at Quantum Mechanics":

All attempts to *literally* "translate" statements about, say, electrical charge into statements about so-called observables (meter readings) have been dismal failures, and from Berkeley on, all *a priori* argu-

5. Michael Dummett, "Truth: Deniers and Defenders," in *Truth and the Past*, 97–116; quotation from p. 114.

6. I am thinking in particular of the essays I collected in the first two volumes of my *Philosophical Papers*, which were published in 1975 by Cambridge University Press. (A third volume, *Realism and Reason*, published in 1983, represents my subsequent "internal realist" position—a position I now regard as a false start to dealing with the very real problem of the normativity of language use.)

ments designed to show that all statements about unobservables must ultimately reduce to statements about observables have contained gaping holes and outrageously false assumptions. It is quite true that we "verify" statements about unobservable things by making suitable *observations*, but I maintain that without imposing a wholly untenable theory of meaning, one cannot even *begin* to go from this fact to the wildly erroneous conclusion that talk about unobservable things and theoretical magnitudes *means the same* as talk about observations and observables.[7]

Although I pointed out in that essay that Carnap had given up the attempt to reduce statements about unobservables to "observation language," I criticized him in "Explanation and Reference," for an "idealist" tendency manifested in the fact that according to the theory of the meaning (or "partial interpretation") of theoretical terms in science he defended in his late writings, every change in the total scientific theory amounted to a change in the reference of every one of those terms, so that theoretical terms were not treated as names of, say, unobservable things and forces concerning which scientists change their minds, but as merely parts of a machine for predicting "observations," parts which have no meaning in themselves apart from their role in the particular theory.[8]

The term "idealism" in those essays was virtually synonymous with "phenomenalism." Prior to my reading Dummett's William James Lectures, the only "idealism" I knew was Berkeley's, and the only "antirealism" I knew was antirealism about unobservables (and, in the case of phenomenalism, about "middle sized dry goods," which were treated as unobservables by phenomenalists). Thus it was an eye-opener that "realism" and "antirealism" could be understood as positions about the nature of truth itself, and not simply as positions about the reducibility or nonreducibility of "theoretical terms" to "observation terms" or of "thing-language" to "sense-datum language."

7. Hilary Putnam, "A Philosopher Looks at Quantum Mechanics," in *Mathematics, Matter and Method*, vol. 1 of *Philosophical Papers* (Cambridge: Cambridge University Press, 1975), 130–158, quotation from p. 131.

8. Hilary Putnam, "Explanation and Reference," in *Mind, Language and Reality*, vol. 2 of *Philosophical Papers* (Cambridge: Cambridge University Press, 1975), 196–214.

What I then called "idealism" is better called *reductionism*, Dummett taught me.[9] Reductionism, with respect to a class of statements, is the philosophical theory that statements in that class are "made true" by facts described by statements in what is claimed to be some epistemologically or metaphysically more "basic" class. For example, the phenomenalist view that statements about tables and chairs and other ordinary "material objects" are made true by facts describable in a sense-datum language is a reductionist view of the kind I called "idealist."

If a view is reductionist with respect to assertions of one kind, only to insist on a "correspondence" notion of truth for statements in the reducing class, then that view is, according to Dummett, metaphysically realist at base. A truly nonrealist view is nonrealist all the way down.

I say that this redefinition of realism (and antirealism) was an "eye-opener" because it seemed to open a way out of the difficulties I had been having in thinking about the model theoretic argument against metaphysical realism—an argument that had occurred to me *before* Dummett's William James Lectures, but that I could not see my way clear to either accepting or rejecting at that time, which is why I did not present it publicly until 1976.[10]

Not surprisingly, Dummett's redefinition of "realism" and "antirealism" was contested: most vehemently, perhaps, by Michael Devitt.[11] According to Devitt, the realism issue is simply, "Is there a mind-independent reality or not?" *(thump)* and there *that* question has nothing to do with semantics. This short way with the issue reminds one of Lenin's (disastrously incompetent) polemical book against Machian positivism.[12] Lenin simply claimed that positivists, since they took human sensations as the class of truth-makers for all propositions (I am using present-day terminology, not Lenin's, of course), could not

9. The views I am referring to were those in the William James Lectures (see note 1, above). They were set out more briefly in "What Is a Theory of Meaning? (I)," and "What Is a Theory of Meaning? (II)," respectively published in *Mind and Language*, ed. S. Guttenplan (Oxford: University Press, 1975), 97–138, and in *Truth and Meanings: Essays in Semantics*, ed. Gareth Evans and John McDowell (Oxford: Oxford University Press, 1976), 67–137.

10. See note 4 for details.

11. Michael Devitt, *Realism and Truth* (Oxford: Blackwell, 1984); see Drew Khlentzos, *Naturalistic Realism and the Antirealist Challenge* (Cambridge, Mass.: MIT Press, 2004) for a convincing criticism of Devitt's response to Dummett.

12. V. I. Lenin, *Materialism and Empirio-Criticism* (Moscow: Foreign Languages Publishing House, 1952).

accept the statement that the solar system existed before there were human beings.[13] This argument simply assumes—what positivists of course deny[14]—that the positivists cannot *interpret* "the solar system existed before there were human beings" in their rationally reconstructed "language of science."

But what of the word "independent" in "the behavior of the stars is independent of human sensations and thoughts and beliefs"? (This is what Devitt portrayed antirealists as *denying*.)

Well, there are many kinds of independence. Presumably causal independence is what Devitt was talking about, since *logical* independence is a property of *statements* (or, perhaps, of events *under a description*), and whether statements are or are not logically independent is certainly a question about their *semantics*, which Devitt claimed to be irrelevant to the realism issue. But then Devitt's argument once again simply assumes—what antirealists of course deny—that the antirealist cannot *interpret* the sentence "the behavior of the stars is independent of human sensations and thoughts and beliefs" in a "justificationist" way, interpret it so that it is "true" (in the antirealist sense). Devitt cannot, after all, say, "But that's not what the sentence *means!*" without engaging in a discussion of—guess what?—semantics.

I remain convinced that Dummett has made a truly lasting contribution to our appreciation of the *depth* of the realism/antirealism issue, just as Berkeley did at an earlier time. Devitt's dismissive attitude is as unphilosophical as Samuel Johnson's stone-kicking.

The Antirealist Tries to Steer between Scylla and Charybdis

But can one really develop a defensible antirealist account of the semantics of our language? When I reread what I wrote in *Reason, Truth and History* (especially in chapters 3 and 5), I see my former self as trying

13. Indeed, Devitt seems to have read Lenin closely—at least his first published attack on *my* "internal realism" was titled "Realism and the Renegade Putnam," a clear play on the title of Lenin's famous article "Marxism and the Renegade Kautsky."

14. For example, Carnap discusses this sort of statement (his example is "If all minds (or all living beings) should disappear from the universe, the stars would still go on in their courses"), without mentioning Lenin, however, in "Testability and Meaning," Part II, *Philosophy of Science* 4 (1937): 37–38, and concludes that it is both cognitively meaningful and well confirmed.

to steer between the Scylla of solipsism and the Charybdis of metaphysical realism, and when I read Dummett's *Truth and the Past*, I find that I have the same feeling. But this takes some explanation, I know.

In §16 of *Experience and Prediction*,[15] Reichenbach considered and rejected a form of verificationism that he described as "the choice of an egocentric language" (a language in which things can meaningfully be said to exist only when observed to exist by the subject, and can meaningfully be said to have only the properties they appear—to that same subject—to have). According to this form of verificationism (Reichenbach is clearly thinking of a position held by members of the Vienna Circle at a certain point), all cognitively meaningful assertions that seem to be about times or places the speaker never observes are to be reinterpreted as asserting that if the speaker were to do so-and-so, then she would experience such-and-such. As we recalled in Chapter 6 ["Hans Reichenbach: Realist *and* Verificationist"], Reichenbach argued that such a reinterpretation is unable to express the rationale for certain "actions concerned with events after our death, such as . . . [purchasing] life insurance."[16]

One obviously doesn't buy life insurance so that one will oneself have certain experiences if one does so (or if one has the experience of doing so)! Let us see now how a similar difficulty might confront a "justificationist" philosopher.

Suppose that this philosopher maintains that what it is for a statement (*any* statement) to be true is for the statement to be justified by experiences she has or will have in *her* lifetime. If what makes the statement true is also supposed to be what the statement "means"—what it asserts to be the case—she is a solipsist. If not, an unacceptable gap seems to open between what a statement *says* and what *makes it true*. In either case, Reichenbach's observation has force: she cannot intelligibly rationalize buying a life insurance policy.

A verificationist who denies that there is such a thing as logically conclusive verification of an empirical proposition may nonetheless face a similar problem. If my understanding of my own sentences is alleged to consist in my ability to assign them a degree of verification on the

15. Hans Reichenbach, *Experience and Prediction* (Chicago: University of Chicago Press, 1938).

16. Reichenbach, *Experience and Prediction*, 150.

basis of my own experiences, then, in particular, my *understanding* of the prediction that my family will be better off after my death if I buy life insurance now consists in the knowledge that certain experiences I have or could have in my lifetime justify asserting that sentence to this, that, or the other degree. Again, if the justificationist says, "Oh, but I didn't say claim that the sentence is *about* those experiences," she creates a gap between the semantics of the sentence—since what makes her a *justificationist* philosopher, in Dummett's sense, is precisely that her program is to give the semantics of the sentence in terms of justification—and what she claims sentences *mean*. But how can *semantics* not be about what sentences *mean?*

Avoiding Scylla: Step One

The first step in avoiding the Scylla of solipsism is one that Dummett and I both took at different times. That step was simply to insist that the justificationism or verificationism that we advocated was *social* and not *individualistic* in nature.[17] Dummett puts it very clearly in *Truth and the Past:*

> What is the concept of truth appropriate to a justificationist theory of meaning? Plainly it must turn on the notion of our being justified in asserting a statement. It is evident at the outset that the word "our" must be taken in a collective, not a distributive, sense.[18]

Avoiding Scylla: A Second Step

In chapter 3 of my *Reason, Truth and History*, this first step was combined with a further one: replacing talk of verification with *idealized* verification:

> Truth is an *idealization* of rational acceptability. We speak as if there were such things as epistemically ideal conditions, and we call a statement "true" if it would be justified under such conditions.

17. Dummett uses the term "justificationism" in *Truth and the Past;* I spoke of "verificationist semantics" in my first internal realist writing, "Realism and Reason," my American Philosophical Association (Eastern Division) Presidential Address of 1976, collected in my *Meaning and the Moral Sciences* (London: Routledge and Kegan Paul, 1978), 123–138.

18. Dummett, *Truth and the Past*, 41.

"Epistemically ideal conditions," of course, are like "frictionless planes"; we cannot really attain epistemically ideal conditions, or even be absolutely certain that we have come sufficiently close to them. But frictionless planes cannot really be attained either, and yet talk of "frictionless planes" has "cash value" because we can approximate them to a very high degree of approximation.[19]

Perhaps it will seem that explaining truth in terms of justification under ideal conditions is explaining a clear notion in terms of a vague one. But "true" is *not* so clear when we move away from such stock examples as "Snow is white."

The simile of frictionless planes aside, the two key ideas of the idealization theory of truth are (1) that truth is independent of justification here and now, but not independent of *all* justification. To claim a statement is true is to claim it could be justified. (2) Truth is expected to be stable or "convergent"; if both a statement and its negation could be "justified," even if conditions were as ideal as one could hope to make them, there is no sense to thinking of the statement as *having* a truth-value.[20]

The Roar of Charybdis Is Heard in the Near Distance

The foregoing account of truth made use of the counterfactual conditional as well as of the notion of epistemically ideal (or "close to ideal") conditions. *S* is true, according to this view, just in case the following counterfactual is true:

S would be justified if epistemic conditions were good enough.[21]

But how is this counterfactual to be understood? As I put the difficulty in my Dewey Lectures,[22] explaining my reasons for giving up the whole approach:

---

19. Putnam, *Reason, Truth and History*, 55.

20. Putnam, *Reason, Truth and History*, 55–56.

21. I employed a similar counterfactual in *Representation and Reality* (Cambridge, Mass.: MIT Press 1988), 115.

22. "The Dewey Lectures 1994: Sense, Nonsense, and the Senses: An Inquiry into the Powers of the Human Mind" (special issue of *Journal of Philosophy* 91, no. 9, 1994); these are collected as part I of *The Threefold Cord* (pp. 3–70).

Unlike Dummett's "global antirealist," I did not suppose that empirical propositions could be *unalterably* verified or falsified.[23] And I was bothered from the start by the excessively "idealist" thrust of Dummett's position, as represented, for example, by Dummett's flirtation with strong antirealism with respect to the *past*, and I avoided that strong antirealism by identifying a speaker's grasp of the meaning of a statement not with an ability to tell if the statement is true now, or to tell whether it is true under circumstances the speaker can actually bring about . . . but with the speaker's possession of abilities which would enable [any] sufficiently rational speaker to decide if the statement is true in sufficiently good epistemic circumstances.

To the objection that this is still an "idealist" position, I replied that it certainly is not, on the ground that while the degree of confirmation speakers actually assign to a sentence may simply be a function of their sensory experiences . . . the notion of *sufficiently good epistemic circumstances* [was] a "world involving" notion. That is why the totality of actual human sense experiences does not, on this position, determine the totality of truths, even in the long run.

On my alternative picture (as opposed to Dummett's), the world was allowed to determine whether I actually am in a sufficiently good epistemic situation or whether I only seem to myself to be in one—thus retaining an important idea from commonsense realism—[but] the conception of an epistemic situation was, at bottom, just the traditional epistemological one. My picture still retained the basic premise of an interface between the knower and everything "outside." But while the need for a "third way" besides early modern realism and Dummettian idealism is something I feel as strongly as ever, such a third way must . . . *undercut* the idea that

---

23. Although Dummett is not unaware that the verification of an empirical statement is typically corrigible, as a rule, he tends to prescind from this fact. This tendency may spring from his expressed desire to carry Brouwer's intuitionist logic, a logic designed by Brouwer in connection with an antirealist philosophy of mathematics, over to empirical language. The simplest possible way to make such a carryover is to extend the notion of "proof," which is the basic notion in the intuitionist semantics for mathematical language, to a bivalent predicate 'verified'" applicable to mathematical and non-mathematical language alike, and this is what Dummett does. In this quotation, only the first italic (*"unalterably"*) was in the original text.

there is an "antinomy," and not simply paste together elements of early modern realism and elements of the idealist picture.[24]

As mentioned earlier, the "idealization theory of truth" was presented in chapter 3 of *Reason, Truth and History*. In chapter 5, the problem of the understanding of counterfactuals like "*S* would be justified if epistemic conditions were good enough" was addressed, however, by adopting a verificationist account of how we understand counterfactuals. I said simply that a "nonrealist" or "internal realist" regards conditional statements as statements that we understand (like all other statements) in large part by grasping their justification conditions. This does not mean that the "internal" realist abandons the distinction between truth and justification, but that truth (idealized justification) is something we grasp as we grasp any other concept, via a (largely) implicit understanding of the factors that make it rationally acceptable to say that something is true" (122–123). The dilemma I faced (but was not aware that I faced at that time) was this: let us suppose, as seems reasonable, that whatever makes it rational to believe that *S* makes it rational to believe that *S* would be justified were conditions good enough. If my understanding of the counterfactual "*S* would be justified if conditions were good enough" is exhausted by my capacity to tell to what degree it is justified to assert it, and that is always the same as the degree to which it is justified to assert *S* itself, why did I bother to mention the counterfactual at all? Why did I not just say that my understanding of *S* is just my capacity to tell what confirms *S* to what degree, full stop? It seems that the whole appeal to "idealized" verification, to counterfactual verification, was an unnecessary shuffle. But then the jaws of the Scylla of solipsism close on me! On the other hand, if I repudiate the justificationist account of our understanding of counterfactuals, the Charybdis of the metaphysical realism I was trying to avoid sweeps me into its whirlpool. It was the impossibility, as I now think it to be, of steering an antirealist course between the Scylla of solipsism and the Charybdis of metaphysical realism that led me to develop and defend what I believe to be an unmetaphysical version of realism in *The Threefold Cord: Mind, Body and World*. It is time now for us to see if

24. Putnam, "The Dewey Lectures," 14–15.

Michael Dummett has a found a way where I failed, to steer between Scylla and Charybdis.

Dummett's Way

As was already said, the first step in avoiding the Scylla of solipsism was simply to insist that the justificationism that we both advocated was *social* and not *individualistic* in nature, or as Dummett put it, that the word "our" in "our being justified in asserting a statement" must be taken "in a collective, not a distributive, sense." Whether this is something that Dummett *can* say without doing violence to his own justificationist principles, and what it means when understood in a justificationist way, is what we must now ask.

The question is important because of its connection with another question, the question to which, indeed, *Truth and the Past* is devoted: how to avoid antirealism about the past. I referred earlier to Dummett's "flirtation with antirealism about the past"; he himself says that this is a topic that troubled him for years, and that this new book is an attempt to see if a justificationist can repudiate "the view that statements about the past, if true at all, must be true in virtue of the traces past events have left in the present." He still not does find that view incoherent, but he does say it is "repugnant."[25] The way in which Dummett proposes to reject antirealism about the past involves simply counting past observers as fully on a par with present observers. The details of this proposal are complex, and it would take a much longer essay than this to examine them in detail. But the essential ideas are (1) that the semantically crucial verification of a statement about the past is not the present "indirect" verification, via a memory, or, in the case of the distant past, via a historical trace, that the statement is true, but the verification by a witness at the time ("Dying does not deprive anyone of the status either of an observer or of an informant");[26] and (2) that while that "direct" verification may be transmitted to us via a trace, it counts as a verification whether it is transmitted or not ("For all the messages

---

25. Dummett, *Truth and the Past*, ix. I believe that Yuval Dolev has successfully argued that, contrary to Dummett, antirealism about the past *is* incoherent. See Dolev's "Dummett's Antirealism and Time," *European Journal of Philosophy* 8 (2000): 253–276.

26. Dummett, *Truth and the Past*, 68.

that have been lost, it remains that statements about the past must count as having been directly established, and therefore as true, if someone observed them to be true at the, or an, appropriate time").[27]

The problem, however, is that while language is indeed social, *competence* is individual. Earlier I quoted Dummett as asking (rhetorically) "How could we learn what it is for assertions to be true independently of any means we have for establishing their truth?" but one can also ask "How could" an individual language learner learn to understand Dummett's "we." Dummett, indeed, tells us that:

> A child who had learned only when he was right to come out with simple assertoric utterances, such as "Doggie" when a dog was in sight, would serve as an extension of adults' range of observation, but could not yet be credited with saying that anything was so; he can be credited with that only when he has learned to treat the utterances of others as extending *his* range of observations. It is intrinsic to the use of language that we accept the testimony of others: to believe what we are told is the default response. Language binds us into society.[28]

I agree that it does, of course. But Dummett moves too rapidly from the child's acquisition of the practice of accepting the testimony of others—an idea the justificationist seems clearly entitled to—to the child's "treating the utterances of others as extending his range of observations," where this "treating" must amount to something quite different from a mere disposition to accept sentences that the child hears if it is to account for the child's grasp of the thought that a statement about the past may be true even though *no* testimony is available (to the child). (Dummett also speaks of the child's forming a mental "grid" that shows the relations of other places and times to one another and to the child's present location.)

The Alternative to Antirealism

In *The Threefold Cord*, discussing the antirealism about the past that Dummett once defended (or experimented with), I wrote:

27. Dummett, *Truth and the Past*, 68.
28. Dummett, *Truth and the Past*, 41.

If we accept it that understanding the sentence "Lizzie Borden killed her parents with an axe" is not simply a matter of being able to recognize a verification in our own experience—accept it, that is, that we are able to conceive of how things that we cannot verify *were*—then it will not appear as "magical" or "mysterious" that we can understand the claim that that sentence is *true*. What makes it true, if it is, is simply that Lizzie Borden killed her parents with an axe. The recognition transcendence of truth comes, in this case, to no more than the "recognition transcendence" of some killings. And did we ever think that all killers can be recognized as such? Or that the belief that there are certain determinate individuals who are or were killers and who cannot be detected as such by us is a belief in magical powers of the mind?[29]

I believe that Michael Dummett would agree with this. But I think that he would still say that we cannot *rest* with the commonsense thought that being able to think about past events that we cannot verify (being able to locate them in our mental "grid") is an ability that we acquire as we acquire language and all the skills that language brings with it. He believes that we need to show that that ability can be accounted for in a "justificationist" way. (Perhaps he thinks this because he thinks that antirealism about the past is only "repugnant" and not actually "incoherent"). But, first, I don't see that he *has* accounted for that ability in a justificationist way, for the reasons I have just briefly laid out, and, second, I *do* think that antirealism about the past is incoherent.[30]

29. Putnam, *Threefold Cord*, xxx.

30. See Yuval Dolev's "Dummett's Antirealism," cited previously. Dummett himself pointed out that if one holds the antirealist view that statements about the past, if true at all, "must be true in virtue of the traces past events have left in the present," then it must be that the meaning of every empirical statement about the past changes every time the reference of "the present" changes—that is to say, must change at every moment. But, as Dolev points out, any attempt to say what a statement about the past meant *a moment ago* must then likewise be semantically unstable—indeed, the change in question will be *indescribable*.

8

When "Evidence Transcendence" Is Not Malign

$\mathcal{A}$s always, I learned from Wright's "Truth as Sort of Epistemic: Putnam's Peregrinations,"[1] and I am sure that the points on which we still disagree will provide fruitful material for future discussions. I can only express my heartfelt gratitude for the careful reading and the enormous amount of thought that obviously went into the writing of this essay. In many ways, Wright is the ideal reader I had in mind when I wrote the papers and books he discusses.

In what follows, I have found it easiest to discuss Wright's points in roughly the reverse of the order they occur in his paper. I begin with a quote from the final paragraph of his paper:

> It is essentially the interface picture that we need to make sense of the idea that "There are no intelligent extraterrestrials" might be true beyond all evidence available in principle, beyond the verdict of even the very best possible empirical theory.[2]

To explain why I don't agree with this, let me go back a few paragraphs in Wright's paper to some remarks in which Wright lays out in a clear

---

1. Crispin Wright, "Truth as Sort of Epistemic: Putnam's Peregrinations," *Journal of Philosophy* 97 (2000): 335–364.
2. Wright, "Truth as Sort of Epistemic," 364.

and very general way the position for which he is arguing. Wright makes the point that there are benign forms of evidence-transcendence:

> This benign form of evidence-transcendence is conceived as going with—in the broadest sense—*contingencies of epistemic opportunity:* in all cases where we have a conception of this kind of how the truth-value of a particular statement could be unverifiable, a developed specific account of that conception will consist in detailing limitations of opportunity, or spatio-temporal situation, or perceptual or intellectual capacity, which stop us from getting at the relevant facts but to which we, or others, might easily not have been subject—or at least, to which we can readily conceive that an intelligible form of investigating intelligence need not be subject.[3]

In the paragraphs that follow, Wright contrasts this benign form with the "malign" kind of evidence-transcendence posited by interface conceptions, writing:

> On this type of view, evidence-transcendence is a product not of contingencies of opportunity, or of contingent limitations of our powers, but of *metaphysical* shortcomings and divides: consciousness—unless it is the consciousness of God, of which we have no satisfactory conception—is necessarily and essentially insular.
>
> The essence of metaphysical realism, we might say, is thus *interface-realism.* And the evidence-transcendence of truth which metaphysical realism brings in train is a malignant kind, the kind that goes with an interface-conception of mind's interaction with the world. About these ideas there is nothing "natural" or "commonsensical." Rather, it is supposed to take philosophical sophistication to appreciate them.[4]

I agree with Wright that the sorts of evidence-transcendence that we can explain as resulting from "contingencies of epistemic opportunity" in the broadest sense should be admitted to exist by any philosophy that

---

3. Wright, "Truth as Sort of Epistemic," 360.
4. Wright, "Truth as Sort of Epistemic," 361.

aims to do justice to the natural realism of the common man (as Dummett's antirealism about the past evidently did not).[5] But unlike Wright, I believe that "There are no intelligent extraterrestrials" might conceivably be true; that this too should be admitted by any philosophy that aims to do justice to commonsense realism; and that the evidence-transcendence of the truth of this proposition should be classed as "benign" and not as "malignant."

To see why, let us compare it with a "Fitch-example" (Wright calls it *F*) whose truth is also evidence-transcendent, but in a way Wright considers "benign":

Q and no and one will ever rationally believe that Q.

Here let *Q* be any empirical proposition that it might happen that no ever rationally believes, say, *There is a gold mountain one mile high.*[6]

According to Wright, we can give a truth-condition for *F*, in the fashion of a Carnapian "reduction sentence" (Wright calls it a "Provisional Biconditional"). The condition is:

(1) If *F* was to be appraised under sufficiently good circumstances, *F* would be true just in case it was believed to be true.[7]

But there is a catch! As Wright notes, there are only two sorts of circumstances in which it is possible to "appraise" the truth-value of *F*: these are (1) circumstances in which it is possible to know that *Q* is false, and (2) circumstances in which it is possible to know that someone rationally believes that *Q* is true, and in both sorts of circumstances *F* is false (because either its first or its second conjunct is false). In sum, what (1) captures is the fact that *F* is *falsifiable*. *But it isn't verifiable.* If we say that *F* might be true, we must presuppose our hearer's possession of an idea of what constitutes *F*'s being true which (1) does not capture. This would become crystal clear if the "sufficiently good circumstances" in (1) were spelled out "constructively," in Wright's sense, for

---

5. My internal realism was never committed to this position of Dummett's.

6. I used this very example, not knowing of Fitch's earlier argument, in Hilary Putnam, "Logical Positivism and the Philosophy of Mind," in *Mind, Language and Reality*, vol. 2 of *Philosophical Papers* (Cambridge: Cambridge University Press, 1975), 441–451.

7. Wright, "Truth as Sort of Epistemic," 357.

then it would be obvious that the "circumstances" in question are all circumstances in which *F* is false. A "reduction sentence" in Carnap's sense leaves the extension of the concept it "reduces" *undetermined* when the test condition mentioned in the antecedent is not fulfilled— something Carnap and Hempel both emphasized.[8] Wright's Provisional Biconditional is meant as a reduction sentence for the predicate "true," one which partially specifies its extension as applied to *F*, and it leaves the extension of that predicate *undetermined* in every case in which the "sufficiently good circumstances" do not obtain—including all the circumstances in which *F is* true.

Thus, one of the following two remarks by Wright must be wrong:

(a) A moderate internalist conception of truth [in Wright's sense] is friendly to . . . classes of potentially recognition-transcendent truths, typified by . . . Fitch examples.[9]

(b) In all cases where we have a conception of this kind of how the truth-value of a particular statement could be unverifiable, a developed specific account of that conception will consist in detailing limitations of opportunity, or spatio-temporal situation, or perceptual or intellectual capacity, which stop us getting at the relevant facts but to which we, or others, might easily not have been subject—or at least, to which we can readily conceive that an intelligible form of investigating intelligence need not be subject.[10]

To spell this out: if Wright's "moderate internalist conception of truth" does indeed allow that some Fitch propositions can be true (I take this to be what is meant by the reference to the "friendliness" of the conception to this class of potentially recognition-transcendent truths), it had better not assert (b)! For it is not the case that our conception of how a Fitch proposition might be true (as opposed to our conception of how it might be *false*) enables us to say how "we, or others" might have been able to recognize its truth.

<hr>

8. C. G. Hempel, "The Empiricist Criterion of Meaning," *Revue Internationale de Philosophie* 4 (1950); collected in A. J. Ayer, *Logical Positivism* (New York: Free Press, 1959). See, for example, *Logical Positivism*, 120.

9. Wright, "Truth as Sort of Epistemic," 358.

10. Wright, "Truth as Sort of Epistemic," 360.

To make matters even stranger, the situation is exactly the same if instead of F, which Wright sees as exemplifying "benign" recognition-transcendence of truth, we take N: "There are no intelligent extraterrestrials," whose (possible) recognition-transcendent truth Wright sees as "malign." For that proposition is falsifiable-though-not-verifiable just as F is. Its truth-value, like F's, can be "appraised under sufficiently good circumstances"—circumstances in which it is false! For if N is false, then there are intelligent extraterrestrials, and we may easily imagine there being observers who know this. We can even formulate a "Provisional Biconditional" for N—simply replace F by N in (1)!

This brings us to the question: given that he doesn't think that "Fitch examples" involve any sort of an interface conception, why does Wright say that "It is essentially the interface picture that we need to make sense of the idea that 'There are no intelligent extraterrestrials' might be true beyond all evidence available in principle, beyond the verdict of even the very best possible empirical theory?" Earlier in the paper, he writes:

If moderate internalism can accommodate the example [our N] as a truth-apt claim, then the view has to be that under such informationally fortunate circumstances [knowledge of the conditions for the evolution of intelligent life, and "enough understanding of the distribution and diversity of matter in the cosmos to allow the assignment of a well-grounded probability to the supposition that such conditions are replicated elsewhere besides on this earth"], thinkers would take the correct view of the question.[11]

It is the idea that thinkers would *not* take the correct view of the question under such circumstances that Wright analogizes to belief in a metaphysical "interface." But this is obviously a confusion.

To see the confusion, let us assume, as is reasonable on present knowledge, that the "very best possible empirical theory" that Wright speaks of tells us that the cosmos, or at least the part of space-time that might contain intelligent life, is finite, and that there is no one place within that finite region from which one can survey (or even receive causal signals from) the entire region. Let us suppose, with Wright, that the theory, call it P, provides "enough understanding of

11. Wright, "Truth as Sort of Epistemic," 353.

the distribution and diversity of matter in the cosmos to allow the assignment of a well-grounded probability to the supposition that such conditions are replicated elsewhere besides on this earth," and let us even suppose that the probability in question is quite high, say .999 or .9999. Now, it is a conceptual truth (what Wright calls an "a priori" truth)[12] that *what is highly probable does not always happen.* Thus it is *internal to physical theory itself (to P)*—and not the product of some metaphysical conception of "the kind that goes with an interface-conception of mind's interaction with the world"—that *N* may be true. If "moderate internal realism" requires us to believe that all those propositions that our best theory regards as highly probable (but no more than that) are in fact *true*, then "moderate internal realism" must certainly be rejected!

What then *is* the source of the recognition-transcendence of true Fitch propositions and true negative existentials similar to *N?* The answer I offer both in the Dewey Lectures and in a paper I believe Wright may have missed[13] is that while it is indeed the case that our ability to perceptually verify them under favorable circumstances is part of what is comprised in our understanding of such atomic descriptive propositions as "Here is a chair" (and thus I do not need to be persuaded by Wright that we should not "recoil" so far in the direction of metaphysical realism as to think of truth as recognition-transcendent in the most ordinary cases), the use of logical connectives and quantifiers does frequently lead to recognition-transcendence for reasons that are clear from the logical structure itself. (Note that even the Fitch examples involve negative existentials!). Nor is the principle of bivalence what is involved here. Just as the logical structure of a Fitch example makes it clear that what is supposed in such an example—and I see no reason to regard it as inconceivable, or "metaphysical," or "confused"—is something that, if it happens, we cannot verify, so the logical structure of *N* makes it clear that what is supposed in this example—say, that something improbable (if it *is* improbable) simply happens—is something

---

12. My qualms about "a priori" stem from the long-standing association of the notion with the idea of *unrevisability*, not with any rejection of the idea of conceptual analysis. Compare with Hilary Putnam, "Pragmatism," *Proceedings of the Aristotelian Society* 95, part 3 (1995): 291–306, especially pp. 299–302.

13. See Putnam, "Pragmatism," 291–306.

that if it happens we cannot verify.[14] Both sorts of example (and, of course, there are others) spell disaster for any elucidation of truth in terms of rational acceptability, even by means of reduction sentences (Provisional Biconditionals).

Much of Wright's paper is concerned with interpretation of and improvement on the theory presented in my *Reason, Truth and History* (which I no longer accept for the reasons given in my Dewey Lectures).[15] I will only venture three brief remarks on what I believe I meant in the insufficiently clear passage that Wright wrestles with so insightfully.

(1) What I had in mind was the following: for a statement P to be true (on the "internalist account"), there must be a set of conditions C that are "good" (say, if we indulge in the fiction that there are numerical degrees of goodness, to some degree g) for appraising P, such that P is assertible under conditions C, and such that it is the case that if conditions C' were still better (say, the degree of goodness for appraising P were g' instead of g) then P would still be assertible under C'. That we can treat conditions that are close to (but not the same as) some ideal conditions I as if they were the ideal conditions (as if the incline were frictionless) if improving the approximation wouldn't affect the result is a principle that governs all use of idealizations in solving practical problems (hence the example of "frictionless planes"). I believe, in fact, that my internalist notion of truth coincided with the notion that Wright calls "superassertibility" in his *Truth and Objectivity* (although that is not how *he* interprets me!), if we prescind from possible differences over the notion of "assertibility."

14. More precisely, the conjunction $P\&N\&S$, where S is the statement that an observer cannot verify whether there is intelligent life in a region of space-time that that observer is unable to receive causal signals from, P is the "possible empirical theory" that tells us that (1) causal signals do not travel faster than light, (2) it is physically possible (and highly probable) that there are intelligent extraterrestrials, but (3) it is also physically possible that there aren't, and (4) there are large regions of space-time that any particular physically possible observer is unable to receive causal signals from, is a statement that it is *logically* impossible to verify if true, and yet it is a statement that P tells us could be true (and even assigns a probability to).

15. These are collected in Hilary Putnam, *The Threefold Cord: Mind, Body and World* (New York: Columbia University Press, 1999), 3–70.

(2) I did not and do not, however, think that one can survey in advance what one might reasonably come to understand by "sufficiently good epistemic conditions," even for a particular topic. Certainly there is no fixed set of "standards" associated with language that could enable one to do this. (This is the possible difference over the notion of "assertibility" to which I just referred.)

(3) Wright is quite correct in supposing that I did not consider the problems posed by the Conditional Fallacy in any of my formulations. I agree that they are serious—indeed, I do not think that Provisional Biconditionals can meet them either (precisely because, like all reduction sentences, they leave the extension of the predicate that they "elucidate"—Carnap's term was "reduce"—undetermined with respect to cases in which the test condition is not fulfilled, and this is precisely what we *don't* want in the case of recognition-transcendent truths). I at least want to say that, for example, *N* can be *true* in such cases, not that it is indeterminate. Even in the case of truths that are not recognition transcendent but simply such that (contingently) the test condition is unfulfilled, it is not enough to specify via a provisional biconditional what the truth value would have been if the recognition condition had been fulfilled, for this leads right back to the problems of the Conditional Fallacy. My conclusion is that the problem Wright poses for my former view is also an (unsolved) problem for Wright's own "moderate internalism."

PART IV

Naive Realism, Sensation, and Apperception

9

Sensation and Apperception

*T*HE REFLECTIONS about the topic of perception and its relations to conception that follow are the product of more than seventeen years of thinking about John McDowell's great book *Mind and World*. If I find myself forced to disagree with him at certain points *(Amicus Plato, sed magis amica veritas)*, that does not alter the fact that his book was a pathbreaking one in the highest sense of the term. For that reason I shall begin the present chapter by reviewing some its arguments, and explain my own view as a correction of his.

John McDowell's Reasons for Thinking That Experience Is Conceptualized

I once wrote,

> What McDowell means by saying that our conceptual powers are "drawn on" in experience, albeit "passively," is not anything mysterious, nor is this to be construed as psychological speculation of some kind; it is articulated by the work that this idea has to do: to show *how* experience involves "openness to how things anyway are."
>
> If we put aside temporarily McDowell's difficult (and fascinating) discussion of experiences with "inner accusatives" (e.g.,

experiences of pain, or of after-images) and confine our attention to experiences of how it is "out there," what McDowell is saying is that such experiences, when they are experiences in what McDowell calls "the demanding sense" (when they function in the justification of belief), are intrinsically about the outer world, and the possibility of having them depends on the possession of the relevant world-involving concepts.

They are not inner signs with a magical connection to the outer world, but takings in of how it is (in the best case), or how it seems to be (in more problematic cases), with the outer world.[1]

I confess that I no longer understand how I could have thought that McDowell's claim that the possibility of having perceptual experiences "depends on the possession of the relevant . . . concepts" can be anything *but* "mysterious."

However, McDowell means exactly what he says, as is shown by other things he says. For example, in *Mind and World*, he writes, "*No subject could be understood as having experiences of color* except against a background of understanding that makes it possible for *judgments endorsing such experiences* to fit into her view of the world."[2]

And he makes clear that this is supposed to apply to inner experiences such as the experience of "seeing red" produced by a blow on the head, or even the judgment that I have a pain. According to this view, experiences *must* be conceptually articulated.[3] What I want to explore

---

1. "McDowell's Mind and McDowell's World," in *Reading McDowell on Mind and World*, ed. N. H. Smith (London: Routledge, 2002), 174–190; quotation from pp. 176–177.

2. John McDowell, *Mind and World* (Cambridge, Mass.: Harvard University Press, 1994), 30 (emphasis added).

3. In "Avoiding the Myth of the Given," in his *Having the World in View* (Cambridge, Mass.: Harvard University Press, 2009), 256–272, McDowell gives up the claim that the experiences of language-using human beings (which he refers to by the Kantian term "intuitions" in this chapter) presuppose that the subject *already possesses* the concepts (including demonstrative concepts, like "this shade") needed to describe their content, but he takes the ability to *form* such concepts to be "in play" when one has those experiences, and he explicitly describes such abilities as "discursive" abilities. Thus, McDowell still takes the learning of a language to be a prerequisite for having experiences in the sense in which rational beings—beings that can understand and respond to requests for justifications for their judgments—have experiences. Hilla Jacobson and I discuss this revised version of the thesis that experiences are "conceptualized" in "Against Perceptual Conceptualism," *International Journal of Philosophical Studies* (forthcoming).

is how McDowell arrived at this metaphysical position! What follows is a very brief account.

McDowell Believes the Space of Reasons Cannot Be Reduced to Facts about the Causation of Our Beliefs

McDowell is not satisfied with a merely reliabilist account of justification and other epistemological notions. And I agree with him. Such an account, if offered in a reductionist spirit, presupposes many notions that the reductionist naturalist is not entitled to, for instance, intentional notions such as reference and truth, not to mention the use of counterfactuals, often accompanied by talk of "possible worlds" *a là* David Lewis, as well as being open to a number of counterexamples.[4]

McDowell must be understood as seeking to produce an account of experience compatible with the idea that perceptual experience justifies beliefs about the layout of the world around one and doesn't merely causally "trigger" true beliefs a high percentage of the time. This is the *first* thing one needs to know about *Mind and World*.

This idea, that perceptual experiences *justify* accepting and rejecting beliefs about the world and do not merely trigger noises and subvocalizations is what McDowell calls "minimal empiricism." McDowell clearly identifies this claim with the claim that "impressions" can do this, and I will come back to this identification later.

James Conant has distinguished between two varieties of skepticism, which he calls "Cartesian skepticism" and "Kantian skepticism."[5] Cartesian skepticism, in Conant's sense, is skepticism about the possibility of knowledge of things and events "outside" the mind. Kantian skepticism is a puzzle about the very possibility that one's thoughts, whether seemingly about an external world or even about one's own sense impressions, can have content at all. Cartesian Skepticism assumes our thoughts about the world are genuine thoughts, that is, that

---

4. See my criticism of Fodor's attempted causal theory of reference in Hilary Putnam, *Renewing Philosophy* (Cambridge, Mass.: Harvard University Press, 1992), 35–59.

5. James Conant, "Varieties of Skepticism," in *Wittgenstein and Skepticism*, ed. Denis McManus (Abingdon, United Kingdom: Routledge Press, 2004): 97–136. Conant claims that in my work *The Threefold Cord: Mind, Body and World* (New York: Columbia University Press, 1999), I failed to see that Kantian skepticism was McDowell's target, and not Cartesian skepticism. I think that McDowell, in fact, attacks both targets in that book.

they are true or false, and only worries about whether we can ever really know that any of them are true. Kantian skepticism threatens to undercut even Cartesian skepticism. This poses a problem for empiricism, in that it is not clear how merely saying that our judgments come from experience explains how any of them have *content*, as opposed to being merely what Rorty called "marks and noises." "Come from" needs to mean something more than "are caused by," McDowell tells us, if experience is to be a "tribunal" before which our judgments are to stand.[6] The *second* thing we need to know to understand McDowell is that he is concerned with Kantian, not Humean, skepticism in *Mind and World*.

McDowell's Way into the Problem

McDowell's way into the problem is via an interesting interpretation of Wittgenstein's Private Language Argument, which he reads in the light of Wittgenstein's remarks on the supposition that words acquire meaning by "ostensive definition."

Wittgenstein's point can be illustrated thus: Russell (as of 1912) thought that we acquire our basic concepts by "acquaintance by introspection" (in effect, by a sort of inner pointing to our private impressions).[7] But concepts are general, as Russell well knew. So to get the concept *red* (as applied to sense data),[8] because I obviously can't direct my attention to all my red sense data, including the future ones, I have to "abstract" the appropriate quality. In other words, I need a private ostensive definition. But all ostensive definition (e.g., holding up a glass and saying "glass" to teach someone the concept) presupposes that the pupil possess at least implicit knowledge of the relevant sortal concept (e.g., "implement" as opposed to "material"). So ostensive definition can't be the way we acquire *all* our concepts. That is, pointing to "bare presences" can't explain how language and minds "hook on to the

6. "We can coherently credit experiences with rational relations to judgment and belief, but only if we take it that spontaneity is already implicated in receptivity; that is, only if we take it that experiences have conceptual content." McDowell, *Mind and World*, 162.

7. Bertrand Russell, *The Problems of Philosophy* (Oxford: Oxford University Press, 1912), 47.

8. How we can possibly acquire concepts that apply to anything besides sense data was a puzzle for classical empiricism.

world." (In addition to Wittgenstein, McDowell attributes this insight to Sellars and Davidson.)

A way out that McDowell doesn't discuss would be to say that some concepts are innate. (Think of Quine's "similarity spaces.") But innate similarity spaces in the behaviorist sense are just innate patterns of response, dispositions to be caused to respond (say, with the noise "red"), and if that's *all* we have, the corresponding judgments are merely conditioned responses to make certain noises, and we lose the fact that our concepts are *concepts*. And if this behaviorist story isn't what the nativist has in mind, then it isn't clear what an "innate concept" is. (Chomsky, today's best-known nativist, rejects the question of how words *refer* as too unscientific to discuss.)[9]

I agree with McDowell, Davidson, and Sellars that appealing to "bare presences" can't provide an answer to the question as to how concepts and experiences are connected, or, in McDowell's terms, how experiences can rationally constrain beliefs. That confrontation with bare presences can do this is what Sellars meant by "The Myth of the Given," and what Davidson meant by the idea of "content" in the phrase "dualism of scheme and content," according to McDowell. (Davidson should have said that what he rejected was the dualism of conceptual scheme and Given, on McDowell's interpretations.) These are fascinating and plausible interpretations, needless to say.

Davidson

Davidson—who evidently despaired of finding a rational linkage between concepts and experiences (or impressions—we need to keep an eye on McDowell's identification of experiences with impressions!) held (reviving an idea of Neurath's) that justification begins with beliefs (which, for Neurath, were just *sentences*) and not with experiences. But how sentences about experiences can be justified by other sentences is just as problematic! (The coherence of the whole system does the work? How do we know it isn't "spinning in the void?") And if observation sentences (Neurath called them "protocols") aren't justified by anything, how can they in turn justify anything? Davidson responds to

9. Noam Chomsky, "Language from an Internalist Perspective," in *New Horizons in the Study of Language and Mind* (Cambridge: Cambridge University Press, 2000), 134–163.

the problem that bothers McDowell by giving up minimal empiricism. But that can't be right, McDowell feels. Nor can the answer be to just recoil back to the Given. We saw that that didn't work. So what way out is left?

McDowell's Way Out

McDowell's way out is to say that perceptual experiences *aren't* just the products of our sense organs. According to McDowell our *conceptual capacities* are "in play" in experience. Impressions "already possess conceptual content." Since both beliefs and "impressions" are conceptually articulated, there is supposedly no obstacle to the idea that impressions can rationally justify, and not merely "trigger," beliefs. Thus, McDowell claims that we can "dismount from the seesaw" that threatens to keep us oscillating between the Myth of the Given and an equally untenable "coherentism."

It seems to me that McDowell, far from giving a philosophical worry peace by "exorcizing the question," has worked himself into an unbelievable metaphysical position! What I find unbelievable is not the claim that *some* of our experiences are conceptualized (in *some* sense of "conceptualized"), nor the claim that conceptualized experiences are epistemologically fundamental, but the claim that *all* experiences, indeed all sensations, involve and presuppose our conceptual powers. Surely, the reader is going to want to know, how exactly is it supposed to be the case that my conceptual capacities are "in operation?"[10] A prima facie difficulty is that any given experience has an enormous number of different aspects.[11] Moreover, as McDowell recognizes, "demonstrative expressions" have to be used to describe many of those aspects;[12] it is not the case that one always has the appropriate concept *before* having an experience that falls under that concept. McDowell (as of

10. "Experiences in general are states or occurrences in which conceptual capacities are passively drawn into operation" (McDowell, *Mind and World*, 30). "Conceptual capacities must be in play in experience if we are to avoid the Myth" (McDowell, *Having the World in View*, 262).

11. The *Stanford Encyclopedia of Philosophy* refers to this as the problem of "the richness of experience." Susanna Siegel, "The Contents of Perception," *Stanford Encyclopedia of Philosophy*, March 18, 2005, www.illc.uva.nl/~seop/archives/spr2009/entries/perception-contents/.

12. McDowell, *Mind and World*, 58.

Mind and World) was clearly wedded to the idea that one could not have a particular *sensation* ("impression") if one did not have the concepts under which that sensation falls. But how could one's conceptual abilities be "in play" when one has a sensation (say, a particular color-sensation) if one didn't *previously* have that concept?

McDowell's view is clearly in flux here. In *Mind and World*, the answer to this question was that one forms the demonstrative concept *and* one has the sensation *at the same time*. In *Having the World in View*, however, the view McDowell defends is that to have a sensation it suffices that one *could have formed* the appropriate demonstrative concept; it is conceded that in many cases one does not, in fact, form it. Yet the claim that "conceptual capacities are in play" in *all* experiences is not given up, and that includes the claim that *one could not have any particular sensation if one did not have the ability to form a concept under which it falls.* But why not? Let us grant that it is a conceptual truth that one could not have the experience of *recognizing* that one is having a sensation that falls under a particular concept if one did not have that concept (or form it on that occasion, in the case of a demonstrative concept). But it does not *seem* to be a conceptual truth that one cannot have the sensation of seeing a particular color (or of seeing red flashes because one has been hit on the head—a McDowell example),[13] or feel a particular sort of pain unless one has, or has the ability to form, a demonstrative concept of precisely that color (or precisely that sort of "red flash"), or precisely that sort of pain.

Why should our human conceptual abilities (which McDowell identifies with "discursive abilities"—that is, the abilities that enable us to use language and speak about "reasons") be required to feel pains or see red flashes when one is struck on the head? And why are brain science and cognitive psychology supposed to be irrelevant to these questions? McDowell's supposed "exorcism" of the questions only leaves this reader *more* puzzled.

A natural place to look for an account of the extent to which human discursive abilities affect sensation would be a sophisticated and nonreductionist cognitive science. But for McDowell, there is *one thing* that is *the natural-scientific kind of intelligibility*, and that he identifies with "bald naturalism," that is, the sort of naturalism that seeks a reductionist

13. See McDowell, *Mind and World*, 30.

account of normative epistemic notions, and there is a *different thing* that is philosophical understanding, and never the twain shall meet.[14] But what I have elsewhere called a "liberal functionalism,"[15] a nonreductive investigation of the functional roles of biological and psychological processes, has no reason to eschew normative notions (e.g., the notion of the "normal function" of an organ or a capacity itself involves normative judgment) or intentional notions. Moreover, the whole idea of a sharp line between philosophical speculation and empirical hypothesis is one I find extremely uncongenial.

In any case, I propose that if we are willing to think about the philosophical problem of how experience can have rational bearing on belief and the cognitive psychological question as to what a reasonable picture of the extent to which our conceptual powers are be "in play" in experience together, we are more likely to make progress than if we assume from the beginning that philosophy is philosophy and natural scientific intelligibility is natural scientific intelligibility, and the two have nothing to do with each other.

A Brief Sketch of an Approach

The approach I propose depends on drawing a distinction that William James employed, but that McDowell's claim that all experiences and / or impressions (he sometimes uses the terms interchangeably) are conceptualized in effect denies, the distinction between "sensations" and apperceptions. James did not, indeed, invent this distinction; at least since Kant's *Critique of Pure Reason*, the distinction has been a standard one in the psychological literature, but Kant also thought that a sensation that was not accompanied by apperception would be "nothing to us,"[16] and this is perhaps the basis for McDowell's denial that there can

14. The possibility stressed by Tyler Burge (discussed in Chapter 1 of this book) that cognitive science might use and be entitled to use a concept like representation goes missing in McDowell's picture, of course. [Note added July 7, 2015.]

15. See "Corresponding with Reality," chapter 3 of *Philosophy in the Age of Science: Physics, Mathematics, and Skepticism*, ed. Mario De Caro and David Macarthur (Cambridge, Mass.: Harvard University Press, 2012) and "How to Be a Sophisticated 'Naïve Realist'," chapter 37 in the same volume.

16. "The *I think* must be capable of accompanying all my presentations; otherwise something would be presented to me which could not be thought at all, which means no less than: the presentation would be either impossible, or at least nothing to me . . . Conse-

be such a thing. James did not deny this, but he recognized that the line between sensation and apperception is *sometimes* fuzzy; in fact, he asserted that in the case of a

> presented and recognized material object . . . Sensations and apperceptive ideas fuse here so intimately that you can no more tell where one begins and the other ends, than you can tell, in those cunning circular panoramas that have lately been exhibited, where the real foreground and the painted canvas join together.[17]

In *The Threefold Cord*, I attempted to use James' notion of "fusion" as a way of taking the metaphysical strangeness out of McDowell's notion that perceptual experiences are conceptualized (while also restricting that claim to the case of a "presented and recognized material object [or event]").[18] But this was a misinterpretation of McDowell on my part; in "Avoiding the Myth of the Given," McDowell makes it clear that while he is willing to abandon the claim that sensations are conceptually articulated he is *not* willing to give up the claim that in *all* (mature human) experience, our discursive abilities are "in play." In some sense, thus, McDowell still thinks that sensations (or "impressions") must be conceptualized.

However, *pace* McDowell, and also *pace* Kant, there is no paradox involved in the idea that we are *aware* of some *unconceptualized* sensations. In *short-term memory*, at least, we can access sensations we had a moment ago that we did not conceptualize at the time. Our present *memory* of those sensations is conceptualized, to be sure, but *they* weren't. Indeed, I have one or two vivid visual memories of sensations I had when I was just learning to talk and had virtually no concepts available for most of the things in the remembered "scene."

That "apperception"—recognition of what one is perceiving—involves concepts was already stressed by Kant. This is also something that the phenomenological school, beginning with Husserl, likewise

---

quently every manifold of perception has a necessary relation to the I think, in the same subject in which the manifold is found." Immanuel Kant, *Critique of Pure Reason*, §15 and §16, B 131.

17. William James, *Essays in Radical Empiricism*, ed. R. B. Perry (Cambridge, Mass.: Harvard University Press, 1976), 16.

18. Putnam, *Threefold Cord*, 158.

emphasized: I see a building as something that has a back, Husserl pointed out, even when I don't see the back.[19] (This is something also emphasized today by the philosopher and cognitive scientist Alva Noë.)[20] Such perception is fallible, to be sure, but so is the perception that something is red or circular.

But pointing this out isn't going to convince McDowell that he should confine the claim that our experiences are conceptualized to apperceptions, because he believes that giving up "minimal empiricism" would make skepticism unanswerable, and minimal empiricism, as he understands it, requires that *impressions* belong to the "tribunal" before which all our judgments have to stand.

On "Fusion"

The phenomenon that interested James is that on some occasions the phenomenal character of a sensation is actually *changed* by conceptualization. For example, the phenomenal character of the sensation of seeing a word in an alphabet one doesn't know certainly changes when one learns to read texts in the relevant language. When literate English speakers see the word STOP on a traffic sign, our awareness of the letters and our awareness that they "say" *stop* are, as James said, "fused." But there are some concepts that need to be distinguished here.

First, there is a difference between *attending* to something and conceptualizing it. If a child feels pain she certainly attends to the pain, whether she applies concepts to it or not. The psychological literature strongly indicates that all experiences are altered to some degree by the particular way in which attention is focused, and Hilla Jacobson and I have argued, on the basis of those findings,[21] that counterfactuals to the effect that a subject *would have been* able to apply the appropriate demonstrative concept to a sensory experience *if she had attended to* it presuppose an untenable "snapshot model" of sensory experience, that

19. According to Ned Block, "Seeing-As in the Light of Vision Science," *Philosophy and Phenomenological Research* 89 (2014): 560–572, cases of what I am calling (visual) "apperception" are cases of "secondary seeing," combinations of both primary visual representation (in Burge's sense of representation) and ensuing conceptualization. I find this plausible. [Note added July 7, 2015.]

20. Alva Noë, *Action in Perception* (Cambridge, Mass.: MIT Press, 2004).

21. We argue this in "Against Perceptual Conceptualism," cited in note 3 above.

is, a model in which a given sensory experience would have been just the same if one had attended to it, just as a tree would have been the same if one had photographed it. (McDowell employs such counterfactuals to explain the sense in which our experiences are allegedly "conceptualized" in "Avoiding the Myth of the Given.") The phenomenal character of a red patch or a pain are different when one attends to them, but I don't believe that they are *necessarily* different when one *recognizes* the color as red or the pain as a pain (although sometimes they may be) and hence I don't need to deny that an animal or a child who has not learned to talk and I ever have "qualitatively" the same or similar feelings of pain or sensations of red (even when we both attend to those feelings or visual sensations). But I do maintain that I have conceptualized awareness that the red I experience is *the color of a surface* (or the result of a blow on the head, as the case may be), and that the pain is *an unpleasant sensation*, that the prelinguistic child and the animal lack.[22]

Using Kantian terminology, we may say that the prelinguistic child and the animal see red and feel pain, but they do not *apperceive* pain, that is, they do not recognize pain as pain. The kind of awareness that constitutes a mature human being's apperceptive awareness of a sensation is *like* a belief, in that it can be accepted or rejected (whereas it makes no sense to accept or reject the mere sensation!), and it presupposes we have the requisite background of concepts, but it is not an explicit judgment, although it can justify a judgment.

To repeat, apperceptions are conceptually shaped, and they can justify judgments. But they are not the same as perceptual beliefs. I may have an apperception or, better, a seeming apperception that one "shaft" is longer than the other in the Müller-Lyer illusion, but I do not *believe* what I seem to be apperceiving. One can seem to oneself to apperceive when one knows that one does not (successfully) apperceive, but one cannot seem to oneself to *believe* when one does not believe. The distinction between sensations and apperceptions is not the same as the distinction between sensations and perceptual beliefs.

I say this because I fear that otherwise this will sound to McDowell like Gareth Evans's story, according to which "the informational

---

22. Although if Burge is right, the prelinguistic child and even the animal may enjoy *representations* of the fact that the color is on a surface and the pain is unpleasant that are more primitive than conceptualizations. [Note added July 7, 2015.]

system" supplies inputs, which causally trigger (but do not justify) the relevant beliefs.[23] This, McDowell might say, is Davidson and Neurath all over again. But while this is right as a criticism of Evans's account, it is not right as a criticism of the account I just proposed (and not only because apperceptions can be *rejected*; they do not automatically "trigger" beliefs, although that is an important point about them). What Evans was doing was speculating about the brain's hardware; thus his account was a *reductionist* account. In my view, talk about what the organism does in *intentional* terms is not reducible to "hardware" talk.[24] To be sure, any intentional state, such as knowing the meaning of the word "ephebe," has to be realized in "hardware" *somehow*. But intentional states are realizable in a practically infinite number of different ways, and the fact that a particular piece of hardware *is* a realization of a particular intentional state is only visible from the intentional level, not from either the neurological or the computational level by themselves.

Amodal Apperception

When my apperception is not of something that produces a sensation but of something "amodal,"[25] it is even clearer that an apperception is different from a sensation. Amodal apperception includes awareness of aspects that are "present in absence" such as my awareness of a tomato that I am looking at as having another side. Alva Noë accounts for such apperception in terms of sensorimotor expectations,[26] but he does also mention *shaping by thought* as a possibility. And it is more than a mere possibility, in fact; my awareness of the computer in front of me as a computer does not consist just of "sensorimotor" expectations.

---

23. For McDowell's description of Gareth Evans's view, see *Mind and World*, 47–63.

24. This is something I argue in many papers; among them are Hilary Putnam, "Meaning Holism," in *The Philosophy of W. V. Quine*, ed. L. E. Hahn and P. A. Schilpp (La Salle, Ill.: Open Court, 1986), 405–431; reprinted in *Realism with a Human Face* (Cambridge, Mass.: Harvard University Press, 1990), 278–302; and Hilary Putnam, "Functionalism: Cognitive Science or Science Fiction?," in *The Future of the Cognitive Revolution*, ed. D. M. Johnson and C. E. Erneling (Oxford: Oxford University Press, 1997), 32–44; reprinted in my *Philosophy in the Age of Science*, ed. Mario De Caro and David Macarthur (Cambridge, Mass.: Harvard University Press, 2012), 608–623.

25. On "amodal" awareness, see Alva Noë, *Action in Perception* (Cambridge, Mass.: MIT Press, 2004), 77–79.

26. Alva Noë, *Action in Perception*, 7–9, and throughout the volume.

Still, I think we should agree when Noë writes that

> the *way* the coin's circularity is present to me when I view it from a single point of view, is *as available to me* thanks to my implicit understanding that were I to move in these and these ways its apparent shape would change correspondingly . . . The way in which the strictly unperceived circularity of the coin is present is decidedly not the way inferred objects are judged to be present. This is demonstrated by the fact the coin would look no less circular even if one knew, for a fact, that it was elliptical. This is a familiar occurrence when we look at pictures. What is drawn is an ellipse, but we experience it as the outline of a plate, say.[27]

In fact, all the claims McDowell makes about perceptual experiences are true of apperceptions, including these amodal apperceptions: they are conceptualized but noninferential, and they can be judged as wrong even though they seem right.

Of course, there are many questions to be investigated if the picture I suggest is right, including the contribution (overstressed by Noë, but undoubtedly important) of sensorimotor skills. But that is all to the good; these are questions that a broad-minded and nonreductionist cognitive science should investigate. It is all to the good that a philosophical account should link up with plausible research programs in "natural science."

What will probably make my story unacceptable to McDowell is that it isn't our *sensations* that are conceptualized on my account. And that means that sensations aren't the "tribunal." But that I think is precisely right. If "minimal empiricism" insists otherwise, then "minimal empiricism" is too empiricist. Apperceptions are the tribunal, not sensations.

27. Alva Noë, "Real Presence," in *Varieties of Presence* (Cambridge, Mass.: Harvard University Press, 2012), 54, 51.

10

Perception without Sense Data

$\mathcal{B}$ECAUSE THE LAUENER PRIZE was bestowed upon me for my entire "oeuvre" in analytic philosophy, it would be appropriate for me to say something about all of my past work, but a lecture that covered all that would be much too long. Instead, because that seems a more reasonable task, I shall mostly confine my discussion to my views in the philosophy of mind as they developed and are still developing after I gave the Dewey Lectures at Columbia University in 1994.[1]

Those lectures, I have to say, were often read in a way that I found disappointing. Many analytic philosophers saw them as a "capitulation" to Wittgensteinian or Austinian ordinary language philosophy. At the same time, what I myself thought was most important in those lectures, namely, the explanation of my reasons for giving up the "internal realist" views I defended in *Reason, Truth and History*[2] (and subsequently, in several papers written between 1976 and 1990),[3] went almost unno-

---

1. Hilary Putnam, "Sense, Nonsense, and the Senses: An Inquiry into the Powers of the Human Mind," *Journal of Philosophy* 91 (1994): 445–517; reprinted in *The Threefold Cord: Mind, Body and World* (New York: Columbia University Press, 1999), 3–70.

2. Hilary Putnam, *Reason, Truth and History* (Cambridge: Cambridge University Press, 1981).

3. Most of those papers are collected in Hilary Putnam, *Realism and Reason*, vol. 3 of *Philosophical Papers* (Cambridge: Cambridge University Press, 1983), and *Realism with a Human Face* (Cambridge, Mass.: Harvard University Press, 1990).

ticed, or, when noticed, those reasons were often misunderstood. Obviously I was not as clear in the Dewey Lectures as I should have been. Let me begin by saying something about these points, before I turn to philosophy of mind.

To take the second point first, it appears that a reason that many people continued to describe me as an "internal realist" is that they confused two different doctrines: conceptual relativity, a doctrine I continue to defend, and internal realism, a doctrine that now I regard as mistaken. Conceptual relativity is the claim that sometimes two scientific theories have different "ontologies" in the familiar Quinian sense, that is, "taken at face value" their quantifiers range over different sorts of objects, and yet there is a systematic way of interpreting each theory in the language of the other that renders them (not just empirically equivalent, but) explanatorily equivalent—that is, the translation of any explanation of a physical phenomenon provided by one theory is a perfectly good explanation of the same phenomenon in the language of the other theory (but one that is very different, at least at "face value"). Internal realism, however, was the claim that what truth amounts to is justification under epistemically ideal conditions. At one time I thought that the existence of cases of conceptual relativity was an argument against metaphysical realism and hence for "internal realism" (which I took to be the only reasonable alternative to metaphysical realism). But that was a mistake.

It was a mistake because one can perfectly well be a metaphysical realist (as, perhaps to your surprise, I now admit to being) in the simple sense of believing that there is a real world that is largely independent of our mental workings, beliefs, or concepts, and many truths about that world that outrun what we can possibly verify, without denying the existence of the phenomenon I call "conceptual relativity." If, for example, it turns out, as according to some quantum physicists it already has,[4] that a theory in which certain particles are fermions and a theory in which the same particles are bosons are simply two "representations" of the same facts, then the moral will be that what is fundamental, at least in the ontology of physics, is not particles but states of affairs. If what are different ontologies in the familiar (Quinian) sense I referred

---

4. For example, C. F. Burgess and F. Quevedo, "Bosonization as Duality," *Nuclear Physics B* 421, no. 2 (1994): 373–390.

to above are just different representations of the same states of affairs, then that may be a problem for the Quinian ontologist, but I no longer think it is fatal for metaphysical realism. I repeat, one can accept the possibility of conceptual relativity and simultaneously reject internal realism. *A fortiori*, they are not the same thing.

On the other hand, the charge that my Dewey Lectures represented a "capitulation" to Wittgenstein and / or Austin is partly but not wholly right.

In my "Wittgenstein: A Reappraisal,"[5] I criticized a view that Wittgenstein undoubtedly held, the view that metaphysics is, in some very literal sense of the term, *nonsense*—that is, completely devoid of linguistic meaning, as claimed by the "New Wittgensteinians," or in violation of the "grammatical conditions for making sense" as claimed by more traditional Wittgensteinians. But I do not find, when I read Plato, or Aristotle, or Maimonides, or Kant, or even Hegel, that I am literally reading nonsense, although there is much about their thought that I cannot imagine believing. Some of my talk about "unintelligibility" in the Royce Lectures now seems wrong to me. Although those lectures were published together with the Dewey Lectures, Wittgenstein figures in the Dewey Lectures themselves in a much more modest role, although I do engage in some metaphysics bashing.

Austin, however, was clearly front and center in the Dewey Lectures. But so was William James. They both figured, not as metaphysics bashers, but because the main point of the Dewey Lectures was that philosophy of perception needs to return to the view of the man and woman on the street, that is, to a view in which we actually perceive shoes and ships and sealing wax and cabbages and kings and many of the other items in the passing show—the view that Russell dismissed as "naive realism." And I saw Austin and James as allies because (albeit in different ways) they both criticized the traditional epistemological paradigm, under which what we "directly perceive" are just our own sense data, and external objects are known by "inference," if they indeed exist as something more than logical constructs out of sense data or "permanent possibilities of sensation." [*Note:* In this essay, I shall use

---

5. Chapter 28 in Hilary Putnam, *Philosophy in an Age of Science: Physics, Mathematics, and Skepticism*, ed. Mario De Caro and David Macarthur (Cambridge, Mass.: Harvard University Press, 2012), 482–492.

"sense data" to refer to experiential phenomena that are supposed to be mental but nonconceptual, and to occur in our "private spaces" (following Russell, not Moore).]

That we need to reject that paradigm is something I still believe. However, I went further and opted for "disjunctivism," which is the view that, in veridical perception—say, seeing objects in one's vicinity as they actually are—there are no such objects as sense data at all. According to disjunctivists, even a "perfect hallucination"—for instance, a hallucination produced by an "experience machine" that causes one's visual cortex and all the other relevant parts of the brain to be in exactly the state that they would be in if one were perceiving, say, a white cat on a blue sofa—and the veridical experience one would have in that state have no common elements. It is true that the two experiences cannot be distinguished on the basis of how things seem to one visually, but, according to disjunctivists, one cannot say that they are indistinguishable *because* they have the same phenomenal quality or qualities. One can only say that they are indistinguishable, *Punkt.*

It is no accident that reading Austin's *Sense and Sensibilia* influenced me in the direction of disjunctivism. Although a close friend of Austin's, J. M. Hinton, is usually credited with being the father of disjunctivism, Austin surely deserves to be called at least its grandfather. For, although most of Austin's *Sense and Sensibilia* consists of arguments against Ayer and other traditional epistemologists, if one tried to extract a positive claim about perception from that book, it would surely be in the general ballpark of disjunctivism. And it now seems to me that the disjunctivist view cannot be right. But neither can Russell's view according to which the colors we see when we look at a table (and the smoothness we feel when we touch it, etc.) are in our own "private spaces," that is, colors and textures and shapes are just our own sense data, and objective, physical colors, textures, shapes are inferred properties of, in effect, noumenal objects.[6]

---

6. This is argued in the first three chapters of Bertrand Russell's *Problems of Philosophy* (Oxford: Oxford University Press, 1912). In chapter 1, Russell proposes that "we give the name 'sense data' to the things that are immediately known in sensation: such things as colors, sounds, smells, hardness, roughness, and so on" (12) [I have Americanized the spelling]. By chapter 2, we have learned that "the sense data are private to each separate person" (20) and in chapter 3 we are told, "Now our sense-data are situated in

In my Dewey Lectures, I defended disjunctivism with a skeptical argument: I claimed (following Wittgenstein) that there could no be such things as sense data (aka "qualia") because there is no criterion for intersubjective sameness here, or even sameness of sense data at different times for one subject.

The particular form of disjunctivism I sympathized with in the Dewey Lectures is due to John McDowell (although, in an afterword to the volume in which I collected those lectures,[7] I refused to endorse the claim that all experiences are conceptualized, which figured large in *Mind and World*).[8] I now believe, for example, that the best "mesh" of phenomenological considerations and neuroscientific ones will involve recognizing that many of our experiences are not conceptualized in any of the senses that McDowell has proposed, and will also involve rejecting the idea (advocated by Wittgenstein and later by Hinton) that there is no possibility of a scientific criterion for sameness and difference of, say, color experience of different subjects in which intersubjective spectrum inversion is an intelligible possibility. In sum, I believe that there is a qualitative and nonconceptual dimension of experience that can be scientifically investigated. To use a term revived by Ned Block, there are *qualia*, and progress can be made and *has* been made in saying something about their neurophysiological basis.[9] But if so, the problem becomes how does one criticize the Russellian conception I described in which what we perceive are just our own qualia?[10]

The ramifications of this question are large, precisely because one dogma of empiricism is still very much with us, and that is the dogma that perception begins with sense data.[11] If disjunctivism were right,

---

our private spaces" (30) and not in "one all-embracing physical space in which physical objects are" (31).

7. In *The Threefold Cord*, I wrote, "My own 'Girondist' position is that while it may be that some experiential content is nonconceptual in the sense of not being conceptualized, such epistemologically important content as recognizing something as an object of a certain kind is *irreducibly* conceptual" (156–157). In the note to that sentence I added that, "I find McDowell's talk of our conceptual powers being in play uncomfortably reminiscent of faculty psychology" (218n24).

8. John McDowell, *Mind and World* (Cambridge, Mass.: Harvard University Press, 1994).

9. I first saw it in the writings of C. I. Lewis.

10. I shall use Russell's term at times to bring out the traditional roots of the current debates about perception, but I will not distinguish between "qualia" and "sense data."

11. Note that following David Chalmers, *The Conscious Mind* (Oxford: Oxford University Press, 1996), but not Block, I do not take talk of *qualia* to rule out "adverbial" views of phe-

the problem of avoiding the errors of empiricism would be solved—just deny that there are any such things as "sense data." Voilà, perception without sense data! But for the sorts of reasons I just referred to, I think this dismissive strategy is misguided.

Indeed, it may seem obvious that, if there are sense data, then they are what knowledge of the world is "based on." What else do we have, after all? Even before we try to see more clearly what the alternatives before us really are, here is a point to keep in mind: the fact (if you agree with me that it is a fact) that our experience has a qualitative and nonconceptual dimension does not entail that we perceive qualia. Indeed, Moore himself thought that it is difficult to perceive qualia, and Shoemaker has argued that we cannot perceive them. As Block writes,

> Shoemaker's view is shared by Fred Dretske, Gilbert Harman, Michael Tye, and many others who advocate what G. E. Moore termed the diaphanousness (or sometimes the transparency) of experience. Harman puts the point by saying that the more one tries to attend to one's experience of the tree, the more one attends to the real tree instead. Although Moore is sometimes cited as the originator of this point, he did not actually accept it. I have heard him quoted saying "the moment we try to fix our attention upon consciousness and to see what, distinctly, it is, it seems to vanish: it seems as if we had before us a mere emptiness. When we try to introspect the sensation of blue, all we can see is the [objective] blue; the other element [the quale] is as if it were diaphanous." But these words are followed by what I regard as a more significant truth: "Yet it can be distinguished if we look attentively enough, and know that there is something to look for."[12]

---

nomenal qualities, that is, views under which they are modifications of experiences rather than "mental paint," and ditto for "sense data." A variant—one I prefer, in fact—of adverbialism, due to Wilfred Sellars, "The Adverbial Theory of Objects of Sensations," *Metaphilosophy* 6 (1975): 144–160, treats "I have a red sense datum" as better analyzed as "I sense redly." In this view, it is the case, as urged by Reichenbach in *Experience and Prediction*, that what correspond to sense data / qualia are states of the subject, not properties of mental particulars (see p. 100n5).

12. G. E. Moore, "A Reply to My Critics," in *The Philosophy of G. E. Moore*, ed. P. A. Schlipp (New York: Tudor Publishing, 1952), 546. The words in square brackets are my interpretations of Moore's expressions.

Hilla Jacobson and I are currently working on a book on the quest for naive realism in contemporary philosophy of mind. We hold neither Shoemaker's view that there is no such thing as attending to one's qualia nor Block and Moore's view that we have to perform a special act of "looking attentively enough" (unless what they mean to point out is just that we have to conceptualize differently when we attend to the qualitative aspect of what is presented in an experience as opposed to its representational content). We can attend both to the objective color (for example) of something (that shirt is blue) and to the "look" of that color, and, indeed, to various "looks" that it (potentially) has—how it looks from here, for example, or how it looks in the daylight, and also to more subjective looks. In the case of veridical perception, all of those looks are genuine properties of the object seen. I have been aware since I was a very young man that the look of colors is different if I close my right eye and if I close my left eye (a very common phenomenon, accounted for by differences in the two macular areas). So one of the many looks I can attend to is the look of the shirt with my right eye closed, and another one is the look of the shirt with my left eye closed. Those looks are properties, albeit relational ones, of the shirt in question. Experiencing "phenomenal qualities" is inseparable from perceiving properties of things "out there," but it isn't simply receiving information about how things out there are *independently* of being perceived (*contra* "representationalist" philosophers of perception). The *qualia* are different. And *contra* the disjunctivists, if we produce those looks without the aid of an object that has the appropriate objective colors (e.g., via the sort of experiments famously performed by Edwin Land), then we do not perceive a color property of anything external to ourselves, but we can still attend to the qualitative dimension of the experience, and we can perceive its similarity to the qualitative dimension of a corresponding veridical experience. But Block is right to concede, as indeed Moore already does, that in most cases we perceive one or more of the objective properties (that shirt is blue, that shirt has such and such a look in artificial light, etc.) and do not conceptualize or "apperceive" the subjective aspect.

With the above in mind, let us now consider three different models of perception. The empiricist model, in which perception is based on "sense data" (aka "impressions and ideas") is still with us, but there are many other models that simultaneously attract both laypersons and philosophers. Two of the most important are Quine's "surface-irritation" model, and the Kantian model favored by McDowell (although I discern the influence of the empiricist model at times in his writing, such as the times he uses "experiences" and "impressions" interchangeably, and emphatically insists on the importance of preserving "minimal empiricism").

I. The Empiricist Model

Bertrand Russell vacillated over the years, but in his great little book, *The Problems of Philosophy*, he held that colors are in our own minds, just as Berkeley and Hume thought, and that we infer the existence of physical colors, physical shapes, and so on, from the properties of these mental entities, and this is a standard empiricist view (sometimes dolled up with the idea that the inferences are "unconscious," or that we don't really make them but it is enough that we could make them, if we were sufficiently "rational"). Many have criticized this view on metaphysical and epistemological grounds, and with good reason, but today I want to look at this and the other two models I mentioned from the standpoint of psychology. From that standpoint, the immediate problem is that we obviously don't make the sorts of inference that Russell described in *The Problems of Philosophy*—not unless we are Bertrand Russell! (Nor did he think we made them; in his view most people are utterly ignorant of their epistemological predicament.) Indeed, the idea that we make such inferences is incompatible with the traditional empiricist claim that (unless we have been educated by philosophers like Russell) we simply project our qualia onto the external world without realizing that there is a difference between those objective properties and our qualia.

What about the dolled-up version, according to which we make such inferences "unconsciously"? At best, this is a hypothesis about subpersonal mechanisms, and I believe that we also need an acceptable personal-level description of perception, and not only an account of the subpersonal mechanisms that subserve perceiving, thinking, deciding, and so forth. But even at the subpersonal level, we now know of many more kinds of computation that the brain is capable of using than propositional inference, so even as a subpersonal account, "unconscious inference from our sense data" is out of date.

Moreover, the inputs to the brain are not qualia, but not because qualia aren't features of brain events (I believe that they are, and, in any case, they certainly supervene on brain events). The idea of qualia as inputs might have been at least partially vindicated had it turned out that Fodor's "modularity" view, on which phenomenal appearances are simply outputs of perception-modules, turned out to be right. In that case qualia might be identified with those outputs, and those outputs in turn identified with the first stage of cognitive processing. But the consensus in neural science today favors a much more complicated story. On the modularity hypothesis, perception was supposed to be an entirely "bottom up" affair, but today it is becoming clear that that perception is both "bottom up" and "top down." When I see a tomato, for example, many parts of the brain are involved, and interactions (reverberating circuits) take place between cortical and precortical functions. If there are "inputs" to the brain, they begin with the eyes— much earlier than the formation of "qualia."

One might try to bypass this objection by adopting a dualistic view of the unconscious mind, and posit that while the inputs to the brain are neural stimulations, beginning in the eyes, the inputs to the unconscious mind are "mental" qualia, but at this point all contact with both science and phenomenology would have been lost. The "unconscious inference" story was cutting edge psychology at one time,[13] but it is not tenable as either personal level or subpersonal level psychology today.

What about the version according to which the story about inferences from qualia to material objects is supposed to be a "rational reconstruction"? When we make explicit the steps in a proof that are left implicit in a mathematics journal, for example, we are engaged in rational reconstruction, but in such a case the steps could have been made explicitly to begin with (the article would simply have been boring to read). But to say why I believe that there is a computer in front of me as I type these words by (1) describing all the relevant "sense data" and (2) providing an inference from all that information (assuming it exists, and assuming it could all be stated) to "there is a computer in front of me" is not something I could really do. At best (and assuming we ignore all

---

13. H. L. Helmholtz, *Handbuch der physiologischen Optik*, vol. 3 (Leipzig: L. Voss, 1866); repr. 3rd ed., with extensive commentary by Allvar Gullstrand, Johannes von Kries, and Wilibald Nagel (Hamburg and Leipzig: L. Voss, 1896), 28–29.

the objections that critics of traditional epistemology have raised), all that the "rational reconstruction story" could show is that a person with literally superhuman capacities for phenomenological description, retention of information, and rapid reasoning would be justified in believing that there is a computer in front of him or her, and not that persons like ourselves are justified in our perceptual beliefs. Perhaps in such a case justification is not needed—justification comes to an end, as Wittgenstein said in *On Certainty*[14]—but providing such a justification was precisely the purpose of the "rational reconstruction"!

II. The Surface-Irritation Model[15]

Although in some of his writing in the 1950s Quine occasionally spoke of "sense data," his considered position was that (1) "sense data" are "posits," just as much as say electrons or genes, and not the subject of a kind of knowledge that is independent of theory, as the sense datum philosopher claims and (2) unlike electrons and genes they are bad posits.[16] What, then, is Quine's picture of perception?

The answer is a straightforward causal story. Light from the window and the desk lamp strikes the computer and is reflected to my eyes, neurons in my eyes are stimulated, my optic nerves are stimulated, my brain does various things, and as a result I acquire a set of "linguistic dispositions" I didn't have before, such as the disposition to assent if Quine (or whoever) points to the computer and utters the "occasion-sentence" *computer*.[17] To the charge that this is not a story on which my belief that there is a computer there is justified, Quine ought not to respond, as he sometimes did, by speaking of the stimulations of those neurons as "evidence" and of my saying "yes" to the query "Is that a computer in front of you?" and the like as "warranted beliefs"; he should simply have said that such notions as "warrant," "belief," and "evidence"

---

14. Ludwig Wittgenstein, *On Certainty*, ed. G. E. M. Anscombe and G. H. von Wright (Oxford: Blackwell, 1969), §192.

15. The term "surface irritation" was famously used by Quine for the triggering of sensory receptors in "The Scope and Language of Science," in W. V. Quine, *The Ways of Paradox and Other Essays*, rev. ed. (Cambridge, Mass.: Harvard University Press, 1976), 228–230.

16. Here I follow Peter Hylton's *Quine* (Abingdon, United Kingdom: Routledge, 2007), 87.

17. The notion of an "occasion sentence" was famously used by Quine in *Word and Object* (Cambridge, Mass.: MIT Press, 1960).

do not belong in science. But that even he was not willing to consistently go that far reveals how unappealing the position is, as McDowell and others have pointed out.

III. The Kantian Model

Kant's great contribution was to call to our attention the ways in which what we perceive is dependent on what we conceive. For example, to perceive—in the sense of recognizing the fact that—one event happened later than another requires possessing the notion of an objective time order, and that notion, Kant claimed (I believe rightly), is dependent on (or rather interdependent with) such conceptual resources as the notions of cause and effect. It is not enough that I experience events in a certain subjective order; I must also know that in certain cases I could have perceived them in a different order (I could have walked around the house in the reverse direction, for example, and still perceived the front, the sides, the chimney, etc.), and in other cases I could not have perceived them in a different order (I could not have perceived that boat sailing away from the bridge before I perceived it approaching the bridge). Conceptualization is a precondition for full-blown perception.

In *Mind and World*, McDowell, however, takes Kant's point to be that *all* experiences are apperceptions (recognitions that something is so and so). This may have been Kant's view too; at least, he writes that an "intuition" to which we do not prefix the "I think" would "be nothing to us," and this could be interpreted as meaning that, as far as we can know, our whole mental life is apperceived by the ego. If so, I believe that Kant made a mistake, and that McDowell makes the same mistake.[18] I think we are aware that there is a great deal of detail in the scene presented to our eyes at any given moment that we do not apperceive, and some of that detail can be recalled by us a moment or two later. But one does

18. I also have problems with McDowell's "minimal empiricism." I quote from *Mind and World* (Cambridge, Mass.: Harvard University Press, 1994): "Empirical judgments in general—whether or not they are justified at all, perhaps less substantially than knowledge requires—had better have content of a sort that admits of empirical justification, even if there is none in the present case (say in a quite unsupported guess)" (6). As it stands, this reads like a "verifiability" requirement, and if that is not how McDowell understands it, it is noteworthy that he does not feel it necessary to explain why it does not mean that every "empirical judgment" must be confirmable or disconfirmable by experience.

not have to speculate about this; there is good experimental work to support the view that what we attend to in experience is far from being the whole of experience. The idea that what is presented in experience outruns what is attended to, conceptualized, and so on, is not simply an illusion, as some have tried to claim. (Of course the point applies also to senses other than vision.)

The point is not trivial, because claiming that only creatures capable of fully conceptualized apperception—that is, of apperception whose content they can formulate in language—can have experiences of the sort we have posits an enormous, and I believe untenable, gulf between our experiences and those of animals and even those of children who are not yet masters of a language.

Seeing apperceptions and not bare qualia as the basis of empirical judgment involves a fundamental shift in perspective.

The fact is that when we have an apperception (or a seeming-apperception—think of the Müller-Lyer illusion!), no particular "impression" is essential. Block and others have pointed out that there is considerable empirical evidence that different subjects experience different qualia when they look at a particular color; but, unless they are color blind, they can all be truly said to see (apperceive) that the traffic light is red, when it is. The apperception or seeming-apperception that the traffic light is red is not the same as an "impression" in the sense of a sensation. Nor is it the same as a perceptual *belief.* (There is no such thing as it seeming to me that I believe something when I know that I don't believe any such thing, but there is such a thing as seeming to apperceive something when I know that I don't.) When we look for a justification for a particular empirical judgment, apart from the very special case in which the judgment is about qualia, what we cite as observational support are *apperceptions* and not qualia (or "sense data").

Of course, McDowell also does not think we do cite sense data (in the sense of qualia) as empirical support for our judgments; he thinks there are no such things as qualia, and that visual impressions, for example, are simply takings-in of properties of the objects we see. If I see a red book, the "impression" that the book is red is just a taking-in of the fact that the book is red. This is not idealism, as some critics of McDowell have charged; however, it is simply wrong. What it is is an attempt at an account of perception without any reference to sense data at all. I agree with McDowell that qualia cannot do the epistemic work of supporting our empirical judgments. In my view, that work is done by our apperceptions and seeming-apperceptions. In fact, perceiving something is sometimes not accompanied by any special qualia. Perceiving that I raised my arm intentionally (as opposed to its just "going up") is something I often do, but there is no "quale" of "voluntariness." Moreover, there are—as Alva Noë has stressed—many forms of "amodal" awareness. The awareness that I am seeing a tomato includes both the awareness that the side toward me has a certain color and the awareness that it has a soft interior and a side I do not see.[19] But the fact that knowledge is grounded in apperceptions and seeming-apperceptions and not in unconceptualized sense data does not imply that the latter do not exist. For our experience is rich in qualia, most of which we do not conceptualize, although many of them can be conceptualized to some extent both when they occur and after they occur. Qualia can even play an epistemic role, when they are what we apperceive. But so can tables and chairs and cats when they are what we apperceive. I am arguing that qualia, as opposed to apperceptions, play no *special* epistemic role, but disjunctivists are wrong to deny their existence.

To summarize, the Kantian picture of perception that McDowell defends in *Mind and World* is simply this: our impressions are already conceptualized.[20] Also, disjunctivism guarantees that our "impres-

---

19. See Alva Noë, *Action in Awareness* (Cambridge, Mass.: MIT Press, 2004). While Noë perhaps overemphasizes the role of sensorimotor expectations in such "amodal" awareness, they are without doubt a significant part of the story.

20. In John McDowell, "Avoiding the Myth of the Given," in *Having the World in View: Essays on Kant, Hegel, and Sellars* (Cambridge, Mass.: Harvard University Press, 2009), he gives up the requirement that experiences *must* be "articulated" or at least "articulable" like propositions, and sums up some key elements of his current view as follows:

> Even though the unity-providing function is a faculty for discursive activity, it is not in discursive activity that these capacities are operative in intuitions. With much of the content of an ordinary visual intuition, the capacities that are in play in one's having it as part of the content of one's intuition are not even susceptible of discursive exercise. One can make use of content's being given in an intuition to acquire a new discursive capacity, but with much of the content of an ordinary intuition, one never does that. (Think of the finely discriminable shapes and shades of color that visual experience presents to one.) Nevertheless an intuition's content is all conceptual, in this sense: it is in the intuition in a form in which one *could* make it, that very content, figure in discursive activity. That would be to exploit a potential for discursive activity that is already there in the capacities actualized in having an intuition with that content. (265)

sions" are not mental entities ("qualia") common to veridical perceptual experiences and certain illusions and hallucinations. Instead, they are simply takings-in of how it is in the environment (in the case of vision, for example). If I see a white rabbit, that there is a white rabbit there is a fact about the world, and it is the conceptual content of some of my visual impressions. Naive realism is the personal level account of perception we need. The only task for philosophy is to explain that this is the case. Neural science is fine in its place, but what it studies is merely subpersonal mechanisms, and philosophers don't need to know anything about them. (A view that understandably infuriates some philosophers, who think that philosophy of mind needs to be scientifically informed.)

If you are like me, it will seem to you that none of these models can suffice. The empiricist model was deeply infected with Berkeleyan idealism from the start; the surface-irritation model does express our need to understand the mechanisms of perception, but it ignores the environment outside the skin (except for those "gavagai," whatever they are) and says nothing about the nature of the subpersonal processing as well as the specific nature of the environment–organism transactions. The Kantian model, as "naturalized" by McDowell, purports to defend commonsense realism, but it embraces a "disjunctivism" that is anything but commonsensical. And all three models ignore a point (stressed by both Dewey and Wittgenstein—an unlikely couple!) that what we perceive depends on what we do. Action and perception are interdependent. (Not that any of these models deny that, to be fair. But their authors evidently didn't think it important.)

Liberal Functionalism

In closing, what I want to do isn't to present a fourth model of perception, but to describe a way of thinking about the topic that can help us see how studies of perception at many levels and with many tools—perceptual psychology (including, importantly, the kind of psychology pioneered by Gibson), evolutionary biology, neural science, behavioral science, and conceptual analysis—can fit together, and how personal-level psychology, subpersonal neural science, and studies of organism–environment transactions at more than one level can all fit together. The aim is metaphysical in the best sense of the term, trying to understand "how things, in the widest possible sense of the term, hang together," and is also scientific without being reductive.

Over the years, I have used the term "functionalism" in both a narrower and a wider sense. In the narrower sense, functionalism held that the mind is simply a computer, one with "inputs from the sense organs" (like Quine's "surface irritation") and outputs to "suitable motor organs," and that to understand our mental functions it would suffice to find the right description of the "program" of the computer. This computer model of the mind led me to the "verificationist semantics"[21] that I mentioned at the beginning of this essay, and that semantic theory was the axle around which "internal realism" rotated.

That form of functionalism, computational functionalism, I gave up even before I gave up internal realism,[22] and in the Dewey Lectures (written after giving up internal realism) I argued that it is hopelessly solipsistic. In fact, my finding solipsism unavoidable in any picture that limits mental life to what happens inside our heads was the impetus for seeking a way to come closer to naive realism without coming so close as to deny the phenomenal characters of experience. And in my Prometheus Prize Lecture in 2010,[23] I proposed a naturalist but antireductionist view I called "liberal functionalism."[24] That view agrees with my former computational functionalism that the question psychology needs to address is the description of the various functions (or rather function*ings*) of an organism, rather than the question of its physical or biological makeup, but it rejects completely both the restriction to computer programs as the sole admissible way of describing those functions (which is not to say that computer programs can never be relevant); it also rejects the idea that what goes on between the "sensory

---

21. This connection is explicit in Hilary Putnam, "Computational Psychology and Interpretation Theory," in *Artificial Intelligence: The Case Against*, ed. Rainer Born (London: Routledge, 1987), 1–17; reprinted in my *Realism and Reason*, vol. 3 of *Philosophical Papers* (Cambridge: Cambridge University Press, 1983), 139–154.

22. Compare with Hilary Putnam, *Representation and Reality* (Cambridge, Mass.: Harvard University Press, 1987).

23. My Prometheus Prize Lecture, "Corresponding with Reality," is collected in De Caro and Macarthur, *Philosophy in an Age of Science*, 72–91.

24. The term "liberal functionalism" was suggested by Mario De Caro and David Macarthur's use of "liberal naturalism" in the introduction to their *Naturalism and Normativity* (New York: Columbia University Press, 2010).

receptors" and the "signals from the brain to the motor organs"[25] is *all* that psychology is concerned with, as my computational functionalism assumed.

Instead, liberal functionalism holds that we have naturally evolved functions for dealing with specific environmental contingencies,[26] as well as functions that develop in the maturational history of each individual—in the case of humans, functions that depend on and in turn condition the sort of language we understand and use. Rather than view what happens between the object we see and eye as simply a matter for physics, for example, a liberal functionalist will follow Gibson's pioneering lead in seeking for a description of the complex relations between the properties of the object in question, the organism's repertoire of actual and possible sensory-motor transactions with the object, and the ways in which the object is perceived. And the vocabulary to be used in describing those functions will not be circumscribed in advance. As I wrote in my Prometheus Prize Lecture,

> An up-to-date liberal functionalist shouldn't think she has to *reduce* all the notions she uses to non-intentional notions. It is true that we have no idea how to reduce the predicate 'refers to' to non-intentional predicates, but that does not mean that talk of certain organisms using signs to refer to certain sorts of things and certain sorts of events should be considered talk of 'occult' entities or properties. Psychologists and anthropologists and sociologists and linguists have long been investigating sign behavior, and most of them do not eschew talk of what signs *refer to*.[27]

25. This is approximately the language I used in "The Mental Life of Some Machines," in *Intentionality, Minds and Perception,* ed. Hector-Neri Castañeda (Detroit: Wayne State University Press, 1967), 177–200; reprinted in Hilary Putnam, *Mind, Language and Reality,* vol. 2 of *Philosophical Papers* (Cambridge: Cambridge, University Press, 1975), 408–428.

26. These are what Ruth Millikan, *Language, Thought, and Other Biological Categories* (Cambridge, Mass.: MIT Press, 1984), has called "normal functions" or "proper functions." I agree with Millikan on the importance of the notion, but not on the claim that we can reduce intentional notions such as reference with its aid.

27. Noam Chomsky is an exception. He thinks talk of reference has no place in serious study of language, and he adds that we can have no intuitions about reference because "the terms extension, reference, true of, denote, and others related to them are technical innovations which mean exactly what their inventors tell us they mean." See his *New Horizons in the Study of Language and Mind* (Cambridge: Cambridge University Press, 2000), 148.

Thus, unlike the functions I spoke of in "The Mental Life of Some Machines," which were restricted to ways of processing inputs (and digitalized ones at that!) from our sensory receptors and sending (digitalized) outputs to our "motor organs," the functions the liberal functionalist will be interested in include ways of perceiving and ways of dealing with elements of the environment beyond our "surfaces," elements as far away as human thought and action can reach. These are, verily, functions with long arms.

As organisms in a world and a culture, we are able not only to perceive the "quality space" of which Quine speaks in *Word and Object*, but also to perceive that, for example, something is a "smart phone" and that something "feels like a trackpad" and that someone "said that there was an earthquake in Thailand," and many other things that require more and less sophisticated conceptual resources to describe. McDowell's claim that our senses provide us with forms of "openness to the world" is right (apart from his confusion of apperceptions with "impressions") but insufficient; what it needs is supplementation with details as to how they do that. But this is not a program to be carried out by empirical investigation alone; as my *Doktorvater* Hans Reichenbach taught me, scientific investigation and philosophical analysis need to go hand in hand. That is as much or more the case in cognitive science as it is in mathematical physics.

⌐ *11*

"Naive Realism" and Qualia

$\mathcal{I}$N "12 PHILOSOPHERS—and Their Influence on Me,"[1] I described how certain teachers and, later, certain things that I read and certain philosophical friendships that I formed, had an influence on the development of my philosophical views. Apart from Rorty, whom I was very fond of, but whose impact I described as "inspiring me to refute his account of pragmatism," all of those influences are described in positive terms. If that lecture had to be given now, rather than in 2007, a thirteenth philosopher would be added:[2] Ned Block. And although John McDowell would still be on the list, I would not write today, as I did then, that it is "the 'disjunctivist' school in the philosophy of perception" that shows us how it is possible to defend what William James called "the natural realism of the common man." The reason for both of these (counterfactual) changes is the same: the impact, over a period of a couple of years, of two papers by Ned Block—a lecture titled "Wittgenstein and Qualia," which I heard Block deliver

---

1. "12 Philosophers—and Their Influence on Me," Dewey Lecture to the Eastern Division of the American Philosophical Association, December 2007, *Proceedings and Addresses of the American Philosophical Association* 82, no. 2 (2008): 102–115.

2. Lest the reader worry that "13 is an unlucky number," let me point out that this is a specifically Christian superstition (arising from the fact that there were 13 at the table at the Last Supper, according to the New Testament), and neither Block nor I are Christians. In the Jewish tradition, 13 is the number of the attributes of the deity!

at the "Putnam Fest" conference in my honor in Dublin in March 2007,[3] and a paper of his titled "Consciousness, Accessibility, and the Mesh between Psychology and Neuroscience,"[4] which appeared later in the same year. In the course of the last few years, these papers have had an impact on my thinking about the phenomenology of perception comparable to the impact on my later philosophy of mathematics that reading Quine's "On What There Is" (1948) and "Two Dogmas of Empiricism" (1951) in my twenties turned out to have. The present essay is an attempt to describe that impact.

Is "Sameness" Well-Defined in the Case of Qualia?

Block's "Wittgenstein and Qualia" did not *immediately* convince me, however. One of its theses I had already accepted: namely, that the view (which I called "externalism" in *The Threefold Cord: Mind, Body and World*[5]) according to which the phenomenological character of a "veridical" perceptual experience (say, the experience someone has when seeing a white cat on a blue sofa) can be exhaustively described by describing the relevant observable properties of the presented scene in the usual public language—such as the shade of blue of the sofa, the kind of "white" in the case of the cat—is untenable.[6] Indeed, as I mentioned in the discussion that followed Block's lecture,[7] I have long maintained that the way the color of something appears to a subject depends on the properties of the perceiving subject as well as on the properties of the something in question. As a young man, I noticed that when I would lie on a beach with one eye shut (as would occasionally happen when

3. The papers read at this conference, including "Wittgenstein and Qualia," are collected in *Reading Putnam*, ed. Maria Baghramian (Abingdon, United Kingdom: Routledge, 2011).

4. Ned Block, "Consciousness, Accessibility, and the Mesh between Psychology and Neuroscience," *Behavioral and Brain Sciences* 30 (2007): 481–548.

5. Hilary Putnam, *The Threefold Cord: Mind, Body and World* (New York: Columbia University Press, 1999), 221n50.

6. In fact, I already argued that "externalism" was untenable in *The Threefold Cord:* "The fact that even if color properties . . . are conceived of as properties of 'external' objects they must be admitted to be *perspectival*, to have different *looks*, including looks that depend on the condition of the perceiving subject, should not be denied (as it has been, unfortunately, by certain 'externalist' philosophers of mind" (169).

7. Block mentions my remarks in that discussion in the (later) version of "Wittgenstein and Qualia" that appears in Baghramian, *Reading Putnam*, 275–318.

one side of my face was lying on the sand) that the beach looked a slightly less intense shade of yellow if the left eye was the open eye and if the right eye was the open eye. But I wouldn't have said that it seemed to be yellow when viewed through my left eye alone, and gray when viewed through my right eye alone. The difference was not that extreme. And it wouldn't have affected my "matching" performance on a color chart. No matter which eye is shut, if the beach matches "yellow$_{32}$" with the left eye shut, it will match "yellow$_{32}$" with the right eye shut. The difference is "ineffable" in Block's sense.[8] But it is not inexplicable; as Block mentions, it is easily accounted for by differences in the maculae of the two eyes. This is not even an "abnormality," for most people report the same phenomenon if they are asked to make the test.[9] And to ask, "Is the sand *really* the shade it looks to your left eye or the shade it looks to your right eye?" is meaningless.

However, at the Dublin conference, I also rejected the idea (which is central to Block's defense of "qualia" talk against Wittgensteinians) that the relation of "sameness of qualitative character" could be fixed by finding out *which brain-states* qualia are (i.e., by showing that a "mind–brain identity theory" is correct for "qualia"). I said in the discussion,

> Now, [Block's paper] certainly suggests that some straightforward identification of qualia with certain brain states is going to be discovered. But if there were such an identification, knowing *which one it is* is a probably unsolvable epistemological problem.[10]

And I referred to an argument I gave for this claim in *Reason, Truth and History*,[11] and I could also have referred to *The Threefold Cord: Mind, Body and World*.[12] Although that book rejected the "internal realism"

8. By "ineffable" Block does not mean "indescribable in principle" but indescribable in ordinary language with the terms used to describe objective appearances, for instance, "such a shade of red."

9. You do not have to go to the beach or wait for summer; just stand 50 feet or so away from a light-colored wall (far enough away so that parallax is not significant) and then close first one eye and then the other. Everyone I know who has tried this has reported a subtle but noticeable difference in the apparent color of the wall.

10. I also remarked that this is a point I argued for in chapter 4 of *Reason, Truth and History* (Cambridge: Cambridge University Press, 1981).

11. Putnam, *Reason, Truth and History*, chap. 4, 75–102.

12. Putnam, *Threefold Cord*, 162–169.

that I defended in *Reason, Truth and History*, it also rejected "qualia" talk, on the grounds that sameness and difference of subjective experiences is something for which there are only ordinary language criteria (for example, if a fully competent speaker of the language says her experience was the same on two occasions, then, other things being equal, that counts as its being the same). The question as to whether the experiences of different people, or even one person at different times, are "really" the same, when there is no basis for doubt in the ordinary use of "same experience" talk, could not, I claimed, be scientifically investigated. There is no "well-defined" relation of phenomenological sameness *there* for science to investigate.

This claim of mine, that qualitative sameness, supposing there is such a thing, is epistemologically inaccessible was directly rebutted by Block in the second of the two papers to which I referred earlier.[13] It is worth our while to review the issues at stake. Here is part of what I said in Dublin after Block delivered "Wittgenstein and Qualia." (I have already quoted the first sentence.)

But if there were such an identification [of qualia with brain-states], knowing *which one it is* is a probably unsolvable epistemological problem. I think we should give up the assumption that sameness of qualitative character is well-defined even for one person at different times or different people at the same time, let alone for nonconspecifics. I don't think that there is a fact of the matter, albeit an ineffable one, about whether the qualitative character is the same or different in such cases. I think that we should give that assumption up. I think that there are no good candidates in present day neurology for a relation of "identity of qualitative character."

If it seems strange that one can be wrong about there being a well-defined relation of identity here, an example from the history of science may help. It naturally seems to us that there is a fact of the matter about what is happening somewhere ten light years from here *right now*. But after Special Relativity we've had to abandon that natural belief. We have learned that "right now" is not well defined when astronomical distances or high relative velocities are involved. Similarly, it may be that "identical phenomenal quality" is not well defined. Nagel's famous question, "Is the

---

13. Namely, Block, "Consciousness, Accessibility, and the Mesh Between Psychology and Neuroscience."

bat's phenomenal experience the same as mine, or not?," may be as meaningless as "What is happening on the sun *this second?*"

At this point, I gave the following argument in support of the idea that the supposed relation of "identity of phenomenal character" (of experiences of a subject at different times) is, if it exists at all, epistemologically inaccessible: Gerald Edelman once invited me to spend a day in his laboratory. In the course of that fascinating visit, he said that when we visualize, say, a colored sheet of paper, part of what happens is that the part of the visual cortex that was active when the original experience occurred is reactivated. Suppose that the recognition of "patterns" (thinking of shades of color as species of "patterns") is modularized. (Edelman also told me that pattern-recognition "modules" tend to "recruit" additional neurons, if they are frequently stimulated, and to lose neurons to adjacent modules if unused compared to the adjacent modules.) Consider the speculation that the slightest change, say the loss or gain of a single neuron, "changes the quale." *Could the subject tell?*

In *Philosophical Investigations*, Wittgenstein wrote, "Always get rid of the idea of a private object in this way: assume that it constantly changes but that you do not notice the changes because your memory constantly deceives you."[14] What Edelman told me suggested to me that if the changes Edelman described did cause a change in the "qualia" that we (supposedly) have when a given module is stimulated, *we would never know* because *when we tried to remember how the sheet of paper* (or whatever) *looked before the neurons were added or subtracted from the module the memory image would seem as if there were no change in the "qualia"*; memories would change as the correlated qualia changed. And this shows at the very least that the supposed "sameness / difference" of qualia is epistemologically inaccessible, and perhaps that the very idea that there *is* such a relation, a relation of *really being the same* (as distinct from the relation of "seeming the same as far as I can tell now by relying on my memory and my mastery of the language") is as much of a mistake as supposing that there is such a relation of "really happening this very second on the sun" (as opposed to happening this second in a given reference frame). Wittgenstein's and Edelman's remarks seemed to fit together like hand and glove.

14. Ludwig Wittgenstein, *Philosophical Investigations*, trans. R. Rhees and G. E. M. Anscombe (Oxford: Blackwell, 1953), II, p. 207.

Problems with My Argument against Qualia

Obviously, I took a remark of Edelman's and ran with it, and I probably ran farther than he would approve. To conclude from the experiment with a colored sheet of paper he described that we can *never* remember what our experiences were like prior to changes in the visual cortex, as I did in that discussion, was a *big* inferential leap. If someone becomes red–green color blind as a result of brain damage, is it really the case that she will not be able to remember what red and green objects *used to look like?* That's certainly not something I know! But there were fatal problems with my argument beyond the uncertainty of the empirical premise it assumed.

Even if its premise were correct, that would only show that if a subject's spectrum became "shifted" as a result of changes in her visual cortex,[15] she would not be aware of it, and hence others could not confirm the shift on the basis of her *reports*. In "Consciousness, Accessibility, and the Mesh between Psychology and Neuroscience," Block argues that identification of the brain-parameters responsible for "qualia" need not depend simply on subjects' reports. In general, mind–brain connections have to be confirmed by arguments from the consilience of a hypothesis with different kinds of evidence rather than from direct "tests" (a situation familiar from present-day physics, for example), as well as from a comparison of the explanatory power (or lack thereof) of various alternative hypotheses, as is common in other sciences. In "Consciousness, Accessibility, and the Mesh between Psychology and Neuroscience," Block outlines how such an approach is likely to go in the case of visual phenomenology. On studying that paper I was completely convinced.

As a by-product of reading that paper I was also enabled to see what was wrong with a key argument in J. M. Hinton's classic paper "Visual Experiences"[16] (the foundational paper for what is today called "dis-

15. Of course, "shifts" due to insertion of color-changing lenses, or changes in the pigmentation of the maculae, or changes in the optic nerves exterior to the brain itself could still be detectable if changes due to changes in the relevant "modules" themselves were not. But while the possibility of shifts whose causes are (literally) "in the head" but not in the brain itself is enough to show that pure "externalism" with respect to color-qualia is untenable, it does not seem to me that they are fatal for Wittgenstein's skepticism about "the private object," or my more empirically grounded attempt to defend it.

16. J. M. Hinton, "Visual Experiences," *Mind* 76 (1967): 217–227.

junctivism") that I had long found fishy. Hinton scoffs at the idea that someone has "experiences" that are the same when she has a hallucination and when she has a corresponding (indistinguishable by her) veridical experience. Call such a common factor her "psi-ing" on both occasions. We could not find out what "psi-ing" is by empirical investigation, Hinton argues, because we would *first* have to be clear on what psi-ing is; his picture is clearly that an empirical identity, say, "As are really Bs" can only be confirmed if one is *totally* clear in advance on what one *means* by "As." Here is the passage:

> If there is no such thing as (Q) [the supposed common factor—*HP*] then there is—of course—no such thing as my psi-ing for the following statements to be about. (i) My psi-ing is one and the same event as some happening that is describable in the language of physics and / or physiology including neurophysiology.[17]

The problem with Hinton's argument, in a nutshell, is that when an identity ("As are really Bs") is a matter of theory (say, "Gravitational attraction is really a 'tidal force' [a deformation of space-time]") rather than a simple observational report such as "that man is my son," becoming clear on what A means (what we mean by "gravitational attraction") and confirming the claimed identity as the best explanation (via the consilience of various lines of data, the fact that it has the highest explanatory power of all the proposed explanations, and the like) proceed simultaneously; one does not come before the other. If qualia are successfully identified with brain-states, then we can expect to become clearer on, not exactly what we "mean" by "qualia," but on *what we ought to mean* by the term. (What we mean today by "water" is not, in fact, exactly what we meant before we discovered the chemistry of water. For Locke, ice and water were two different substances, albeit one frequently turned into the other.) In 1967, Oxford "ordinary language philosophy" was still riding high; the argument of Hinton's that I just quoted represents the weak side of that proudly scientifically unsophisticated philosophical school.

17. Hinton, "Visual Experiences," 219.

"Naive" Realism

The idea that the mass of mankind is quite mistaken in thinking that the colors, textures, and other "secondary properties" of the objects they claim to perceive are "out there," in the things themselves, when they are really just our own "sense data" is an old one.[18]

For Russell it was quite clear when he wrote *The Problems of Philosophy* in 1912 (and still clear in 1940, even after a flirtation with direct realism in *The Analysis of Mind*),[19] that we do not observe physical objects at all. He wrote,

> When, in ordinary life, we speak of *the* color of the table, we only mean the sort of color which it will seem to have to a normal spectator from an ordinary point of view under usual conditions of light. But the other colors which appear under other conditions have just as good a right to be considered real; and therefore, to avoid favoritism, we are compelled to deny that, in itself, the table has any one particular color.[20]

About ten pages later, Russell has shown to his satisfaction that the table we see lies in our own private visual space, and the table we feel lies in our own private touch space, and so on.[21] And furthermore, we do not perceive the external, physical, table at all:

> My knowledge of the table as a physical object, on the contrary, is not direct knowledge. Such as it is, it is obtained through acquaintance with the sense data that make up the appearance of the table . . . There is no state of mind in which we are directly aware of the table; all our knowledge of the table is really knowledge of truths, and the actual thing which is the table is not, strictly speaking, known to us at all.[22]

---

18. See book I, section II, part IV of Hume's *Treatise of Human Nature*, for example.

19. Bertrand Russell, *The Analysis of Mind* (New York: Macmillan, 1921).

20. See Bertrand Russell, *The Problems of Philosophy* (Oxford: Oxford University Press, 1912), 10.

21. Russell, *Problems of Philosophy*, 29.

22. Russell, *Problems of Philosophy*, 47.

Finally, our knowledge of the table must be via *inference:*

> Thus it becomes evident that the real table, if there is one, is
> not the same as what we immediately experience by sight or
> touch or hearing. The real table, if there is one, is not *immedi-*
> *ately* known to us at all, but must be an inference from what is
> immediately known. Hence, two very difficult questions at once
> arise; namely, (1) Is there a real table at all? (2) If so, what sort of
> object can it be?[23]

Nor is the Russell view wholly dated. Although philosophers who will
say that what we perceive are our own sense data are no longer thick
on the ground, there are respected contemporary philosophers who
deny that colors are "real" (Larry Hardin, for example),[24] and if colors
are not real, then much of what we take ourselves to see is not there to
be seen!

Moreover, a search of the Internet under "naive realism" will reveal
that quick "refutations" of naive realism, many of them two or three
centuries old, are all over the place. For example,

> If naive realism is to be taken seriously, and colors are out there in
> the world, then apples regularly change color depending on how
> much light is around them. It is much more plausible, though, to
> think that the apples are the same as they ever were, that all that
> has changed is our experience of them.[25]

This refutation assumes that the naive realist cannot maintain that
dispositions to have certain appearances to human beings cannot be "out
there in the world." In fact, even naive realists would include *disposi-*
tions to have certain a certain look depending on the lighting conditions
and the position of the viewer among the objective properties of the
objects viewed.

---

23. Russell, *Problems of Philosophy*, 11.

24. C. L. Hardin, *Color for Philosophers: Unweaving the Rainbow* (Indianapolis: Hackett, 1988).

25. See Tim Holt, "Naive Realism," *Theory of Knowledge*, n.d., www.theoryofknowledge .info/naiverealism.html.

Yet today there *are* philosophers who are proud to call themselves naive realists.[26] Obviously, this new use represents a reaction against views like Russell's. And clearly the "externalism" that I argued against earlier represents a sort of return to naive realism, as does my own call in *The Threefold Cord* for a "second naiveté" in the philosophy of perception. But rather than try to survey all the contemporary views that represent (more or less) a defense of naive realism, what I shall do for a moment is look at Russell's position and see at what points a defender of any degree of return to naive realism might reject it.

Russell's Position Again

In the previous quotations from *The Problems of Philosophy*, the following propositions are obviously assumed to be true:

(1) We perceive our sense data. (But the man and woman on the street mistakenly think that what they are perceiving are physical things.)

(2) We don't actually perceive physical objects.

(3) What we know about physical objects we know by inference. The premises for those inferences come from observing our own sense data.

Some Ways of Rejecting Russell's Picture

It is easy to find grounds for rejecting one, two, or all three of these Russellian propositions, but, as we shall see, some of the ways of rejecting them hardly do justice to what William James called the "natural realism" of the ordinary person. Many of those ways amount to little more than an appeal to ordinary usage—not a bad thing when it is just one of a number of points made in a philosophical discussion but hardly a satisfactory response by itself to a deeply thought out and complex metaphysical *cum* epistemological position such as Russell's.

For example, one might reject proposition 1 by saying, "We don't *perceive* visual 'sense data,' we *have* them." And one might then reject

26. For instance, "disjunctivists" in the philosophy of perception. See, for example, M. G. F. Martin, "On Being Alienated," in *Perceptual Experience*, ed. Tamar Szabo Gendler and John Hawthorne (Oxford: Clarendon Press, 2006), 354–410.

proposition 2 by saying, "When we have the appropriate visual sense data, and we unconsciously and automatically infer that there is a table in front of us, then that is what we ordinarily *call* 'seeing a table.'" Obviously, this is not a rejection of Russell's metaphysical picture at all but simply a recommendation that Russellians find a way of expressing their view that is more charitable to ordinary ways of speaking. However, propositions 2 and 3 would be rejected by some philosophers on more interesting (and controversial) grounds: a widely held view today is that the justification of observational beliefs, at least about such fundamental sensible properties as color, shape, texture, hardness, and the like, is simply a "reliabilist" one; we have been programmed by evolution so that when any of those beliefs is caused by impacts on our sense organs (an event that reliabilists identify with *perceiving* the objects, when the causal chain is of the right sort), the belief is very likely to be correct. This "reliabilist" ground for rejecting propositions 2 and 3, unlike the "ordinary language" grounds for rejecting propositions 1 and 2, does involve a serious disagreement with Russell's metaphysics; today's naturalistic reliabilists (rightly in my view) see perception as beginning with external things, and transactions involving both those things and the organism, and not with "sense data"; but it would theoretically be possible to produce a version of reliabilism more friendly to at least part of Russell's picture. I can imagine a philosopher who simply replaces "caused in the right way by impacts on our sense organs" with "caused in the right way by appropriate sense data," leaving it an open empirical question whether the "right sort" of causation is inference (perhaps unconscious inference, as Helmholtz believed).[27]

Another common ground for rejecting propositions 1, 2, and 3 is the so-called transparency of perceptual experience. Here is how Block, who accepts the view as a description of *part* of the phenomenology of perception,[28] describes it in "Wittgenstein and Qualia":

Shoemaker's view is shared by Fred Dretske, Gilbert Harman, Michael Tye and many others who advocate what G. E. Moore termed the diaphanousness (or sometimes the transparency) of

---

27. H. L. Helmholtz, *Handbuch der physiologischen Optik*, vol. 3 (Leipzig: L. Voss, 1866); 3rd ed., repr. with extensive commentary by Allvar Gullstrand, Johannes von Kries, and Wilibald Nagel (Hamburg and Leipzig: L. Voss, 1896), 28–29.

28. However, Block rejects the idea that we are *unable* to *ever* attend to our own qualia.

experience. Harman puts the point by saying that the more one tries to attend to one's experience of the tree, the more one attends to the real tree instead.[29] Although Moore is sometimes cited as the originator of this point, he did not actually accept it. I have heard him quoted saying "the moment we try to fix our attention upon consciousness and to see what, distinctly, it is, it seems to vanish: it seems as if we had before us a mere emptiness. When we try to introspect the sensation of blue, all we can see is the blue; the other element is as if it were diaphanous." But these words are followed by what I regard as a more significant truth: "Yet it can be distinguished if we look attentively enough, and know that there is something to look for.[30]

Any inference from *it seems to us that we attend to "the real tree"* to *"we actually perceive the real tree"* would, of course, be questioned by Russell, and with reason. The "diaphanousness" of (much of)[31] perceptual experience is simply a fact about the phenomenology of perceptual experience, but accepting it as such is not sufficient to overthrow or even present a clear alternative to Russell's picture.

Externalism as a Break with Russell's Internalist Picture

Theories like Russell's are *internalist* theories in the sense that (1) the inputs to perception, "the sense data," like Hume's "ideas and impressions," are entirely inside the subject's mind, and all the cognitive processing takes place inside the mind, where (2) the mind is conceived of as either inside the brain (by materialists like Hans Reichenbach)[32] or as totally immaterial (by Berkeley, and, arguably, by Hume as well; Russell's view seemed to have wavered between materialism and immaterialism over the years). Such views represent what I called an "interface conception" in *The Threefold Cord*, because they allow us no truly

---

29. G. M. Harman, "The Intrinsic Quality of Experience," *Philosophical Perspectives* 4 (1990): 31–52.

30. Block, "Wittgenstein and Qualia," 280.

31. I say "much of" because I agree with Block that we can and sometimes do attend to our qualia as such.

32. According to Reichenbach, "impressions" are our own internal states. See Hans Reichenbach, *Experience and Prediction* (Chicago: University of Chicago Press, 1938), 172.

cognitive access to the world, at any rate to the world outside the brain. But there is no good reason for a present-day naturalist philosophy of mind to be internalist.

In a way, this is something I already argued in "The Meaning of 'Meaning'."[33] A central thesis of that essay was that we need an externalist and anti-individualist account of what it is to understand the words of a natural language.[34] To think about gold, or water, or grass, or most of the things we think and talk about, is to engage in an activity that presupposes complex interactions with our environment and with other people. In "The Meaning of 'Meaning'," I expressed this by saying that "Meanings aren't in the head," but as a number of people later pointed out, I should have said "The mind isn't in the head." It is not, I hasten to add, that "the mind" is *somewhere else;* the mind isn't a thing with a location at all (so it is not simply the brain under another name), but a system of *world-involving abilities and exercises of those activities.* This view is, I believe, now accepted by a majority of philosophers of mind and cognitive scientists.

This is the view of the mind I have had for a long time, but in the last few years I have realized that it also captures what was right in "functionalism." It is true that I originally gave the name functionalism to an internalist view; in "The Nature of Mental States,"[35] the mind was identified with brain, which was described as a computer, and our mental states were identified with computational states of that computer. That was wrong,[36] but the idea that mental capacities and activities are *ways of functioning* was right, provided we allow that those ways of functioning may involve the environment and other people, and provided

---

33. Hilary Putnam, "The Meaning of 'Meaning'," in *Language, Mind and Knowledge*, ed. Keith Gunderson, *Minnesota Studies in the Philosophy of Science*, vol. 7 (Minneapolis: University of Minnesota Press, 1975), 131–193; collected in Hilary Putnam, *Mind, Language and Reality*, vol. 2 of *Philosophical Papers* (Cambridge: Cambridge University Press, 1975), 215–271.

34. By an "externalist" account of understanding, I mean here one that makes essential reference to things in the environment, as the account of meaning in "The Meaning of 'Meaning'" did, *not* one that insists that the phenomenological character of a "veridical" perceptual experience can be exhaustively described by describing the relevant observable properties of the presented scene.

35. Hilary Putnam, "The Nature of Mental States," in *Mind, Language and Reality*, 429–440.

36. I explain why I say it was wrong in Hilary Putnam, *Representation and Reality* (Cambridge, Mass.: MIT Press, 1988).

we do not limit the language used for the description of those ways to the language of computer science. For that reason, in a lecture I gave not long ago,[37] I referred to my present position as "liberal functionalism," and to functional "states" in this liberal sense as having "long arms" (arms that reach out to the environment). In this terminology, "The Meaning of 'Meaning'" is a liberal functionalist view of cognition, or an "externalist" view if we do not give "externalist" the meaning I gave it in *The Threefold Cord*—the meaning according to which an "externalist" view of perception requires us to hold that the phenomenological character of a veridical perceptual experience can be exhaustively described by describing the relevant observable properties of the presented scene in the usual public language—but simply take an "externalist" view to be one that allows at least some of our mental states to be at least partly externalistically identified.

I said earlier that an externalist conception of thinking (in this sense of "externalist") is now widely accepted in cognitive science and philosophy of mind. But once this has become the case, as it obviously had not in Russell's day, nothing stands in the way of extending externalism to *perceptual* states as well.[38] But now a problem arises.

The Problem

From here on, I shall discuss McDowell's views in *Mind and World* as an example of a position diametrically opposed to Block's and to the whole idea of qualia, that is, of nonconceptual phenomenal characters common to both veridical and nonveridical experiences.[39] To see the problem to which I just alluded, let us recall that McDowell motivates

---

37. Hilary Putnam, "Corresponding with Reality," in *Philosophy in an Age of Science: Physics, Mathematics, and Skepticism*, ed. Mario De Caro and David Macarthur (Cambridge, Mass.: Harvard University Press, 2012), 72–90.

38. A great deal in this direction has been done by Tyler Burge in *Origins of Objectivity* (Oxford: Oxford University Press, 2010).

39. Block himself usually takes "representationalists," particularly "intentionalists" like Tye, as his chosen targets; however, these philosophers are not in total disagreement with Block because they do believe veridical and hallucinatory experiences (to take the extreme case of the nonveridical) have a common phenomenal character, although they identify that phenomenal character with information; disjunctivists such as McDowell are in *total* disagreement with Block's views because they deny both that sensory impressions are nonconceptual *and* that there is such a "highest common factor."

his complex chain of arguments in *Mind and World* by laying down two requirements for a satisfactory philosophy of perception. The first, which he calls "minimal empiricism," is that sensory impressions must be a "tribunal" before which our beliefs about the world can stand,[40] and much of the controversy connected with that book has to do with McDowell's claim that this requirement can only be fulfilled if those impressions are themselves *conceptualized*.[41] The second (which is supposed to follow from the first) is that "reliabilism" must be rejected, because in the reliabilist view, McDowell charges, experience only "exculpates" the subject from criticism for having the beliefs her impressions cause her to have, but fails to *justify* those beliefs. This is the central argument of *Mind and World:* sense impressions (the "tribunal" before which all our beliefs have to stand) can justify beliefs only if those sense impressions are themselves justified.

In opposition to McDowell's views, Hilla Jacobson and I have argued, on both empirical and conceptual grounds, that the phenomenal characters of perceptual experiences are not (in any case, not always) conceptualized in any of the senses McDowell has proposed;[42] hence, if McDowell is right, they cannot be a "tribunal," whether or not those phenomenal characters are identical with qualia. So, if McDowell is right, skepticism threatens us. Moreover, qualia, Block taught us, are brain states, and hence *internalistically identified*. We might, of course, say that having (appropriate) qualia only counts as *perceiving* something when they are caused in the right way; but didn't I criticize that idea previously when I wrote that to say, "When we have the appropriate

---

40. Minimal empiricism, which McDowell endorses, "makes out that the very idea of thought's directedness at the empirical world is intelligible only in terms of answerability to the tribunal of experience, conceived of in terms of the worlds impressing itself on perceiving subjects." Quote from John McDowell, *Mind and World* (Cambridge, Mass.: Harvard University Press, 1996), xvi. Note the (nonaccidental) similarity of "impressing itself" and "impressions."

41. McDowell generally uses "impressions" and "experiences" interchangeably (he also sometimes uses the Kantian term "intuitions," particularly in the essays collected as *Having the World in View; Essays on Kant, Hegel, and Sellars* (Cambridge, Mass.: Harvard University Press, 2009). In *Mind and World*, he identifies "intuitions" with "bits of experiential intake" (pp. 4 and 6) and "impressions" with "impacts of the world on our senses" (139).

42. Hilla Jacobson and Hilary Putnam, "Against Perceptual Conceptualism," paper read (by Hilla Jacobson) at the conference "Philosophy in an Age of Science: Conference in Honor of Hilary Putnam's 85th Birthday," Harvard and Brandeis Universities, June 30– July 4, 2011; forthcoming in the *International Journal of Philosophical Studies.*

visual sense data, and we unconsciously and automatically infer that there is a table in front of us, then that is what we ordinarily *call* 'seeing a table'" is "not a rejection of Russell's metaphysical picture at all, but simply a recommendation that Russellians find a way of expressing their view that is more charitable to ordinary ways of speaking?" So it looks as if we have both handed game, set, and match to the skeptic *and* fallen back into Russell's picture.

My present view is almost the complete opposite of McDowell's. (1) Where McDowell requires that "impressions" must be a tribunal, I argued in Chapter 10 that it is *apperceptions* (and seeming-apperceptions) that are the tribunal, and not impressions.[43] Some apperceptions and seeming-apperceptions do, indeed, include the occurrence of qualia (or "impressions," to use McDowell's term, but without assuming the metaphysics that goes with it), but such cognitive states are not the same as qualia, nor, as we argued in Chapter 10, are they simply beliefs "triggered" by qualia.[44] The idea that "impressions" are the ultimate source of the confirmation and disconfirmation of empirical beliefs is a hangover from empiricism that should be jettisoned.

(2) Unlike McDowell, I don't agree that reliabilism must be completely rejected, as I will explain in the next section. That does not mean that we should accept the view I rejected above, according to which perceiving (for example) a rabbit on one's lawn is just having the appropriate visual "sense data" and unconsciously and automatically inferring that there is a rabbit on the lawn in front of one. But this issue deserves a section to itself.

A Relevant Objection to Reliabilism

The version of reliabilism that McDowell considers in *Mind and World* is one on which impressions cause beliefs in a way that McDowell

---

43. See my "Comments on Travis and McDowell," in Baghramian, *Reading Putnam*, 347–358. McDowell would deny that his "sense impressions" are what Block and I call "qualia," but the difference he finds depends on the controversial claims that (1) impressions are always conceptualized; and (2) impressions are not a common factor in both veridical perceptual experiences and hallucinations (even "perfect" hallucinations, in which the brain is in the same state as it is when a veridical perception takes place). I believe that both these claims are untenable.

44. Although awareness of the role of apperception, and its difference from simple sense impressions and from belief, figures largely in the thought of Leibniz and Kant, it simply goes missing in empiricism. That is why talk of "minimal empiricism" is so misleading!

associates with "bald naturalism"—that is, a way that is just a matter of the operation of subpersonal mechanisms, and thus wholly outside "the space of reasons." I agree with McDowell that we want something more than just an account of subpersonal mechanisms. Moreover, Russell's claim that we know about his table (or the rabbit on my lawn) via *inference* is simply unbelievable, if the inference is supposed to be conscious; if it is supposed to be "unconscious inference," as Helmholtz proposed, then what we have is, again, just a hypothesis about subpersonal mechanisms in the brain (at best). Indeed, the hypothesis is not particularly convincing for at least two reasons. (1) Subpersonal mechanisms may perform syntactic operations that we (at the personal level) *interpret* as inferences, such as "writing" (in "Mentalese") both "A" and "B" given "A&B," but "writing" one or two formulas given a third formula as "input" is not *inference*, it is only a syntactic representation of an inference. (2) Now that we know about forms of computation that do not consist of inferences in the traditional sense at all, there are many more possibilities for modeling the subpersonal processes involved in thought and perception than Helmholtz could have thought of. But we do not need to speculate about this; it is enough to see that a story about visual qualia causing beliefs via unconscious mechanisms, however interesting to investigate, is not an account of perception at the level we seek. About that McDowell is right. This is a relevant objection to *one form* that "reliabilism" can take.

Apperception is a phenomenon at the psychological level, the level of rational agency,[45] and there is no reason why there shouldn't be an account of the perceptual transactions of human beings (and other organisms) with their environments at that level. In the human case, such an account will involve also an account of language acquisition and of the role of our linguistic abilities in apperception. A "liberal functionalist," in my sense, can agree with McDowell that conceptualization plays an important role in perception, in a demanding sense of perception. McDowell's mistake is to assimilate all *experience* to perception in the demanding sense.

45. My identification here of the "psychological level" with the level of "rational agency" is something I now [July 2015] regard as a mistake. *Representation*, in Burge's sense discussed in Chapter 1, is a psychological activity (not a *subpersonal* one)—representing something involves the thing represented, and is thus an *externalistically identified* psychological process—but much more primitive than "rational agency," which requires conceptualization. [Note added on July 5, 2015.]

But what of McDowell's claim that *any* form of reliabilism only "exculpates" the subject from criticism for having the beliefs her sense impressions cause her to have, but fails to *justify* those beliefs? What do we do about skepticism?

Two Unsound Objections to Reliabilism

(1) Cartesian Skepticism Unanswerable

James Conant has distinguished between two kinds of skepticism, which he calls "Cartesian skepticism" and "Kantian skepticism."[46] "Cartesian skepticism," in Conant's sense, is skepticism about the possibility of *knowing* anything about an "external world"; "Kantian skepticism" is a worry about *how it is possible that* our thoughts, whether supposedly about an external world or even about our own sense impressions, really have *content* at all. (Note that this is not supposed to be an *epistemological* question.)

Through the years, both Conant and McDowell have taken me to task because, as they see it, in *The Threefold Cord* I mistook the target of *Mind and World* to be the "Cartesian" variety of skepticism, whereas it was actually the "Kantian" variety that McDowell was concerned to exorcise.[47] I know that I was not alone in missing this important distinction, because a criticism of *Mind and World* that I have often heard from students (though not one that I ever made) is that it doesn't "answer" the (Cartesian) skeptic. If this objection applied to McDowell, it would apply even more strongly to the reliabilist, since the latter does not *seek* to answer the Cartesian (or "Humean") skeptic at all. But the criticism seems to me misguided.

It is misguided because the notion of "answering the skeptic" suffers from a fatal ambiguity. If "answer the skeptic" means *give the skeptic a proof that we do know, for example, that there are such things as fireplaces and chairs in front of them that we sit on* (Descartes's example, slightly modified) *which the skeptic herself must accept*, that is, a proof from premises she must grant, then that is evidently impossible. We do find that

46. James Conant, "Varieties of Skepticism," in *Wittgenstein and Skepticism*, ed. Denis McManus (Abingdon, United Kingdom: Routledge Press, 2004), 97–136.

47. See John McDowell, "Responses," in *Reading McDowell: On Mind and World*, ed. Nicholas Smith (London: Routledge, 1994), 267–305.

disturbing, but as Quine famously wrote, "The Humean predicament is the human predicament."[48] The question we nonskeptics *should* worry about is, Is there a proof from premises *we* must accept that we do not know any such things? And I have argued elsewhere that the answer is that there is no such proof, although, to be sure, there is a work of rational reconstruction of our talk about knowledge, justification, and the like that has to go with that answer.[49]

A more legitimate reason for worry about reliabilism is that as an account of our uses of the verb "to know" in general it is open to many difficulties. In particular, reliabilists seem driven to either deny the conceptual connections between knowledge and justification altogether, or else to give implausible accounts of justification. But that does not show that when we come to the question of our knowledge of such elementary perceivable facts as the fact that we see something red in front of us or something square in front of us we really have more to say than "I see it." And "I see it" counts, in most cases, as justification enough simply because we have been evolved to be highly reliable in such cases and with respect to such simple properties at least.[50]

That reliabilism may be right in such basic cases does not mean that it is right in all cases and about all knowledge / justification claims, of course. And this much reliabilism does not commit us to any confusion of the subpersonal and the personal levels of explanation because it is not a story *about* how our recognition abilities work in such cases, or about the nature and the interrelations of concepts and experiences at work in such cases. But that remark clearly does not address the Kantian skeptic, who is McDowell's concern.

(2) Kantian Skepticism Unanswerable

The problem of what to say about Kantian skepticism is quite different, however, as McDowell rightly emphasizes. First of all, there aren't

48. W. V. Quine, "Epistemology Naturalized," in *Ontological Relativity and Other Essays* (New York: Columbia University Press, 1969), 69–90.

49. See the papers collected as section V, "The Problem and Pathos of Skepticism," in De Caro and Macarthur, *Philosophy in an Age of Science*.

50. Note that I did not say that "the putative reliability of the process of seeing" is the justification / the subject's reason for believing that p; the justification is "I see that p" *Period*. But we would not count it as a justification if it were not reliable.

"Kantian" skeptics in the way there are Cartesian (or Humean, or Pyr-rhonian) skeptics. It would be obviously self-refuting to claim that "no thought has any content at all, including this one." What Kant is asking of us is not to refute this claim, since it refutes itself, but to answer a "how is it possible?" question: *How is it possible* that thoughts possess content? And that is a task for all philosophers as well as for psychologists—indeed, for all who theorize about the mind.

That there is a real task here is not an objection to reliabilism, how-ever, because the reliabilism I have endorsed (call it *minimal* reliabilism) does not *purport* to address it. If it seems to McDowell to be an objec-tion to reliabilism that it offers "exculpations" where "justifications" are called for, that is because it does not do what his own answer to the "how can thoughts possess content?" question allegedly does.[51] But I find that answer unacceptable if understood, as I think it is intended to be understood. Strangely, because it is a vital part of McDowell's call for "minimal empiricism," I have been unable to find any real discussion of what he says about content in the literature. The connection to Block's concerns (lest the reader think I have forgotten that this is an essay about Ned Block!) is that McDowell seems to be offering a "tran-scendental argument" that qualia, if there are such things, must be *conceptualized* if our thoughts are to have content at all, a thesis that goes against much of what Block claims.

I just said that "I have been unable to find any real discussion of [McDowell's account of content] in the literature"; in part, this no doubt due to the fact that McDowell presents that account in very few pages,[52] and neither in *Mind and World* nor in *Having the World in View* does he expand on that presentation in any great detail. Indeed, it may be that I misunderstood what McDowell intends, but what follows is how I understand him.

(1) McDowell is a realist (as am I, and as is Ned Block). He criticizes Sellars for denying the reality of the objects of our commonsense world-picture,[53] and, although I could only find one remark to this effect in *Having the World in View* (and none that I recall in *Mind and World*), he

---

51. See McDowell, *Mind and World*, 11–12. McDowell does not use the term "reliabi-lism," but the position he ascribes to Davidson is a version of the reliabilism with respect to perceptual judgments I describe.

52. See especially McDowell, *Mind and World*, 3–13.

53. McDowell, "The Logical Form of an Intuition," in *Having the World in View*, 41–42.

regards the unobservables of modern science as fully real.[54] However, his account of how reference is fixed is primarily an account of reference to things we can perceive with our human senses.

(2) Like Sellars (and, again, this is something I agree with, and I am sure Block agrees with), he accepts the fundamental Wittgensteinian (and pragmatist) insight that grasping concepts that refer to observable things and acquiring a system of beliefs about those things, and ways of acting on them and interacting with them, are interdependent abilities. That is why the mere ability to discriminate (respond differentially to), say, squares and nonsquares, an ability we share with properly conditioned mice, does not suffice to have the concept *square*. Because McDowell believes impressions are conceptualized, he concludes that animals without language (like the mice) cannot have the sort of sensory impressions we have. When we see a square, our sensory impression, as it were, "speaks" to us, and its speech employs the concept *square*.[55] It follows that we cannot even imagine the sensory impressions of a mouse or, for that matter, a prelinguistic infant.[56]

(3) However, once we have acquired the linguistic capacities that are required to have impressions that are not "mute," our impressions present to us (in favorable cases) facts about the things that we look at, touch, listen to, as they are. Our impressions are not *representations* of the goings-on around us; *we are directly aware of the goings-on themselves*. The "transparency" of perceptual experience is a real transparency, not just a point about how it seems to us. (In this respect, the metaphor of impressions "speaking" to us is not the best figure for McDowell's purposes; "intentionalists," who identify phenomenal character with "information," also believe our impressions speak to us, but they speak to us even when they are nonveridical.) For McDowell, as a "disjunctivist," nonveridical impressions aren't impressions at all, at

54. In his Second Woodbridge Lecture, McDowell writes, "Not, of course, that we cannot direct thought at objects that we are unable to bring into view, perhaps because they are too small or too far away." And he adds, "But thought so directed is carried to its object, so to speak, by theory" (*Having the World in View*, 37). He does not discuss reference to such objects as *fields* or quantum mechanical particles or wave functions, which are not the sort of thing that could be "viewed" if they were larger or closer to us.

55. I recall that somewhere—I cannot now find the place—McDowell writes that instead of saying "percepts without concepts are blind" he should have written that "percepts without concepts are mute."

56. I criticize this view in Putnam, "Comments on Travis and McDowell," 347–358.

least not in the case of complete nonveridicality (i.e., complete hallucination). It is the fact that in veridical perception we directly perceive
the world itself that is supposed to make it non-mysterious that we
can refer to things and events in it, and hence non-mysterious that
thoughts about observable things and events have content.

(4) At times, however, McDowell's view seems to amount to the sort
of liberalized verificationism one finds in logical positivism after 1939:[57]
statements about both observables and unobservables, including
"guesses," have content as long as *and only as long as they are confirmable
by perceptual experiences* (which, in the light of the previous point, means
not by private sense data but by events a human could observe). As I
already mentioned in chapter 10, in *Mind and World* McDowell writes,
"Empirical judgments in general—whether or not they are justified at
all, perhaps less substantially than knowledge requires—*had better have
content of a sort that admits of empirical justification, even if there is none in
the present case (say in a quite unsupported guess)*."[58] Since this occurs in
a discussion of the temptation to succumb to "the myth of the Given,"
perhaps it is not McDowell's own view, although it does look as if it is
something that McDowell concedes the philosophers who succumb to
the myth. At any rate, this is not a premise in the argument for the
Given that McDowell ever criticizes.

Point 3 [and point 4, if it is McDowell's view] constitute McDowell's
answer to the "how do thoughts possess content?" question, and as I
indicated earlier, I find this answer unacceptable. I fact, I think both
points 3 and 4 are wrong.

Point 3 is wrong because it is not the case that when we perceive, say,
that something is red, or that something "looks red" in the objective
sense, the objective color, or the objective "looking red" [or whatever
color is in question], is present as the phenomenal character of our "impression," as McDowell's account demands. It is not the case because
the phenomenal character of the "impression" varies from person to
person, as the data cited by Block show (and as my own visual experi-

---

57. After 1939, the logical positivists (or "logical empiricists" as they by then preferred
to style themselves) abandoned sense-datum epistemology in favor of "thing language,"
and they also recognized that theoretical terms could not be "reduced" to observation
terms. I give a brief account of this history in Putnam, *The Collapse of the Fact / Value Dichotomy* (Cambridge, Mass.: Harvard University Press, 2002), 7–27.

58. McDowell, *Mind and World*, 6 (emphasis added).

ence, described earlier in the essay, also shows). The strong form of transparency that McDowell's account needs is just not there; if this is "naive realism," it is *too* naive.

Point 4 is wrong because it is incompatible with what I take to be a proper scientific realism.[59] If we can refer to things outside our light cone at all, as I take it we obviously can, it is not only "guesses" that "admit of empirical justification" that have content, but so do conjectures that it is impossible to justify that have content—for example, the conjecture that "there are no intelligent extraterrestrials anywhere in space-time."[60]

With respect to how our thought can reach to the unobservable, I could find only the single remark (in the Second Woodbridge Lecture) that "thought so directed is carried to its object, so to speak, by theory."

In sum, to the extent that we can understand "how is it possible that thoughts possess content?" as an intelligible question, McDowell has not given an answer we should accept. And, in any case, it is not an objection to what I called "minimal reliabilism" that it does not answer that question.

Some Observations on the "How Is It Possible?" Question

The "how is it possible that thoughts have content?" question that preoccupies McDowell is not a request for a *reduction* of intentionality ("content") to something else. A long time ago, I myself was tempted by the desire for a reductive account when I wrote,

> The brain's "understanding" of its own "medium of computation and representation" consists in its possession of a verificationist semantics for the medium, i.e. of a computable predicate which can represent acceptability, or warranted assertibility or credibility.[61]

59. See Hilary Putnam, "Pragmatism," *Proceedings of the Aristotelian Society* 95, no. 3 (1995): 291–306; "When 'Evidence Transcendence' Is Not Malign" [a reply to Crispin Wright], Chapter 8 in this volume; and "On Not Writing Off Scientific Realism," in *Philosophy in an Age of Science*, 91–108.

60. See Chapter 8 for a defense of this claim.

61. Hilary Putnam, "Computational Psychology and Interpretation Theory," in *Realism and Reason*, vol. 3 of *Philosophical Papers* (Cambridge: Cambridge University Press, 1983), 130–155. The sentences quoted in the present essay are on p. 142.

McDowell's work has been consistently free of all signs of such a temptation. What bothers him is something else. The obvious answer to the "how is it possible?" question, if we prescind from the difficult question of reference to unobservables, is, "What's your problem? Don't we see (touch, handle, etc.) objects in our environment all the time?" But the fact that our perception of such familiar objects as apples and chairs depends on "bits of sensory intake" leads, *if we identify that sensory intake with "impressions," and we identify impressions in turn with unconceptualized "qualia,"* straight to the conclusion that the basis for all our "knowledge of the external world" is our qualia; and it is hard to see how they *can* be a *basis.* Moreover, even if we don't hope for a reductive account of reference and "content," it is reasonable, especially after the rejection of Platonist and Rationalist accounts of the mind, to posit that what we can conceive and what we can refer to depends, at least in its initial stages,[62] on what we have cognitive contact with.[63] And if all we have cognitive contact with, in the initial stages of empirical knowledge, is qualia . . . ?

Surely this is a reasonable worry. And McDowell's principle philosophical claim is that the way to give that worry rest is to reject the idea of unconceptualized qualia altogether. There are "impressions," of course, but they put us in direct contact with the world, *and* they are conceptualized—they *tell us* about that world. But this combination of "externalism" and conceptualism with respect to the phenomenal character of experience is, I have argued, untenable on both empirical and conceptual grounds. So what do I suggest instead?

McDowell is certainly right that appealing to qualia ("bare presences") can't provide an answer to the question as to how concepts and experiences are connected, or, in McDowell's terms, how experiences can rationally constrain beliefs. But to get from that observation to the conclusion that "the content of experience is conceptual,"[64] McDowell needs to assimilate sensory impressions themselves to apperceptions, and that is where we disagree. In fact, there are apperceptions that have *no* accompanying qualia at all. Suppose I raise my right hand. My aware-

62. See Bertrand Russell, "On Denoting," *Mind* 14, no. 56 (1905): 479–493.

63. Of course, any theory has to recognize the possibility of reference "by description." But not all reference can be by description.

64. McDowell, *Mind and World,* 45.

ness that *I raised it* (it didn't simply "go up") is a genuine awareness, a genuine act of apperception, but there is no *quale* of voluntariness. (I think I remember that Elizabeth Anscombe somewhere describes this kind of awareness as "knowledge without observation," but this seems to me to be a misdescription. I would say that I *did* observe that I raised my hand, but this is observation without any particular qualia, or, to use a term employed by Alva Noë, an instance of "amodal awareness.") Similarly, my awareness when I see a tomato that I am seeing something that has a round other side and a soft seedy inside involves amodal awareness and not only qualia. McDowell thinks he has to say that *impressions* warrant beliefs, and that is the reason that he needs them to be conceptually articulated; my view is that it is *apperceptions* that warrant beliefs. Of course, certain sorts of apperceptions are internally related to impressions. But *it is the apperceptions and not the impressions that do the warranting.*[65] Babies and languageless animals do not have apperceptive awareness in the demanding Kantian or McDowellian sense, but I see no reason to deny them qualia.

Of course,[66] there is as little hope of a *reductive* account of apperception as there is of a reductive account of intentionality; indeed, apperception involves intentionality because it involves *recognizing* things and goings-on for what they are, and recognizing involves applying concepts. Apperceiving some thing or event in my environment is what I have called a "functional state with long arms," a world-involving functional state, in a very liberal sense of "functional state." Under normal conditions *neither* our perceptual experiences *nor* sentences we accept are the beginning of the process of forming a perceptual belief. The beginning is outside our heads; the process of forming a perceptual judgment to the effect that there is a notepad on this table is an exercise of a "function"—in fact, a whole system of functions, some shaped by evolution, and some shaped by cultural processes that connect me to objects and goings-on in my environment (in this case, to the notepad and to the table). Forming beliefs in accordance with our normal biological functions and our linguistic upbringing is not just uttering noises that are mere responses to qualia, although those qualia are a *part* of the causal chain that constitutes the normal formation of

---

65. I spell this out in more detail in Chapter 10.
66. Part of this paragraph is adapted from Putnam, "Corresponding with Reality."

a particular perceptual belief on the basis of seeing something in one's visual field.[67] On a liberal functionalist story, for either our beliefs, or the proto-beliefs of animals and prelinguistic children, to have content is just for them to function as representations of external states of affairs. In brief, a belief about the surrounding environment has content by virtue of being connected to possible states of the world via the externalistically identified functional states of the speaker. This is the classic functionalist account, liberalized by (1) liberalizing functionalism itself (detaching it from its narrow computationalism and reductionism) and (2) making functionalism externalist (functional states can involve tomatoes, and not only the senses and the motor organs). Kant would, of course, say this is a question-begging answer, and I would tell him that the sort of a priori proof that our concepts have content, the proof of the "object validity" of our categories, that he hoped for is a chimera.

The Epistemic Role of Qualia

If qualia cannot play the epistemic role that traditional empiricism assigns to "impressions," and if they cannot be "puffed up" to play that role by attributing propositional content to them, then do they have any epistemic role to play at all?[68] I suggest that they do, but not in all cases of perception (as traditional empiricism insists). And this is a good moment to refer once more to the views of Ned Block. Earlier, I quoted a passage in "Wittgenstein and Qualia" that included the following:

> I have heard [Moore] quoted saying "the moment we try to fix our attention upon consciousness and to see what, distinctly, it is, it seems to vanish: it seems as if we had before us a mere emptiness. When we try to introspect the sensation of blue, all we can see is

---

67. Or at least that is a reasonable hypothesis on the basis of present knowledge. But it isn't *a priori*, as many philosophers seem to think, that the relevant qualia (partially) cause or even temporally precede the cognitive awareness that I am seeing a tomato or a rabbit; it is logically possible that the cognitive awareness and the quale are effects of a common cause, or that the qualia are the effect and the cognitive awareness is the cause. But these questions relate to the subpersonal mechanisms behind awareness; the idea that they are a question for personal-level psychology is *the* central mistake of classical empiricism.

68. This question was put to me by Hilla Jacobson.

the blue; the other element is as if it were diaphanous. But these words are followed by what I regard as a more significant truth: "Yet it can be distinguished if we look attentively enough, and know that there is something to look for."[69]

I agree with Block that we can attend to our own qualia. Moreover, this is not just something that eighteenth- and nineteenth-century introspective psychologists or twentieth-century phenomenologists or the subjects of twenty-first century experimental studies of perceptual experience did and do; there are many moments in life when we are interested in "what it is like" to experience such and such, in a sense that involves attending to our qualia rather than (or, as the occasion demands, along with) attending to the worldly properties that we perceive when we "see through" the qualia as through a transparent window. Qualia themselves are as much capable of being the objects of perceptual experience as, say, trees or rabbits. If it seems shocking to "downgrade" the epistemological role of qualia to the level of the epistemological role of the trees and the rabbits, it is no doubt because the view that knowledge is "based on" qualia has become so deeply entrenched.

In his Second Woodbridge Lecture,[70] McDowell takes Sellars to task for positing "non-concept-involving episodes or states in sensory and specifically visual consciousness."[71] As McDowell reads Sellars, Sellars thinks we need to see the flow of "conceptual representations" in perception as "guided by manifolds of sensations," where the latter are the non-concept-involving episodes or states in question.[72] And, in line with his "naive realist" view of experience, McDowell replies that it is not "non-concept-involving episodes or states" that do the guiding, but the "objects themselves" (the rabbit and the trees, to stick to our examples).[73] I agree with McDowell that the guiding that is *epistemologically* relevant is done by the objects themselves, but I agree with Sellars that part of the guiding that is *causally* relevant—*assuming our current*

---

69. Block, "Wittgenstein and Qualia," 280.
70. McDowell, "The Logical Form of an Intuition," in *Having the World in View*, 23–43, esp. 23–33.
71. McDowell, "Logical Form of an Intuition," 24.
72. McDowell, "Logical Form of an Intuition," 24.
73. McDowell, "Logical Form of an Intuition," 39.

neurological picture—is partly done by qualia. What McDowell cannot contemplate as so much as a possible position is that while qualia ("non-concept-involving episodes or states") are causally relevant to perception, they do not and cannot do the epistemological heavy lifting that the empiricist tradition asks them to do. "Naive realism" is right in insisting that we do perceive external objects and that this is not a matter of drawing inferences from qualia; that is why we need an account of perception that connects perception both with the objects perceived (an "externalist" account) and with the subject's conceptual activity. But "naive realism" is wrong when it denies *any* gap between the properties of external objects and the phenomenal character of experience.

PART V

Looking Back

12

The Development of Externalist Semantics

$\mathscr{M}$Y INTEREST IN LINGUISTICS goes almost as far back as my interest in philosophy.[1] The latter goes back to my high school days, when I and two or three friends started a small philosophy club, and I went on to major in philosophy at the University of Pennsylvania. I don't know how I learned that there was a small autonomous "section" headed by Zelig Harris in the anthropology department called "Linguistic Analysis," but learn that I did, and from my second year in college I took every course that was offered by Harris. (Noam Chomsky was one of my fellow students.) Harris was not at that time teaching his own view of semantics. In any case, what I learned was his techniques for describing the syntax of a natural language, and likewise Chomsky's first famous publication, *Syntactic Structures*, was entirely devoted to syntax. As far as my own experience for a number of years went, "meaning" was a topic discussed by philosophers, not by linguists. The only course on the topic I had as a student, in fact, was a course on

1. This chapter consists of the lecture I gave on November 1, 2011, on the occasion of being awarded the Rolf Schock Prize in Logic and Philosophy by the Royal Swedish Academy of Science for my contribution "to the understanding of semantics for theoretical and 'natural kind' terms, and of the implications of this semantics for philosophy of language, theory of knowledge, philosophy of science and metaphysics." In it I describe the path that led to the work for which I was awarded that prize, including at least one wrong idea that I had to overcome on the way.

Carnap's *Meaning and Necessity* taught by Morton White, who, along with C. West Churchman, was my principal mentor in philosophy at "Penn."

I went to graduate school, of course (at the University of California–Los Angeles), and became an analytic philosopher and philosopher of science (and, mainly on my own,[2] a mathematician as well). My very first published paper (1954) was titled "Synonymity, and the Analysis of Belief Sentences,"[3] and that title might lead you to think that I was already focusing on semantic issues, but that is not the case. That paper grew out of a conversation with Carnap about a criticism due to Benson Mates of a criterion of synonymy (for sentences, not for individual words) that Carnap had proposed. I suggested that Mates's criticism might be met by counting the *logical form* of a sentence as one of its meaning-components, and Carnap urged me to publish this proposal, which I did. But that was all there was to it.

My interest in semantics, although at the time I would not have used that word, really began in 1957–1958, when Herbert Feigl invited me to spend my semester of leave from Princeton at his Minnesota Center for the Philosophy of Science. The following spring, Paul Ziff, who was on leave from Harvard where he was an untenured assistant professor, delivered a seminar in Princeton on what became his book, *Semantic Analysis*,[4] which was attended by myself and a number of my students, including Jerry Fodor and Jerrold Katz, and those two things, the semester at Feigl's Center and the impact of Ziff's course, together led to a turning point in my philosophical thinking.

At the Minnesota Center, I was the only (even partial) defender of Quinian skepticism about the analytic-synthetic distinction, and the only critic of Adolf Grünbaum's "conventionalism" in the philosophy

---

2. The only graduate course in mathematics I had, in fact, was a course in Ideal Theory at Harvard in 1948–1949. I learned mathematical logic by solving problems posed for me by Georg Kreisel, when I became an assistant professor at Princeton University, starting in 1953, and, after publishing a number of papers in logical and mathematical journals, I received tenure in both the philosophy department and the mathematics department at Princeton in 1959.

3. Hilary Putnam, "Synonymity, and the Analysis of Belief Sentences," *Analysis* 14 (1954): 114–122; repr. in *Propositions and Attitudes*, ed. N. Salmon and S. Soames (Oxford: Oxford University Press, 1988), 149–158.

4. Paul Ziff, *Semantic Analysis* (Ithaca, N.Y.: Cornell University Press, 1960).

of geometry.[5] I enjoyed my discussions with all the members of the center (including Paul Feyerabend, who was the other young visitor at the center that semester), but my main activity was to write the first draft of a paper titled "The Analytic and the Synthetic."[6] The conclusions of "The Analytic and the Synthetic" are closely connected with what was later called "externalism."

In those years, the fifties and sixties of the last century, young analytic philosophers tended to be either partisans of logical positivism or partisans of Oxford "ordinary language philosophy." Although my *Doktorvater*, Hans Reichenbach, was a logical positivist,[7] I had come to have serious doubts about both movements. The "ordinary language" philosophers knew little, and for the most part cared less, about science, while the logical positivists thought that terms in scientific theories, including geometrical terms such as "distance," have their meanings fixed by "definitions," which they sometimes took to be operational definitions ("coordinating definitions"), and sometimes theoretical sentences such as "$E = \frac{1}{2}mv^2$" (as a definition of "kinetic energy"). Whenever a scientific revolution forced us to revise those "definitions"—something they recognized had already happened more than once—it followed from their account that the *reference* of those terms changed. For example, in nineteenth-century physics, the kinetic energy of an object was defined as one-half the product of its mass and the square of its velocity, $\frac{1}{2}mv^2$. But according to Einstein's special relativity, the kinetic energy (the total relativistic energy minus the famous mc^2) isn't *exactly* $\frac{1}{2}mv^2$, but that plus a correction which is tiny when the velocity v is tiny compared to the velocity c of light. However, I argued, "kinetic energy" did not refer to *one* physical magnitude in 1899 (namely $\frac{1}{2}mv^2$) and to a *different* magnitude ($\frac{1}{2}mv^2$ plus the relativistic correction) in

---

5. Hilary Putnam, "Memo on 'Conventionalism'," Minnesota Center for the Philosophy of Science, March 22, 1959; first published in *Mathematics, Matter and Method*, vol. 1 of *Philosophical Papers* (Cambridge: Cambridge University Press, 1975), 206–214.

6. Hilary Putnam, "The Analytic and the Synthetic," in *Scientific Explanation, Space, and Time*, ed. Herbert Feigl and Grover Maxwell (Minneapolis: University of Minnesota Press, 1962), 358–397; repr. in Hilary Putnam, *Mind, Language and Reality*, vol. 2 of *Philosophical Papers* (Cambridge: Cambridge University Press, 1975), 33–69.

7. As related in Chapter 6 of this volume, Reichenbach did not like the term "positivist" because he associated it with the view that all scientific concepts referred, however indirectly, to human sense-data, which was something he did not believe. He preferred "logical empiricist."

1905; rather, I said, we were talking about the *same* magnitude in those two years, but we came to have a *more accurate idea of the nature of that magnitude.* And similarly, I argued, when physicists gave up the idea that atoms are little solar systems (the Bohr model), they did not *change the reference* of the term "atom"; rather, they arrived at a better idea of what atoms *are.*

Two points are essential here, if one wants to understand the connection with semantic "externalism": *First,* the idea that terms must have precise and unchanging definitions, and that it is those definitions that fix their reference, has to be given up. *Second,* it is a combination of theories and experiments that tell us what our terms refer to, and not unchanging "definitions." Because the results of experiments depend on the external environment, as does the fate of the theories we use those experiments to test, one way of expressing this is that the terms I discussed in "The Analytic and the Synthetic" (e.g., "energy," "atom") have their reference fixed by the environment itself, and not simply by what is in our heads. But that is not the way I thought about it at the time, which is why ten years had to pass before I arrived at "semantic externalism."

As I mentioned, the first draft of "The Analytic and the Synthetic" was written in 1957–1958; my first explicitly "semantic externalist" paper, "Is Semantics Possible?," was written ten years later.[8] One reason for this substantial time gap is that I thought of "The Analytic and the Synthetic" as a paper only about one limited issue in semantics, namely, what was right and what was wrong in Quine's famous attacks on the analytic-synthetic distinction. The moral I drew was that while Quine was wrong to deny that there are any analytically definable terms in the language at all—I defended, and still defend, the idea that there is a point to saying that "all bachelors are unmarried" is an analytic statement—the notion of analytic truth could not bear the weight put on it by Russell, Frege, and the logical positivists, all of whom claimed that the truths of mathematics were analytic, and some of whom also who thought that "$E = \frac{1}{2}mv^2$" was analytic in classical physics and that Einstein—for good reason, to be sure—"changed the

8. Hilary Putnam, "Is Semantics Possible?" *Metaphilosophy* 1 (1970): 187–201; revised version in *Language, Belief and Metaphysics: Contemporary Philosophic Thought: The International Philosophy Year Conferences at Brockport,* vol. 1, ed. H. E. Kiefer and M. K. Munitz (Albany: State University of New York Press, 1970), 50–63; repr. in *Mind, Language and Reality,* 139–152.

definition." However the idea of theorizing about "semantics" as such was far from my mind. After all, the linguistics I knew did not include any such field, while in analytic philosophy at the time "semantics" mainly referred to the part of logic that deals with Tarski's formal analysis of the notion of truth. To explain how semantics came to be an issue for me, and for some of my students (particularly for Jerrold Katz and Jerry Fodor), I need to describe Paul Ziff's seminar.

Ziff's theory, which we discussed for hours every day in the spring of 1958, has been largely bypassed by the development of linguistics and philosophy of language, but it contained important, if eccentrically formulated, insights.[9] It was not a theory of *understanding*; thus, unlike Quine's *Word and Object* to which it was clearly responding, it did not presuppose Skinnerian or any other psychological theory.[10] Nor did Ziff try to show how semantics could be done without the notion of "meaning," as Davidson tried to do in a famous essay published the same year.[11] Rather, it was concerned with the question of what sort of *evidence* a linguist trying to write a lexicon for a language (either a familiar language, or one previously unknown) might draw on and how that evidence might be organized. (In this respect Ziff's *Semantic Analysis* resembles *Word and Object*, but with a much more realistic idea of what linguistic evidence is.) The idea of trying to describe what an ideal dictionary entry for a word might look like, and what evidence would be relevant, was to be central to my "The Meaning of 'Meaning'" and its predecessor "Is Semantics Possible?," although the conclusions I reached were quite different.[12] But mainly it was the sheer *ambition* of Ziff's project that impressed us. As Jerrold Katz later said of *Semantic Analysis*, it was "a pioneer work, in that it is the first to propose an empirically based

9. One of those insights is that a property may be *linguistically* associated with a natural kind term although the property is only contingently, not analytically, associated with the relevant kind. For example, the properties *striped* and *quadrupedal* are associated with the noun *tiger*, but it is not analytic that all tigers are striped, and possibly not even true that there are no three-legged tigers. "Tigers are striped" and "Tigers are quadrupeds" are "state regularities" in Ziff's terminology. I did not preserve the terminology, but Ziff's observation led me to the notion of a *stereotype* in the "The Meaning of 'Meaning'," in *Mind, Language and Reality*, 215–271.

10. W. V. Quine, *Word and Object* (Cambridge, Mass.: MIT Press, 1960).

11. Donald Davidson, "Truth and Meaning," *Synthese* 17 (1967): 304–323.

12. I mean "ideal" from a strictly linguistic point of view, with no philosophical or behavioristic axe to grind, of course.

theory of meaning to deal systematically with the various topics that are part of the subject of meaning, and to attempt to fit such a theory into the larger framework of structural linguistics."[13]

Following Ziff's seminar, in 1958–1959 and 1959–1960, I worked mainly on a famous mathematical problem, Hilbert's Tenth Problem, and in 1960–1961, having finally received tenure in both mathematics and philosophy at Princeton, I finally had a full year's leave, which I devoted again mainly to mathematical logic. But in 1961 I left Princeton to become professor of Philosophy of Science at the Massachusetts Institute of Technology (MIT), where I also had the opportunity to hire a number of philosophers and to create what was first a "philosophy section" of MIT's humanities department, and later an autonomous philosophy department (and still later one-half of MIT's Department of Philosophy and Linguistics). Among the philosophers MIT hired on my recommendation were the "two Jerries," Jerry Fodor and Jerrold Katz. The question Paul Ziff had raised for us was a main topic of discussion among the three of us: What might a field called "semantics" look like? How could we lay the foundations for (to use Katz's words that I quoted a moment ago) "an empirically based theory of meaning to deal systematically with the various topics that are part of the subject of meaning," that might "fit . . . into the larger framework of structural linguistics"?

Although in the course of time Fodor, Katz, and I all came to propose very different answers to that question, at the beginning we all agreed, and it was my later realization that what we agreed on in those years at MIT must be *wrong* that brought about my move to "externalism."[14] What we agreed on was that the meaning of a word could be given by "semantical rules,"[15] and what we worked on was the problem of saying what such rules might look like. But while that was a full-time worry for Katz and Fodor, I was at that time (1961–1965) doing math-

---

13. Jerrold Katz, "Review of *Semantic Analysis*," *Language* 38, no. 1 (1962): 52–69.

14. I left MIT for Harvard in 1965.

15. "How Not to Talk about Meaning: Comments on J. J. C. Smart," in *Boston Studies in the Philosophy of Science*, vol. 2, ed. R. S. Cohen and M. R. Wartofsky (New York: Humanities Press, 1965), 205–222; repr. in *Mind, Language and Reality*, 117–131. I talk about "semantical rules" in the *Boston Studies* publication (216–222), and in *Mind, Language and Reality* (126–131). This is the text of a talk to the Boston Colloquium in the Philosophy of Science that I gave December 12, 1963.

ematical logic a lot of my time, and also beginning to apply concepts from computer science to the philosophy of mind.[16] So I pretty much dropped semantics for the time being, apart from the conversations I described. But when I decided to teach a course in the philosophy of language at Harvard in 1967, I returned to the subject, and I found that I was dissatisfied with the idea that the two Jerries and I had shared, that one could state semantical rules with the properties that (1) they are in some sense "internalized" by every competent speaker and (2) they determine the meaning of every word in his or her repertoire. Those were the wrong ideas I had to overcome to get to externalism.

Reconsidering those ideas in 1967, I recalled that Locke had once claimed that "gold" is synonymous with "precious, incorruptible, yellow metal soluble in *aqua regia*,"[17] and I reflected that I had no idea what "aqua regia" *is*, so that couldn't *possibly* be what I (or most other English speakers) *mean* by "gold."[18]

The problem I faced was this: if the meaning of the word *gold* is given by a battery of semantical rules, as Katz, Fodor, and I had all been supposing, *what are those rules?* I had ruled out " 'gold' is the name of a precious metal," " 'gold' is the name of a yellow metal"—indeed, everything except " 'gold' is the name of a metal" in "How Not to Talk about Meaning,"[19] and clearly " 'gold' is the name of a metal" isn't sufficient as a description of the meaning of the word.

---

16. Although I had already published "Minds and Machines," in *Dimensions of Mind*, ed. Sidney Hook (New York: New York University Press, 1960), 148–180, while I was at MIT, I wrote "Robots: Machines or Artificially Created Life?" *Journal of Philosophy* 61 (1964): 668–691; repr. in *Mind, Language and Reality*, 386–407.

17. Locke says different things about "our idea of gold" in different places. In one place he writes, "He that will examine his complex idea of gold, will find several of its ideas that make it up to be only powers; as the power of being melted, but of not spending itself in the fire; *of being dissolved in aqua regia* [emphasis added—HP], are ideas as necessary to make up our complex idea of gold, as its colour and weight: which, if duly considered, are also nothing but different powers" (John Locke, *An Essay Concerning Human Understanding*, ed. P. H. Nidditch (Oxford: Oxford University Press, 1975), II, 23, §10). But in another place he has it that the nominal essence of the name "gold" "is that complex Idea the word Gold stands for, let it be, for instance, a Body yellow, of a certain weight, malleable, fusible, and fixed" (III, 6, §2). But the same objection applies: I have no idea what the "certain weight" of gold is, and so, according to Locke, I do not know the "nominal essence," that is, the meaning of the word.

18. Putnam, "How Not to Talk about Meaning," 217–218.

19. Putnam, "How Not to Talk about Meaning," 217–218.

I found myself driven to an idea that was wholly new to me, and apparently to other philosophers as well: *nothing* that is in the head of the average speaker suffices to determine what her word *gold* refers to. Meanings aren't in the head.

Well, if they aren't in the head, where are they? Of course, the brain *is* in the head, and the brain has to undergo appropriate changes (maturation, and all the various effects of acculturation) before one can speak a natural language. "Meanings aren't in the head" doesn't mean that the brain has nothing to do with semantic competence. But what fixes the meanings of a speaker's words is not just the state of her brain; the reference of our terms is generally fixed by two things that classical philosophy of language either ignores or mentions only as an afterthought: *other people and the world.*

You may have noticed that I just shifted from "meaning" to "reference"; they are not the same, but they are closely connected. Consider: typical modern English speakers have only a vague idea of what an elm tree looks like. They depend on other people, especially experts, to determine for them which trees are "elms," and if there is an island somewhere in which a dialect of English is spoken in which the word "elm" is the name of a different species of tree—say, of beeches— then we would say that on that island "elm" means *beech.* For natural kind words, for instance, names of biological species and names of substances, difference in reference *counts as* difference in meaning.[20]

One problem with viewing the reference of my words as something fixed by the way my brain is "programmed" is that such an individualistic account ignores *the linguistic division of labor.* Not only am I unable to reliably distinguish elms from other species of tree; the fact is that *I do not have to be able to do this on my own.* If I need to know whether a particular tree is an elm, I can ask someone who is more knowledgeable than I.

In the case of names of substances—metals, for example—the linguistic division of labor is even more obvious; or it is obvious once pointed out—evidently it wasn't obvious to Locke, with his various attempts to say what the "idea" of gold is that we English speakers sup-

20. The extension of a natural kind term—that is, the set of things it is true of—is one of the components of its "meaning vector," in the theory I proposed in "The Meaning of 'Meaning'."

posedly possess, or to me when I thought the reference of gold must be fixed by semantical rules that every competent speaker tacitly knows. There are plenty of people who can determine for us whether a piece of metal is *really* gold—jewelers, chemists, atomic physicists, among others.

At this point, it is important to see that the experts themselves do not identify substances by unchanging "definitions," unchanging necessary and sufficient conditions. (Recall what I had argued in "The Analytic and the Synthetic," the paper I had first drafted ten years earlier in Minnesota!) Even the criteria used by experts are sometimes badly off the mark. But in cases such as the case of gold, cases in which there are large numbers of what are agreed to be good samples of the pure metal, the deviant examples will be declared to be such when science discovers that their nature is not the same as that of the great majority of the accepted samples. And if a sample is too deviant, we will decide it isn't gold at all, even if it superficially resembles gold. The samples do not literally *speak*, but they have a decisive vote in what counts as a member of the kind. In "The Meaning of 'Meaning'," I referred to samples that play this role as our *paradigms*.

Of course, there are natural kinds that we are all pretty good at identifying without relying on experts, for example, *water*. But it would be wrong to think that the extension of the word "water" is fixed simply by the superficial properties of water—that is, that "water" means "liquid that quenches thirst, has such and such a taste, . . . and so on." And it would be equally a mistake to say that "water" means "H_2O." It is true that most educated people now know (or think they know) that H_2O is the chemical formula for water, but educated speakers and uneducated speakers do not speak different languages. (Moreover, "water is H_2O" is not precisely true![21]) Water has the same meaning in the mouth of an English-speaking scientific ignoramus and the mouth of an English-speaking chemist; they both know the meaning of "water" in English in the sense of possessing the sort of linguistic competence that every person who masters the language is linguistically obliged to have in connection with that word. They refer to the same liquid when they use the word. Moreover, speakers who lived before Dalton

---

21. Normal water is actually a quantum mechanical superposition of H_2O, H_4O_2, H_6O_3 . . . Very little (if any) water is simply H_2O.

introduced the modern notion of a chemical compound referred to the same liquid when they used the term "water." The word does not change its meaning every time we discover a better account of the nature of water. The meaning and reference of "water" aren't what has changed; it is our knowledge about water that has changed. The meaning of "water" isn't fixed by a definition, either in terms of the observable properties of the substance or in terms of the properties mentioned in our latest scientific theory; it is fixed by the nature of our paradigms of water. To be water is to be the same liquid as *this*, where *this* can be (almost) any of the paradigm examples of water.

What I have described is the reasoning that led me to the conclusion that the meaning and reference of the term "water" aren't in the head; they are fixed by what goes on in the world. (Saul Kripke had already entertained similar ideas when he was a member of Harvard's Society of Fellows [1963–1967]. I didn't learn of Kripke's views until 1970, however, when news of his lectures at Princeton spread through the philosophical world.)

I presented my account at the 1968 Summer Institute in Philosophy of Language in Seattle. (David Kaplan, who was present at those lectures, once wrote me, "I remember your quickly disabusing me of the idea that the intension of a natural kind word [that which determines the extension in a possible world—*HP*] is something we 'grasp,' as Carnap would have put it. It ain't in the head, as you put it. And almost as soon as you said it, it seemed right.") I presented a one-lecture version of the theory at the University of Minnesota in 1969, and the first published version appeared in 1970, under the title "Is Semantics Possible?" But it was not until December 1972 that I wrote the first draft of "The Meaning of 'Meaning'." It was then that what became the best-known argument for semantic externalism occurred to me. I refer to the "Twin Earth" argument.

The argument is a simple thought experiment: imagine a planet like earth—call it "Twin Earth"—on which the liquid that fills the lakes and rivers, that people drink, is not H_2O but a different compound, XYZ, with similar superficial characteristics. The Twin Earthers are supposed to be our doppelgängers, and some of them even speak English. Also, I imagine the year to be 1750, so it is before the chemical composition of either water or twater (Twin Earth "water") is known. The English-speaking Twin Earthers naturally call twater "water" (and the French-speaking ones call it "eau," and the German-speaking ones call it "Wasser"). The linguistic intuition of the great majority of people who have considered this thought experiment is that upon learning that Twin Earth "water" doesn't consist of H_2O at all, we Earthers would say "it isn't really water." The word "water" has a different meaning on Earth and on Twin Earth. Twin Earthian Oscar's word "water" and Earthian Oscar's word "water" are homonyms, but not synonyms. They do not have the same meaning—not even if Earthian Oscar and Twin Earthian Oscar happen to be microphysical duplicates!

It is irrelevant that there is no such (possible) compound XYZ, because we can imagine that neither Oscar nor Twin Oscar know this esoteric fact. (Indeed, I am not sure I myself *know* such a thing, unless having been told that this is so by a former chemist-turned-philosopher-of-science counts as "knowing.") The question is what we would say under perfectly imaginable circumstances, not what is chemically or physically possible. Moreover, the example can easily be modified to avoid this (irrelevant) objection, and that is what I did in a later paper:[22] just imagine that Twin Earth water consists of 50 percent water and 50 percent a tasteless and nonpoisonous liquid that does not quench thirst. Of course, Twin Earthers, if their bodies are like ours, would have to drink more of their "water" per day than we drink, but it is plausible to suppose that ordinary speakers do not notice this, and that they would not regard this fact as relevant to the meaning of the vocable "water" if they did notice it. (It used to be the case that Brits ate ten times as much chocolate per year as Americans, but no one regarded this as a difference in the meaning of the vocable "chocolate.") And it is not essential to the Twin Earth thought experiment that Oscar and Twin Earth Oscar be microphysical duplicates, or that their brains be microphysical *duplicates:* it is enough if their brains are in sufficiently similar states with respect to those systems that enable the appropriate use of words.

Because I mentioned Saul Kripke, I should also mention that, in his great book *Naming and Necessity,* his path to similar conclusions was a *via negativa:* if you think that what we mean by a natural kind term (say,

22. Hilary Putnam, "Meaning Holism," in *The Philosophy of W. V. Quine*, ed. L. E. Hahn and P. A. Schilpp (La Salle, Ill.: Open Court, 1986), 405–431; repr. in *Realism with a Human Face* (Cambridge, Mass.: Harvard University Press, 1990), 278–302.

"water" or "gold") is fixed by a definition, *just tell me that definition*. You will quickly find that all the proposed definitions either presuppose esoteric knowledge—the precise weight of gold, in the case of one of Locke's suggestions, or the fact that gold is soluble in aqua regia [whatever that is]—knowledge that most speakers certainly do not possess—or have counterexamples that are easy to find.

Externalism and Perception

Because I am also being awarded the prize for my "contribution to the understanding of semantics for theoretical and 'natural kind' terms, and of the implications of this semantics for philosophy of language, theory of knowledge, philosophy of science and metaphysics," I want to close by saying something about those implications. "The Analytic and the Synthetic" was already an "application of externalist semantics to the philosophy of science," even if I did not think of it that way. As for implications for metaphysics, I believe the area in which there is the most widespread acceptance of externalism, together with fascinating disagreements about what externalism *implies*, is the philosophy of mind, and particularly the philosophy of perception. In "The Meaning of 'Meaning'," I said meanings "ain't in the head." Our verbalized thoughts have meaning only in conjunction with our transactions with objects in our environment and with other speakers. It is in the context of a network of social and physical interactions, and only in such a context, that I can do such a thing as "think that the price of gold has become very high in recent years." If thinking that thought is what I once called a "functional state," it is not (as I mistakenly believed) simply a "computational state" of my brain; the "function" in question is a world-involving function. The thought is no more simply in my "head" than the meaning of the word "gold" is. And if thoughts aren't in the head, then the mind isn't in the head either. The mind isn't a *thing* with a definite location, but a system of world-involving abilities and exercises of those activities. On this all externalists in the philosophy of mind agree.[23]

---

23. I should mention that some implications of externalism for theory of knowledge are explored in my well-known "Brains in a Vat" thought experiment. See Hilary Putnam, "Brains in a Vat," in *Reason, Truth and History* (Cambridge: Cambridge University Press, 1981), 1–21.

Coming to the controversial area of perception, there is also some agreement. The long-maligned "naive realist" view that we have direct cognitive contact with external things and a number of their properties, and not just with our own sense data, is now close to becoming the orthodoxy. To perceive an apple is to be aware of *the apple*, not of sense data, and we are able to be aware of things like apples because we have evolved to respond to the appropriate "affordances," to use Gibson's famous term.

However, serious disagreement sets in is when one asks, "What is the role of the phenomenology of perception, the 'what it's like' aspects, the 'qualia,' in the perceptual transaction with, for example, the apple?" There are "phenomenists" about qualia, such as Ned Block, who would say that while *perception* is world-involving, *qualia* themselves are non-conceptual internal states (a position I myself agree with).[24] There are thinkers who would identify our visual sensations (for example) with properties of the surface of the apple itself (call them "ultra-naive realists") when the perception is "veridical."[25] There are thinkers (Dretske, Tye, and many others) who would identify our qualia with "information" (and who differ among themselves concerning what *sort* of "information"). And there are even thinkers who would say that, just as it is possible for microphysical duplicates to mean different things by their words if their environments are different, so it is possible that Oscar's visual sensation when he looks at the blue sky on Earth is what *I* would call a "visual sensation of blue" and Elmer's visual sensation when he looks at the blue sky on Twin Earth is what *I* would call a "visual sensation of green," even if their brains are in the same state (a position I find highly implausible).[26] But this is not a madhouse, as a skeptic (or a Wittgensteinian) might suspect! Important interactions between researchers in brain and behavioral science and philosophers

24. N. Block, "Mental Paint," in *Reflections and Replies: Essays on the Philosophy of Tyler Burge*, ed. M. Hahn and B. Ramberg (Cambridge MA: MIT Press, 2003), 165–200.

25. For example, see Michael Martin, "On Being Alienated," in *Perceptual Experience*, ed. Tamar Szabo Gendler and John Hawthorne (Oxford: Oxford University Press, 2006), 354–410.

26. For example, see Michael Tye, "Phenomenal Externalism, Lolita and the Planet Xenon," in *Qualia and Mental Causation in a Physical World: Themes from the Philosophy of Jaegwon Kim*, ed. Terence Horgan, Marcelo Sabatés, and David Sosa (Cambridge, Mass.: MIT Press, 2015), 190–208; and Michael Tye and Alex Byrne, "Qualia Ain't in the Head," *Nous* 40, no. 2 (2006): 241–255.

have already resulted from these discussions. No one can be sure what the philosophy and psychology of perception will look like in another fifty years, but that is an indication of the vitality of the field. That my contributions to something as dry sounding as "the understanding of semantics for theoretical and 'natural kind' terms" has helped to revive interest in the metaphysics of perception gives me great pleasure.

≈ 13

Sixty-Five Years of Philosophy

A PARTICIPANT'S THOUGHTS AND EXPERIENCES

$\mathcal{W}$HEN IN 2012 I accepted an invitation from Dr. Rupert Read to be part of a series of Royal Institute of Philosophy Public Lectures on 50 Years of Philosophy, I wrote, "Would it be too narcissistic if we called my lecture 'Sixty five years of philosophy: a participant's thoughts and experiences?'[1] (I would mention in the talk that fifteen years ago I published a piece called 'A Half Century of Philosophy Viewed from Within.'[2] Part of what the talk would describe is how my view of those years has itself changed in this new century. If you don't like the idea, I'll try to come up with something else.)" But when the time to write this lecture came, I quickly realized that what I had suggested was much too ambitious. In 1997, I had strong opinions about where philosophy had been headed in the previous fifty years, and I confidently issued verdicts on which tendencies were positive and which were misguided; today I disagree with some of those verdicts, and I would qualify the verdicts with which I still agree. For example, at that time I wrote:

---

1. This chapter was a lecture delivered via Skype at the University of East Anglia on December 5, 2013, from my home in Massachusetts. The sixty-five years counts from my graduation from the University of Pennsylvania.

2. Hilary Putnam, "A Half Century of Philosophy, Viewed from Within," *Daedalus: Proceedings of the American Academy of Arts and Sciences* 126, no. 1 (1997): 175–208.

213

If what "scientific realism" meant to philosophers like myself at the beginning of the 1960's was simply the rejection of positivism, and, more generally, of the idea that the statements of the natural sciences require philosophical reinterpretation, within a few years it was to develop into an elaborated metaphysical position, or rather a pair of positions (each of which has many versions). The first position, which I shall call "panscientism," holds that philosophical problems are fated, in the end, to be resolved by the progress of the natural sciences, and that the best the philosopher can do is to anticipate that progress, and suggest how the sciences can solve them. The second position, for which I shall employ a term introduced (for his own view) by Simon Blackburn, but which I shall use in a wider sense, I shall call "quasi-realism." This position does not claim that all philosophical problems will be solved by natural science, but it does hold that the complete description of reality as it is "in itself" is given by natural science, and, in most versions of the position, by physics. The idea that there is a sharp distinction between the way things are "in themselves" and how they appear to be, or how we speak of them as being, is characteristic of the position. What distinguishes the second position from the first is the idea that many of the ways we speak, and, indeed, have to speak, do not correspond to the way things are in themselves, but represent "local perspectives." To the extent that philosophy has to clarify and help us understand the status of these local perspectives, it has tasks over and above the tasks of the natural sciences. The "local perspectives" do not, however, have any real metaphysical significance; only natural science has that. Paul and Patricia Churchland, Daniel Dennett, and Jerry Fodor, notwithstanding their substantial disagreements, are all representatives of the first position; as representatives of the second position, in addition to Simon Blackburn, and again notwithstanding their substantial philosophical disagreements, I will cite the distinguished British philosopher Bernard Williams. Of course, not all analytic philosophers are either pan-scientists or quasi-realists; but these two attitudes have very much come to dominate the scene in "analytic metaphysics."[3]

3. Putnam, "A Half Century of Philosophy," 183.

Those of you who are lucky enough to own a copy of my *Philosophy in an Age of Science* know that the scientific realism I presently defend does *not* amount only to the claim that scientific theories don't "require philosophical reinterpretation." In the philosophy of physics, and particularly of quantum mechanics, I argue, the interpretations of contemporary physical theories produced by scientists are neither clear nor unambiguous, and they themselves require—not *re*interpretation, but—interpretation;[4] interpretation not only by philosophers, but by philosophers *and* physicists in dialogue with one another. Of course, I still reject the positivist interpretation(s), but I do not scorn the enterprise of philosophical interpretation of physics. And the scientific realism I defend in *Philosophy in an Age of Science* is not a claim about whether scientific theories do or do not need "reinterpretation";[5] it is the claim(s) that most of the entities postulated by our best scientific theories do exist, and that those theories are approximately true statements about how they behave. Moreover, as I first said in 1975, scientific realism, in this sense, is the only philosophy that doesn't make the success of science a miracle.[6]

I do still reject "panscientism" and "quasi realism." But, whereas the alternative I defended in the 1997 article was a position I ascribed to Wittgenstein, that the real task of philosophy is to lead us to see the "unintelligibility" of philosophical "positions," in *Philosophy in an Age of Science*, I criticize the whole idea that philosophical positions are often, let alone as a rule, literally unintelligible.[7] The characterizations of philosophy I now prefer are very different. As I say there, two definitions of philosophy appeal to me the most, and each definition requires to be supplemented by the other.[8]

4. Hilary Putnam, *Philosophy in an Age of Science: Physics, Mathematics, and Skepticism*, ed. Mario De Caro and David Macarthur (Cambridge, Mass.: Harvard University Press, 2012), chap. 6, "A Philosopher Looks at Quantum Mechanics (Again)," and chap. 7, "Quantum Mechanics and Ontology."

5. See particularly chapter 4, "On Not Writing Off Scientific Realism."

6. Hilary Putnam, *Mathematics, Matter and Method*, vol. 1 of *Philosophical Papers* (Cambridge: Cambridge University Press, 1975), 73.

7. See Hilary Putnam, "Wittgenstein: A Reappraisal," in De Caro and Macarthur, *Philosophy in an Age of Science*, chap. 28.

8. Putnam, "Science and Philosophy," in De Caro and Macarthur, *Philosophy in an Age of Science*, 44.

One definition comes from Wilfrid Sellars's essay "Philosophy and the Scientific Image of Man."[9] "The aim of philosophy," he wrote, "is to understand how things in the broadest possible sense of the term hang together in the broadest possible sense of the term." And the other is Cavell's famous characterization of philosophy as "The Education of Grownups." Neither of these characterizations implies that any part of our language, in or out of science, is only "quasi-realistic" or that all philosophical questions are fated to be either answered or dissolved by future science.

Instead, then, of trying to make large pronouncements as to where philosophy should be going, as I did in 1997, what I shall do today is look back on one part of my own philosophical career, and thereby both recall a part of the "50 years of philosophy" to which this series is devoted and connect that part with questions—particularly about perception and cognition—that occupy me at the moment.

Twin Earth and Brain in a Vat

I long ago discovered that what most undergraduates know about my philosophy is two of my thought experiments: the Twin Earth thought experiment from "The Meaning of 'Meaning',"[10] and the Brain in a Vat thought experiment from *Reason, Truth and History*.[11] I shall talk about the connection between the two as a way of leading into the questions that, as I mentioned, occupy me presently. Some undergraduates also hear about my "functionalism" (a position in the philosophy of mind), but rarely if ever, in my experience, about my modal-logical interpretation of mathematics, my changing positions in the philosophy of quantum mechanics, my writings in ethics and economics, and other

---

9. Wilfrid Sellars, "Philosophy and the Scientific Image of Man," in *Frontiers of Science and Philosophy*, ed. Robert Colodny (Pittsburgh: University of Pittsburgh Press, 1962), 35–78; repr. in *Science, Perception and Reality* (1963; Atascadero, Calif.: Ridgeview, 1991), quotation from p. 37 of the 1991 edition.

10. Hilary Putnam, "The Meaning of 'Meaning'," in *Language, Mind and Knowledge*, ed. Keith Gunderson (Minneapolis: University of Minnesota Press, 1975), 131–193. Collected in Hilary Putnam, *Mind, Language and Reality*, vol. 2 of *Philosophical Papers* (Cambridge: Cambridge University Press: 1975), 215–271.

11. Hilary Putnam, "Brains in a Vat," in *Reason, Truth and History* (Cambridge: Cambridge University Press, 1981), chap. 1.

topics, and I shall not talk about these other interests of mine. So let me describe those two well-known thought experiments of mine.

Twin Earth

Although many of you know about Twin Earth, I need to review the argument in which that thought experiment figured. Imagine a planet like earth—call it "Twin Earth"—on which the liquid that fills the lakes and rivers, that people drink, is not H_2O but a different compound, XYZ, with similar superficial characteristics. The Twin Earthers were supposed to be our doppelgängers; some of them even spoke English. Also, I imagined the year to be 1750, before the chemical composition of either water or twater (Twin Earth "water") was known. The English-speaking Twin Earthers naturally called twater "water" (and the French-speaking ones called it "eau," and the German-speaking ones called it "Wasser"). The reaction of the majority of people who have considered this thought experiment is that upon learning that Twin Earth "water" doesn't consist of H_2O *at all*, we Earthers would and should say "it isn't really water." The word "water" has a different meaning on Earth and on Twin Earth. Twin Earthian Oscar's word "water" and Earthian Oscar's word "water" are homonyms, but not synonyms. They do not have the same meaning—not even if Earthian Oscar and Twin Earthian Oscar happen to be microphysical duplicates!

It is irrelevant that there is no such physically possible compound XYZ, because we can imagine that neither Oscar nor Twin Oscar know this esoteric fact. (Indeed, I am not sure I myself *know* such a thing, unless having been told that this is so by one former chemist counts as "knowing.") The question is what we would say under perfectly imaginable circumstances, not what is chemically or physically possible. Moreover, the example can easily be modified to avoid this (irrelevant) objection, and that is what I did in a later paper:[12] just imagine that Twin Earth water consists of 50 percent water and 50 percent a taste-less and nonpoisonous liquid that does not quench thirst (D_2O, "heavy

12. Hilary Putnam, "Meaning Holism," in *The Philosophy of W. V. Quine*, ed. L. E. Hahn and P. A. Schilpp (La Salle, Ill.: Open Court, 1986), 405–431; repr. in *Realism with a Human Face*, ed. James Conant (Cambridge, Mass: Harvard University Press, 1990), 278–302.

water," is such a liquid). Of course, Twin Earthers, if their bodies are like ours, would have to drink more of their "water" per day than we drink, but it is plausible to suppose that ordinary speakers do not notice this, and that they would not regard this fact as relevant to the meaning of the word "water" if they did notice it. (It used to be the case that Brits ate ten times as much chocolate per year as Americans, but no one regarded this as a difference in the meaning of the word "chocolate.") And it is not essential to the Twin Earth thought experiment that Oscar and Twin Earth Oscar be microphysical duplicates, or that their brains be microphysical *duplicates:* it is enough if their brains are in sufficiently similar states with respect to those systems that enable the appropriate use of words.

The conclusion of this argument is that what our words refer to is, in general, not determined merely by what goes on in our brains, or, more broadly, inside our bodies: the difference that makes a difference between us and the Twin Earthers lies at the "other end" of the causal chains connecting us with the stuff we drink. *Reference depends on causal connection to the extra-bodily environment.* (In "The Meaning of 'Meaning'" I gave other reasons that this is the case, including the social nature of language.)

Brain in a Vat

The similarity of my Brain in a Vat thought experiment and the movies *The Matrix* and *The Matrix Reloaded* has often been remarked. In *The New Yorker*, Adam Gopnik wrote,

> It was, improbably, the Harvard philosopher and mathematician Hilary Putnam who, a couple of decades back, proposed the essential Matrixian setup: a bunch of brains in a vat hooked up to a machine that was "programmed to give [them] all a collective hallucination, rather than a number of separate unrelated hallucinations." Putnam used his Matrix to make a tricky argument about meaning: since words mean what they normally refer to within a community, a member of the vatted-brain community might be telling the truth if it said it was looking at a tree, or, for that matter, at Monica Bellucci. That's because the brains in that vat aren't really speaking our language. What they are speaking, he said, is

"vat-English," because by "a tree" they don't mean a tree; they mean, roughly, a tree image.[13]

The purpose of this argument was to show that a scientifically up-to-date and less solipsistic version of the Cartesian claim that there might be no external world at all, because I might be a disembodied mind deceived by an evil demon, could be refuted. And one premise in the argument was a generalization of the "semantic externalist" conclusion of the Twin Earth argument. That argument showed that, in the case of natural kind terms such as "water," "gold," and "elm," reference depends on causal connection with instances of the natural kind, either directly (i.e., on the part of the speaker herself) or indirectly (i.e., via communication with speakers who have communicated with speakers who have communicated with speakers who . . . leading back eventually to speakers who have causal connection of the right kind with instances of the natural kind). Of course, one can also refer to things no one has interacted with, and things that may not exist; for example, we can refer to the nearest intelligent extraterrestrials. This is what is called "reference by description," but reference by description depends ultimately on "direct" reference. Thus we can generalize the conclusion of the Twin Earth argument as follows: reference to objects in the external world depends on *information carrying causal connection with those objects or at least with objects that have properties in terms of which the objects referred to can be described, and the causal connection has to* involve *the properties in question.* The Brain in a Vat argument depends on this generalization of the conclusion of the Twin Earth Argument.

This is obviously a controversial premise, and it has been controversial almost as long as there has been philosophy, and I will say something about this shortly. But first let me just state the argument. Assuming this premise (which I shall call "semantic externalism"), the Brain in a Vat argument is simply this: to refer, say, to cabbages, or to vats, or to rabbits, mountains, or whatever it is necessary to have causal connection with them, or with objects with related properties. But according to the Brains in a Vat hypothesis, the experiences of the Brains in a Vat are just the experiences they would have if the world they seem to experience were a

---

13. Adam Gopnik, "The Unreal Thing: What's Wrong with *The Matrix*," *The New Yorker*, May 19, 2003, www.newyorker.com/magazine/2003/05/19/the-unreal-thing.

real world, that is, they experience just what non-envatted people would be experiencing. Because it is part of the scenario that the Brains were *always* envatted, so there was never a time when they had information carrying causal interaction with things in the "real world" and their properties, it belongs to the Brain in a Vat hypothesis that people in the vat have no information carrying causal interaction with real cabbages or real rabbits or real mountains, or even real vats (they are causally dependent on one vat, of course, as they would die if it broke, but they do not receive information from it as long as the system functions as it is designed to). Nor do they have information carrying causal interactions with such properties as one thing's being inside another, or being to the south of another, or having a certain color or weight or whatever. Thus, if "semantic externalism" is right, then the Brains in a Vat aren't able to refer to cabbages or kings, or ships or shoes or sealing wax.

This means that although the Brains in a Vat use the same words we do, or at least the same vocables go through their heads, and their Joycean "stream of consciousness" may be the same as that of a non-envatted person, *their words do not have the same meanings as those of a non-envatted doppelgänger.* That was, remember, the conclusion of the Twin Earth argument. Thus, they are not speaking the same language as a non-envatted doppelgänger. Let us call the language of the Brains in a Vat (or of the ones who call their language "English") *Vat English.*

The question as to whether *I* am a Brain in a Vat is the question as to whether the language I speak (I call it "English, of course) is Vat English.

But in my language, the word "cabbage" refers to cabbages. How do I know that?

There is a fundamental logical principle, basically stated by Tarski, according to which *in one's own language* any term *T* refers to, precisely, *T*s.[14] For example, *in my language*, the word "cabbage" refers to cabbages. For me to say in my language, the one I am speaking (or writing or thinking in) now, that the word "cabbage" does not refer to cabbages in that very language would be simply self-contradictory.

---

14. Tarski's disquotation principle (the famous convention T) was stated for truth rather than reference, but the above disquotation principle for reference follows from Tarski's analysis as well; formally, *for all* x, x *satisfies the open sentence* "Tx" *if and only if* Tx ("satisfaction" is the reference relation, in Tarskian semantics).

But we just saw (and again, I am saying all this in my own language) that in Vat English the word "cabbage" does not refer to cabbages. From these two facts together, it follows at once that my language is not Vat English. Hence, I am not a Brain in a Vat.

Instead of discussing the lecture I am going to finish giving, we could of course spend the rest of our time discussing the pros and cons of this argument, why it seems so counterintuitive, and why nonetheless so many people now accept semantic externalism, including this consequence. I will just say one thing: the argument is not meant to convince a skeptic. Skeptics can always reject the premise; they can reject semantic externalism. On the other hand, if the skeptic assumes that semantic externalism is false, the skeptic assumes something I do not believe and do not have to believe. Thus, even if the argument does not show that Cartesian skepticism is wrong, it does show that Descartes, or his imagined contemporary successor who talks about Brains in a Vat rather than disembodied minds, does not have a proof I must accept that skepticism is *right;* or at least not a proof based on the possibility that we are all Brains in a Vat, because I don't have to accept the possibility that *I* am a Brain in a Vat.

A Word about the History of Externalism

Externalism, in the form in which I presented and defended it in "The Meaning of 'Meaning'," is a contemporary position, but the debate between externalists and those who think we are innately capable of referring to things regardless of whether we have had any causal interactions with them or with other things with related properties goes back at least to the times of Plato and Aristotle. Descartes's skeptical scenario (I am a disembodied mind deceived by a demon) assumes that a mind can refer to any sort of object even if the owner of that mind has never had any causal connection with the external world at all. (As I like to express it, Descartes thought we are *semantically omnipotent.*) It is plausible to interpret Plato as having thought the same thing. On the other side, in Aristotle's philosophy of mind, as I interpret it,[15] the only

---

15. "Aristotle's Mind and the Contemporary Mind," in *Aristotle and Contemporary Science*, ed. Demetra Sfendoni-Mentzou, Jagdish Hattiangadi, and D. M. Johnson (New York: Peter Lang, 2000), 1:7–28.

properties we can conceive of are such that either we have *experienced* instances of them, or have experienced other properties in terms of which we can describe the properties we are thinking of. As I interpret him, Aristotle was an "externalist."

What makes externalism attractive today, in my eyes at least, is its consonance with a naturalistic way of thinking about human beings in the world. The idea of us as beings with an intrinsic ability to think about things whose properties we may neither have experienced nor detected with the aid of scientific instruments nor have the ability to define in terms of properties we have interacted with in one of these ways makes reference a magical power, and I believe that referring is a perfectly natural affair.

Externalism and Perception

The Brain in a Vat argument was an opening chapter in a book (*Reason, Truth and History*) concerned with issues about metaphysical realism (but that is another story). I no longer accept the conclusion of that book, which was that the Brain in a Vat argument refutes metaphysical realism.[16] But today I want to apply the semantic externalism that, as I have been explaining, figured both in that argument and in the earlier Twin Earth argument to a very different subject, the subject of *perception* (the subject I am working on now). But before we think specifically about perception, let me smooth the transition by applying the causal connection principle we have been talking about to the philosophy of mind. One such application has already been made by a great twentieth-century philosopher, Donald Davidson: the famous (or notorious) "Swampman" thought experiment.[17]

Davidson's thought experiment is very simple. (I shall modify it so that it is compatible with contemporary physics.) Imagine a swamp

16. See Putnam, "Corresponding with Reality," in De Caro and Macarthur, *Philosophy in an Age of Science*, 72–90.

17. Donald Davidson, "Knowing One's Own Mind," in *Subjective, Intersubjective, Objective* (Oxford: Clarendon Press: 2001), 15–38; originally published in *Proceedings and Addresses of the American Philosophical Association* 60 (1987): 441–458. Davidson later expressed embarrassment at his own thought experiment in his article "Interpretation: Hard in Theory, Easy in Practice," in *Interpretations and Causes: New Perspectives on Donald Davidson's Philosophy*, ed. Mario De Caro (Dordrecht, the Netherlands: Kluwer, 1999), 31–44. I see need for the embarrassment.

somewhere full of warm water and vegetation and thus with atoms, or at least atomic particles, of which in principle a human being could be formed. Suppose that by one of those almost infinitely improbable but not impossible quantum-mechanical scenarios,[18] the particles in the swamp jump together and form a human being with a completely false but reasonably consistent set of memories, as of a human life, including some memories that make sense of the fact that he is now in this swamp. Swampman, of course, might be on Earth, he might be on Twin Earth, or any other planet that has the right sort of atmosphere. No matter what the "water" on that planet actually is, Swampman, if he is a duplicate of an Earthean human being, will say that water is H_2O. But the question is, "What do Swampman's words refer to?"

If semantic externalism is correct, the answer is that *Swampman's words do not refer to anything.* And if his words do not (yet) have any reference, *Swampman has no concepts*; and, *a fortiori*, anything he says is *meaningless.* Of course, after he has been in existence for a while, and has had causal connection with the liquid in the swamp and calls it "water," with the grass in the swamp and calls it "grass," perhaps his words acquire meaning, but initially, *Swampman has no concepts, and hence no thoughts.* Some philosophers of mind would go further and say he has no consciousness; I don't see that conclusion as following, but in any case, it follows from our externalist (or "causalist") premise that Swampman has no concepts. To have concepts it is necessary to have appropriate causal connection with an environment. Semantic externalism implies externalism about the mind; if to have a mind is to have thoughts, then to have a mind it isn't sufficient to have the right goings-on in the brain and the rest of the body; to have a mind you have to be hooked up to an environment in the proper way, or at least to have a mind that can think about an external world, you have to have causal interactions that extend into the environment. One might call this an *anti-solipsist conclusion:* If externalism is right, *pace* Descartes, an isolated disembodied mind would have no thoughts about the world at all, not even false thoughts. In Kantian language, the pseudo-thoughts of Descartes's isolated mind are an empty play of representations and not thoughts at all.

---

18. Davidson, "Knowing One's Own Mind," has this all happening as a result of lightning bolts, which is, physically speaking, impossible.

To put it another way, one suggested many years ago by John Mc-Dowell, if meanings aren't in the head (which is what I said in "The Meaning of 'Meaning'"), then the mind isn't in the head either;[19] that is to say, the mind isn't a thing, it's a set of abilities—abilities that involve the external world from the beginning.

Especially at the University of East Anglia, it is appropriate to say at once that such a view was arrived at by Wittgenstein long before I thought about this question, but Wittgenstein's arguments, while fascinating, are problematic for me. The Twin Earth argument was my own way of arriving at the conclusion that to think of the mind in the traditional epistemological way, as something that is isolated from the world initially and that has to get past a kind of "veil" of its own sensations to get to the world, is wrongheaded from the start.

Enter William James

So far I have argued that the possession of concepts that refer to things in the external world depends on world-involving transactions; without those world-involving transactions, we have only an empty play of representations and not genuine concepts. That is a statement about *conceptualization*, and I said I was going to talk about perception. But the connection between conceptualizing and perceiving was already pointed out by William James, in a remark that has influenced me for many years. The remark was that (in the case of "a presented and recognized material object") "sensations and apperceptive ideas fuse here so intimately that you can no more tell where one begins and the other ends, than you can tell, in those cunning circular panoramas that have lately been exhibited, where the real foreground and [where] the painted canvas."[20] As James indicated, the best example of this phenomenon of "fusion" is the recognition, say, the seeing, of an object, when one sees

---

19. John McDowell, "Putnam on Mind and Meaning," in *Philosophical Topics* 20 (1992): 35–48. McDowell wrote, "The moral of Putnam's thought for the nature of the mental might be, to put it in his terms, that the mind . . . is not in the head either" (36).

20. William James, "Does Consciousness Exist," in *The Works of William James: Essays in Radical Empiricism*, ed. Frederick Burckhardt and Frederick Bowers (Cambridge, Mass.: Harvard University Press, 1976), 3–19, quotation from p. 16.

it not only in the minimal sense of "see,"[21] in which a cat might be said to see a television set, without having a concept or a protoconcept of a television set,[22] but sees it in the sense in which to see a television set is to *see it and know that what one is seeing* is a television set, the case of a full-blown apperception. In such a case, my perceptual experience has a sensational component—it includes what some philosophers call "qualia" that could also be part of the experience of a child who does not yet have the concept of a television set—but it also includes in a way that is real but hard to describe the fact that *it looks like a television set*, the fact that the concept "television set" is in play.

But now we can apply *externalism:* if to see a television set, in the sense in which a master of the relevant part of a language can see a television set, requires concept-possession, and concept-possession requires causal connection to external things, then *seeing* requires causal connection to external things—not just in the trivial sense, that we don't call it "seeing" if no light rays from external objects are striking the eye, but in a much more complicated sense: *seeing, in the sense of perceiving by means of sight, requires a history of language acquisition and language use.* (In fact, according to another part of the argument of "The Meaning of 'Meaning'," it also requires a history of interaction with other speakers, but I do not have time to go into that part of the argument today.) In the demanding sense, Swampman doesn't "see" anything when he appears on the scene; he doesn't *perceive* anything.

How this "externalist" picture contrasts with the traditional epistemological account was already indicated earlier, when I said that on that account the mind has to get past a "veil" of its own sensations to get to the world. I could also have said that in the traditional epistemological picture, knowledge is *entirely* based on experiential qualia, in the sense that everything we know about the world has to be inferred by the subject from those qualia, from the phenomenal character of his or her sensations. Perhaps the best statement of that view in the twentieth century is Russell's classic *The Problems of Philosophy*. In *The Problems of Philosophy*, everything we know about the external world is inferred from

---

21. On the senses of "see," see Ruth Anna Putnam, "Seeing and Observing," *Mind* 78 (1969): 493–500.

22. On the difference between the concepts of humans who have mastered a language and the protoconcepts, as I termed them, of animals, see Hilary Putnam, *Renewing Philosophy* (Cambridge, Mass.: Harvard University Press, 1992), 28–31.

our "sense data," and those sense data are all in our own "private spaces."[23] If the externalist picture I have been defending is right, this traditional picture of us as starting from data available in our individual "private spaces" and inferring that there is an external world at all is hopelessly wrong. If all we have is our own private data, then we are Swampmen. Swampman has sensations, but he cannot infer the existence of an external world—he cannot so much as *conceive* of an external world. Swampman has no concepts, and having no concepts—if we accept what James said about "fusion"—lacking "apperceptive ideas" to fuse with his sensations, means having no perceptions (or, in a different terminology, no "apperceptions"). Knowledge is not the product of interactions with mental objects in a private space, but of transactions between a human organism and an environment, including a history of transactions with a linguistic environment.

23. Bertrand Russell, *The Problems of Philosophy* (Oxford: Oxford University Press, 1912), 29.

Acknowledgments

Many of the papers reprinted here have been lightly edited to correct minor mistakes, avoid needless repetition, and, in cases where the papers were originally given as talks, remove indications of occasional address. Minor additions or deletions to several papers for purposes of clarification have been made. However, in cases where we have added a whole paragraph indicating a significant change in view, this has been indicated in the text by putting it in brackets and giving the date of the remark, when pertinent. We thank the publishers and journals that have granted us the permission to republish some of the papers contained in this book.

1. "Naturalism, Realism, and Normativity." From *Journal of the American Philosophical Association* 1, no. 2 (2015): 312–328. Published online 19 June 2015 (journals.cambridge.org/apa). Copyright © 2015 American Philosophical Association.
2. "On Bernard Williams's Philosophy as a Humanistic Discipline." From *Philosophy* 76, no. 4 (October 2001): 605–614. (Published with the title: "Reply to Bernard Williams' Philosophy as a Humanistic Discipline.") Published by Cambridge University Press on behalf of Royal Institute of Philosophy. Reproduced by permission of Cambridge University Press, Copyright © 2001 Royal Institute of Philosophy.
3. "What Evolutionary Theory Doesn't Tell Us about Ethics." From *Understanding Moral Sentiments: Darwinian Perspectives?*

ed. Hilary Putnam, Susan Neimann, and Jeffrey Schloss (New Brunswick/London: Transaction Publishers, 2014), 203–211. (Published with the title "Not Very Much.") Copyright © 2014 Transaction Publishers, New Brunswick, New Jersey.

4. "Sosa on Internal Realism and Conceptual Relativity." From *Ernest Sosa and His Critics*, ed. John Greco (Malden, Mass.: Blackwell, 2004), 233–248. Copyright © 2004 Blackwell Publishing Ltd.

5. "Richard Boyd on Scientific Realism." From *Reading Putnam*, ed. M. Baghramian (London: Routledge, 2013), 95–100. (Published with the title "Comment on Boyd.") Reproduced by permission of Taylor & Francis Group, LLC. Copyright © 2013 Maria Baghramian, for selection and editorial matter. Copyright © 2013 Hilary Putnam, for contribution.

6. "Hans Reichenbach: Realist *and* Verificationist." From *Future Pasts: The Analytic Tradition in Twentieth-Century Philosophy*, ed. Juliet Floyd and Sanford Shieh (Oxford: Oxford University Press, 2001), 277–287. Reproduced by permission of Oxford University Press, USA. Copyright © 2001 Oxford University Press, Inc.

7. "Between Scylla and Charybdis: Does Dummett Have a Way Through?" From *The Philosophy of Michael Dummett*, ed. R. E. Auxier and L. E. Hahn (Chicago: Open Court, 2007), 155–167. Copyright © 2007 by The Library of Living Philosophers.

8. "When 'Evidence Transcendence' Is Not Malign." From *Journal of Philosophy* 98, no. 11 (November 2001): 594–600. (Published with the title "When 'Evidence Transcendence' Is Not Malign: A Reply to Crispin Wright.") Copyright © 2001 The Journal of Philosophy, Inc.

9. "Sensation and Apperception." From *Consciousness and Subjectivity*, ed. Sofia Miguens and Gerhard Preyer (Berlin: Ontos Verlag, 2012), 39–50. Copyright © 2012 Ontos Verlag.

10. "Perception without Sense Data." Derives from a lecture read at the 5th International Lauener Symposium held in Bern, Switzerland, in June 2012, during which Hilary Putnam was awarded the Lauener Prize for an Outstanding Oeuvre in Analytical Philosophy for that year. The essay will first be published in *Themes from Putnam*, edited by Michael

Frauchiger (series: Lauener Library of Analytical Philosophy, vol. 5) Berlin/Boston: Walter de Gruyter.

11. "'Naïve Realism' and Qualia." Will appear in *Themes for Ned Block*, ed. Adam Pautz and Daniel Stoljar (Cambridge, Mass.: MIT Press, forthcoming).

12. "The Development of Externalist Semantics." From *Theoria* 79, no. 3 (2013): 192–203. Published by John Wiley and Sons. Copyright © 2013 Stiftelsen Theoria.

13. "Sixty-Five Years of Philosophy: A Participant's Thoughts and Experiences." Lecture given as one of the Royal Institute of Philosophy Public Lectures on 50 Years of Philosophy, at the University of East Anglia on December 5, 2013. Published for the first time in this collection.

Index